Comments from readers of the first edition (2007):

"The principles she outlines definitely made me look better. A fun read too."

—Susie

"Reading her book is like having an engaging, lively, and fun conversation with someone you trust."

—Joyce

"Don't even attempt the one-sitting reading. It really needs to be digested in small chunks. I came away with a fresh perspective on much more than fashion."

—Blogger

"Thoroughly enjoyed Ms. Warren's book. Practical, fun and witty."

—Squeal

"It's a tome filled with no-nonsense advice and plenty of insightful solutions."

—*Cleveland Plain Dealer*

"Everything you ever wanted to know about identifying and developing your personal style is packed into this book, from choosing the right colors and clothing to organizing your closet and saving money. Clearly presented, and the questionnaires and illustrations are a nice bonus."

—*Orlando Sentinel*

"She isn't a marriage counselor but she may have saved a marriage or two. Beyond defining style, the book shows women how to shop for purses, shoes, and accessories."

—*NOW Magazine*, Milwaukee Journal Sentinel

it's *so* you!

A LIGHT-HEARTED AND EASY APPROACH TO FIND YOUR PERSONAL STYLE

mary sheehan warren

Scepter

Originally published by Spence Publishing, Dallas, Texas in 2007 and reprinted with permission.

Published in the United States by
Scepter Publishers, Inc.
P.O. Box 211, New York, N.Y. 10018
www.scepterpublishers.org

ISBN: 978 1 59417 141 3

Illustrations by Bethany and Sam Torode
Book design by Sam Torode

Printed in the United States of America

To my mother.
You are beautiful.

contents

acknowledgments

Many people helped to make this book possible, and I am extremely grateful for their support and encouragement.

Thanks to my husband, Robert, for his loving patience and generosity. He was willing to spend Sundays venturing out with our five children to the hotspots of Milwaukee so that I could write this book. Thanks also to my parents, Joseph and Christina Sheehan, who ensured that I received common sense lessons in fashion and style.

I must also thank the two people who helped give me the technical expertise to write this book in the first place. Patti Francomacaro and Jeannette Kendall are not only great powerhouses of fashion skill, but they are the most wonderful teachers I'll ever know.

A warm thank you to my very wonderful illustrators, Bethany and Sam Torode, and to all those people who provided me with valuable input, suggestions, inspiration, or hands-on assistance, especially Jody Phelan, Mary Demet , Mary Anne Wahle, Jim Francomacaro, Ann Molabola, Marybeth Hagan, Anne Rice, Phil Brach, Debbie Duffy, Helena Metzger, Sue David, Beth Griffin, Francine Fiori, Rose Haas, Patti Lowe Weix, Priscilla Zito, Suzanne Pressburg, Cynthia Martin, Annie Lang, Patty Corboy, Frank Sheehan, Liz Brach, Cecilia Escobar, Patrick Griffin, Heather Weibye, Kristen Fulmer, Ruth McGuire, Julia Kearney, Carla Powell, Kate Baird, and Lexington College (Chicago).

Finally, I am extremely grateful to the hundreds of women who throughout the years have taught me about human nature and the special needs of real women. My experiences with them are what bring my points on style to life.

it's *so* you!

introduction

just clothing

What are you wearing right now? What does your outfit *say* about you? Is it *you*?

What's in your closet? Do these items boost your self confidence? Do they flatter you in the ways you had hoped?

Most importantly, do you feel you have a successful style? Or is what you own *just clothing*?

Personal style is a wink at the fashion world. Your style says, *I've got control over you, and you've got nothing over me.*

So why are there so many more tears than winks? The tears flow not only because fashion is so tied to self-esteem, but also because the choices regarding its products and services can become overwhelming, confusing, and, at times, elusive.

Fashion once eluded me. Nearly ten years ago, I would never have dreamed of teaching about personal style. Sure, like many women, I thought I had a style, but I certainly couldn't articulate what it was, how it worked for me, or even *if* it worked for me. I was a typical American consumer, groping at images I liked on others but rarely reflecting on how they appeared on me. All I had was *just clothing.*

And did I ever have clothing! In fact, two closets, two dressers, and half the laundry room floor were stuffed with unwise investments that added up to a small fortune.

True, I looked presentable. Co-workers and friends would often say, "That is a gorgeous dress!" or "Wow, what fancy duds!" at least once a week. But on a deeper level I knew I wanted to hear "*You* look wonderful!" And so I would make even more expensive fashion mistakes in an attempt to fulfill my wish.

I'm no beauty queen – just like most women. But I wanted – and still want – what most women want: a confident and attractive appearance. Confidence translates into personal and professional effectiveness. It's not about vanity, and it's certainly not frivolous.

you look wonderful!

My life radically changed when I began writing for two fashion designers who had teamed up to present fashion seminars to the public. Not surprisingly, the business boomed, and as demand for services increased, I received training in the *elements of style*, the foundation for all successful fashion decisions.

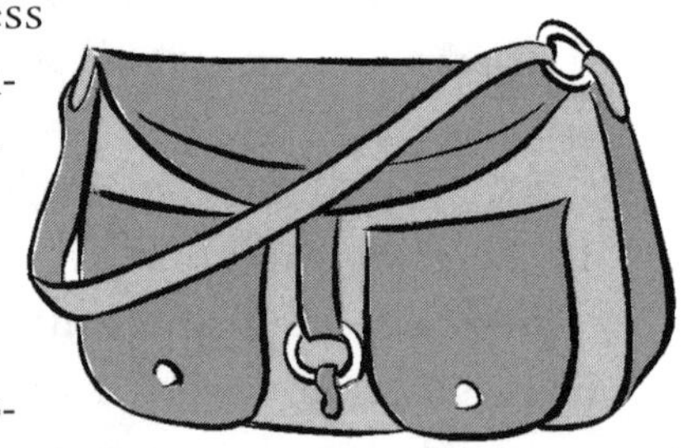

This changed my life.

I discovered that I didn't need to agonize over every decision to have fantastic style. I first needed to step back and take the time to study myself. In fact, no one can approach the marketplace without knowing exactly what she requires from fashion. It was such a simple and refreshing concept that we created *Elegance In Style* (EIS), an educational organization dedicated to helping women take this first step.[1]

Within the first few months of incorporation, EIS was in demand by women who heard we had life-changing measures to share. By the end of the first year we had visited ten states, and by the end of the second, we had trained women from around the world to become fashion consultants. In 2001, we began our sister organization, *Success In Style*, which provides career attire to needy women in the Baltimore area, and our sphere of influence widened even more.[2]

Seminar after seminar and clinic after clinic, we found the same things to be true of women of all ages, incomes, and occupations: too much clothing bought with too little reflection was costing them time, money, and self-confidence, obscuring their natural attributes with costumes rather than enhancing them with style. We found that the office professional with all the money in the world was just as frustrated as the at-home mother with no money and no time. We found that the free-spirited teenager wanted to look as beautiful as much as the senior wanted to look elegant. And we found that the petite-size woman was searching for clothing that worked for her size just as the plus-size woman was desperate for styles which flattered her own. What we witnessed first-hand was the universality of a woman's desire to look her best in the style in which she feels most comfortable.

> *Fashion changes, but style is eternal.*
>
> YVES SAINT LAURENT

This book is a summary of the life-changing and liberating skills I have acquired during these past several years.

how to read this book

It's one thing to read about style. It's quite another to *work* with your own. This book has been designed to do both. You will reflect upon the nature and history of fashion, your life-long use of fashion, and your understanding of style. But also, very early on, you will come to articulate your own style and take action in your closet.

It's So You! is a process, and each chapter builds upon the skills learned in the preceding one. Not only should you read them in order, you should delve into the activities scattered throughout the book. Most of them require you to use a pencil, and many of them prompt you to get up out of your seat. They are:

1. THE FASHION MOMENT OF TRUTH – There are three of these, at the end of chapters two, three, and four. They incorporate the skills you learn in the chapter and walk you through a wardrobe analysis. All three are conducted on the same wardrobe. However, the skills you learn should be applied to every wardrobe you own. By the time you finish all three, you will be ready to begin planning an ideal wardrobe that reflects *your* personal style. (You will also have the cleanest closet of your life!)

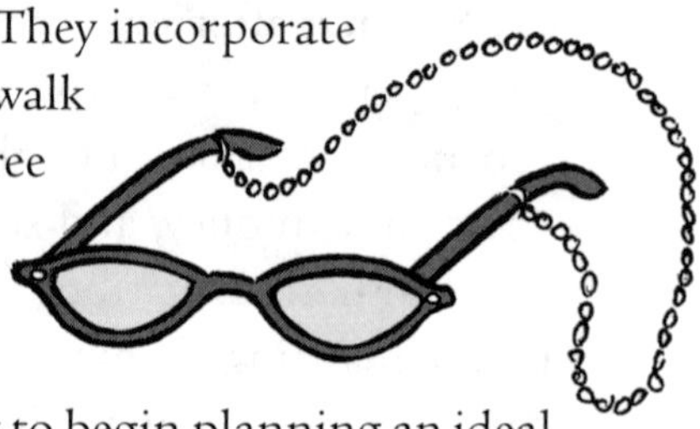

2. THE STYLE PROFILE – These will spark reflection about yourself and your style, providing nothing less than a life-changing revelation or simply prompting you to complete a specific improvement in your wardrobe. There are twenty-four of these activities.

Finally, I have included information on leaving your legacy of style. The most stylish women in the history of fashion *inspired* others to look their best. True success in personal style is not self-serving. It's the ability to help others feel their best as well.

3. THE SEMINAR FAQ — In the ten years my collegues and I have been providing seminars, workshops, and consultations, we have addressed countless questions, concerns, and comments from women in all kinds of circumstances. Each chapter includes answers to one of the more commonly asked questions.

Let's begin with the first *Style Profile*.

STYLE PROFILE #1

my objectives

Something prompted you to begin reading this book. Perhaps you are curious. Maybe you need a little pizzazz in your appearance. Or, maybe you want to change your life. Knowing your objectives for this book will help you to stay focused and encourage you to be completely honest with yourself. (Just remain open to adapting your objectives as you move along.)

Reflect upon what you think this book can help you do. Write an objective for yourself below.

____

____

____

____

____

CHAPTER ONE

my style, your style, their style

how you solve a problem like Maria's

Maria is a wife, mother, accountant, and thoroughly busy woman. She is also, incidentally, a size sixteen, somewhat large in the hips, and a little discouraged by the fashion scene. She'd tell you that when she finally sacrifices her precious time to shop for clothing, she feels limited to finding "big knits" for her casual wear and "reliable" dresses for work. Forget any discussion about clothing as an art form; it's an agonizing, heart-wrenching chore for her.

Make happy those who are near you and those who are far will come.

CHINESE PROVERB

Women like Maria are often so accustomed to their lifelong fashion coping strategies (like big knits) and so paralyzed in a debilitating standoff with the fashion world that seeking help with fashion seems like a frivolous expense – something that only the beautiful people do.

It usually takes a specific event to get a woman like Maria to really, truly look into the mirror. After all, for many, a long hard look in the mirror often begins an un-welcomed emotional chain reaction. Maria's specific event was a new job, and for her the chain reaction ended with the realization that her current work image didn't convey any professional confidence, much less self-assured beauty.

So, where can a thorough self-analysis lead? It *can* lead to a radical makeover!

Maria took her style head-on and found that the fashion world was not as daunting as she had originally thought. She and I worked from *her* needs, and everything just fell into place. With a greater emphasis on self-analysis and meaningful communication than on eye shadow and hair spray, the results were:

- a streamlined and neat silhouette
- consistent, current, and refined styling using garments and accessories
- a healthy glow because garment colors flatter
- a sense of quality because she never settles for the mediocre
- personal and professional confidence
- peace to know that her fashion spending is reasonable
- joy to find her niche in the fashion world

This changed her life.

my style, your style, their style

Barbara had a completely different set of issues. She was a bit more aggressive and often took a feisty approach to her wardrobe enhancements. Once she complained to me that at one point in a long and tempestuous relationship with her clothing she had suddenly decided to remake herself into what she considered to be "serious but sexy." Since I didn't really understand what she meant by that, she had to clarify: "You know, muted earth tone colors mixed with black on serious suits with naughty hemlines."

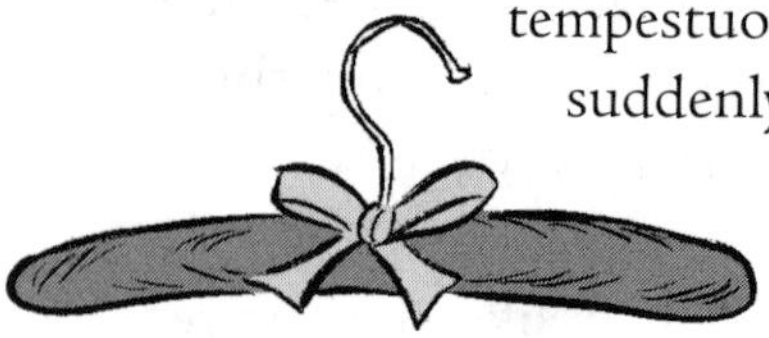

"Oh that," I nodded. So I asked about the results.

"Terrible," she said. "One day, after only two weeks of wearing these – by the way – very expensive clothes, I suddenly realized that the serious in me didn't like the short hemlines, and the sexy in me didn't like the unflattering colors! The whole look just wasn't me."

Just wasn't me. Where have I heard that before?

I eased Barbara's fears about our upcoming consultation, explaining that although she was proactive and decisive about her style, her mistake was that in planning her wardrobe she was attempting to design *herself* for a style, rather than design a style for her *self.* All too often, we mold ourselves to an image that has nothing to do with our tastes, our talents, our personalities, or even our dignity as women.

> *You were born an original. Don't die a copy.*
>
> JOHN MASON

Why do we do this? Usually it boils down to old-fashion imitation. We like beauty when we see it; we try to mimic the beauty we see

- in fashion magazines
- in marketing (not just fashion marketing)
- in the media
- in movies
- on celebrities
- on colleagues at work
- on the idealized image of a professional woman
- on the idealized image of femininity
- on the idealized image of Feminism
- in art
- on heroines
- on friends
- on sisters
- on mothers, aunts, or grandmothers that we admire
- on images we have acquired in our past and have emotionally idealized over time

There's certainly nothing wrong with wanting to imitate the styles of people we admire. After all, we learn a lot of good things from other people. However, in admiring other women for their beauty (and hopefully their talent and virtue as well) we need to draw the lines between *their style, your style,* and *my style.*

a solution for you, me, and barbara

You know what happened to me. Let me tell you how I helped Barbara, who said she wanted "serious but sexy."

The first step was to get her to define "serious" and "sexy" and to have her add any other qualities that she deemed appropriate for her business wardrobe.

Serious, as I found out, really meant professional. She wanted to be understood and respected.

> ***The true mystery of the world is the visible, not the invisible.***
>
> OSCAR WILDE

Sexy, as she revealed, really meant beautiful and feminine. In being professional, Barbara didn't want to lose any part of her womanhood. In her personal time, Barbara wanted also to be attractive as *a woman*. This, she admitted, did not mean emphasizing sexual characteristics, but keeping them a bit mysterious. (It isn't so much that Victoria has a secret: everyone knows what's under the fancy underwear. It's more that she needs privacy so that aspects of her body designed for intimate love are not becoming objectified for anything less.)

She also confessed that she adores bright colors, likes feminine detailing, and wants to be noticed but not scrutinized.

What a little digging can do! Using this information, Barbara and I designed a wonderful wardrobe with gem tone colors that complemented her complexion, tailored pieces which conveyed an appropriate level of convention, styling which flattered her figure, and exotic accessories that added interest and charm to the structure of her suits. All this, incidentally, on a rather tight budget.

Today, Barbara is a happy woman. She knows her style and demands that fashion fit her life.

style, not image

Notice that I use the word *style* throughout this book and not the word *image*. That's because style is something over which you have direct control. Image implies more than your clothing and behavior and is a bit subjective since it is partly defined by how other people see and – yes, it's true – *judge* you. Many dictionaries mention the word "reputation" when defining image. Image is something over which you only have very indirect control.

You can't manipulate the gray matter of other people. They will form opinions about you based upon the experiences they have with you. So, for example, you *do* have control over your own behavior and character. You have the freedom to behave honestly or dishonestly, kindly or cruelly, intelligently or stupidly. Others will then shape an image of your character accordingly.

Style works in a similar way. Style is choice. It's easy to consciously design and manipulate the variables which make up your appearance. You have the freedom to consciously choose particular pieces of clothing, accessories, and combinations of the two. You also have the freedom to dress creatively, professionally, and elegantly. Others will then shape an image of your style accordingly.

But why style? Why not just wear any old thing we choose and forget all this image and style and fashion stuff? Just let the clothes hang how they may, live and let live, and let people "see the real you."

Well, the "real you" is partly a visual experience for others. We look, we watch, we attempt to understand, and we respond (or react). This is how we experience each other.

The real you should come out in your *personal* style. It's personal because each and every one of us is unique in what we like, what we want to say, and in how we want to say it. These things must be carefully combined into a style that recognizes our differences but doesn't overemphasize them, a style that provides a level of comfort but doesn't make us sloppy, and a style that facilitates our talents rather than overwhelms or inhibits them.

Style, which may or may not be the high fashion of the time, should direct attention to *good* things. It should raise the tone of any setting, celebrate our womanhood, and affirm all the other many wonderful attributes which make up our personalities. These are just some of the universally desired attributes of style. Indeed, if there weren't any universals, no one could ever properly plan for a job interview, give a speech, or successfully complete a business transaction or an exchange with the in-laws.

Three specific goals for personal style bear an infinite number of sparkling gems:

CREATIVITY — A thoughtful choice of clothing, accessories, and details. It's the mark of individuality and is done as a gift of self to others. It's saying, "Hey world, I have something unique to offer you!"

PROFESSIONALISM — A liberating restraint. An oxymoron? No, because it's the thing that cultivates our creativity into something that allows for opportunity – no matter what our profession (business, medicine, education, entertainment, homemaking, etc.). It's saying, "Hey world, I am to be taken seriously as a woman!"

ELEGANCE — The dazzle and sparkle that result from a unique combination of creativity and professionalism. It includes poise, modesty, and refinement. It's saying, "I'm beautiful *because* I am a woman!"

Creativity, professionalism, and elegance are certainly life-long aspirations for many of us. Indeed, some who are enthusiastic about fashion may still have a ways to go in personal style. On the other hand, when you see someone who has attained this polished level of style, you know it. You admire it, but you can't imitate it exactly. You must develop your own style and cultivate these qualities in your own way.

STYLE PROFILE #2

free association

Engage in a little free association for a moment. For each term jot down images and words that bring to mind the ideal. Then, consider *your* style, the only style about which we are concerned.

Creativity: ____

____

Professionalism: ____

____

Elegance: ____

____

____

The ways I am creative with my style:

____

____

____

The ways I am professional in my style:

____

____

____

The ways I am elegant in my style:

____

____

____

STYLE PROFILE #3
finding myself in the closet

So, you know a little bit more about yourself and your style. Now, determine what items in your closet just aren't *you*? Take a look. Pull out three things that you generally hesitate to wear because you feel a little uncomfortable in them or you are just never in the "mood" for. Then, reflect upon why you bought them. What was going through your mind when you made the purchase?

Items in my closet that I never wear	*Why I bought them*
1 ____________________	____________________
	____________________
	____________________

2

____________________ ____________________

____

____

3

____________________ ____________________

____

____

So, what were your reasons? Was it in response to clever marketing? Were you inspired by someone else? Were you just not thinking at all when you bought them? Was it all just too good of a "bargain" to pass up?

love and lipstick

girl, I got some draperies in that same pattern as your dress!

While some women may not imitate, others may pursue a look that seems to promise delivery from boredom, drudgery, or temporary disorientation due to a life change. During my first pregnancy, I was constantly grasping for a style – any style – that made me feel comfortable with my changing body and helped preserve the *me* that I thought I was losing. One day toward the end of the pregnancy while I was grocery shopping, my search came to a crisis. Decked out in my Laura Ashley sage green floral corduroy jumper ($98 on sale in 1992) and obliviously assailing the conveyer belt with my provisions, the cashier called out, quite unexpectedly and unprovoked, "Girl, I got some draperies in that same pattern as your dress!"

I froze. Did I really and truly remind this woman of a window treatment? Was it a cozy free association or a gut reaction to an obvious absurdity? And could it be that my style can be summarized with a visit to someone's living room?

When I see people dressed in hideous clothes that look all wrong on them, I try to imagine the moment when they were buying them and thought, "This is great. I like it. I'll take it."

ANDY WARHOL

Well, no. The truth is that I had always felt a little compromising in that jumper, and her comment only brought this to a conscious level for me. The jumper *just wasn't me.*

But the jumper *was* somebody else. A woman with the corresponding personality would have presented herself with confidence, elegance, and romantic grace and probably wouldn't have cared if she conjured up decorating ideas for observant grocery store cashiers. (I suspect, however, that this same woman would inspire wonder, suspending all memory of fabric patterns.)

In this, and many other fashion blunders throughout my life, I wasn't necessarily imitating fashion that I had seen on other people, but capriciously grabbing at images and ideas which happened to make me feel good – at least for a time.

This is one of the most common problems with any woman's wardrobe. It's easy to understand how it might happen, considering that women now have the greatest amount of disposable income in the history of humankind. In turn, the fashion industry spends billions of dollars a year trying to get that money from us. They certainly are the masters of making even the ugliest of garments look stunning with provocative photography and creative packaging. Almost any consumer can get to a point where he or she is convinced that life depends upon acquiring a certain look, an image, or even an ideal.

In the case of my jumper, I can recall all my feelings at the time of purchase. It was so very pretty and romantic. It seemingly gave me a quick solution to losing my sense of youth and femininity. (I think that I also wanted people to recognize my obvious choice for Laura

Ashley and make assumptions about my socioeconomic status.) It's just that after all is said and done, romance and softness were not and still *are* not my fashion personality, and hormonal ups and downs should never dictate anyone's spending patterns.

It's fun to watch the variety of personalities in this world and how each reacts to different things in different ways. We are obviously not mass-produced like something industrial, but hand crafted and packaged with an infinite number of possibilities. This is why personal style is such a key issue in fashion. But before we uncover your personal style, let's get into this packaging and find out *who* you really are.

Know first who you are and then adorn yourself accordingly.

EPICTETUS

you're worth more than you know

A lot of attention has been paid to dressing for success in professional life. That's often why people hire fashion consultants. I'm finding, however, that many more women seek help with fashion for their personal lives. It's very common for me to hear women comment on how they just want to look better for themselves, for the people they love, or for the people they wish to love.

So it's important to dress for success for your *life*, your *complete* life. Your personal style will only be successful if you dress your whole self rather than just yourself as a professional or as a friend or as a mom or as a socialite. You not only want to have success, but you want a successful *life*. Doing this means knowing who you are and how much you are worth.

In considering your value, think of a diamond rather than something cheap like glass. Then think of the difference: Glass is flat, transparent, and plentiful. A diamond is multifaceted, unique, and precious.

MULTIFACETED — Five minutes of familiarity with you is only scraping your surface. There is so much more to be discovered. You have ever-expanding talents, values, attitudes, experiences, aspirations and passions. You grow and change, and any other person in the world attempting to know you can do so only over a long and uninterrupted period of time.

UNIQUE — You are one of a kind. You combine your physical, intellectual, and emotional attributes in a way that has never existed before, does not exist anywhere else, and will never exist again. You will never meet someone and say to yourself, "She is me."

PRECIOUS — You are valuable and irreplaceable. You *are* God's gift to the world. You are worth infinitely more than any single diamond or all the diamonds put together. An understanding of your awesome dignity as a woman is prerequisite to designing your style, and no other foundation is worthy of consideration.

you're a woman

Pretty early on in your life you realized that your body is different from a man's. And no, you're not weird for noticing. This difference has fascinated, inspired, and even frightened people since we ran to gather the fig leaves. Men are attracted to this body, children cling to it, artists replicate it, poets admire it, society reinvents it (in vain), and clothiers cover it. Your body, by original design, is miraculously durable and efficient, aesthetically appealing, potentially life-giving, comforting, and nurturing. Yes, men love your curves. They love them because they speak about life and love.

> *You don't have to show your breasts to be radical. Just having them is radical enough.*
>
> PATTY FRANCOMACARO

Because your body is so much about life and love, it is closely tied to the love you give from your heart. True love is a gift of your *self* to another.

This gift is multifaceted, unique, and precious; it's not a cheap gift. Naturally, you tend to carefully select the people to whom you give of yourself, because in any kind of relationship, we give a little away (and even *a little* is precious).

Each relationship (professional, casual, friendly, familial, and intimate) provides its own level of give and take. So, in the most superficial of these you are barely affected because you give very little away. (You don't love what you don't know.) For the most part, you are unmarked and unchanged.

A sexual relationship affects you in a far more pervasive way because you give your most intimate self. So if you are still wired the way you began, you are given in a wholly emotional way in response to that kind of give and take. (*Sex and the Single Girl* never really got into this stuff.)

How in the world is this related to your style? Dressing for success for your whole life means dressing with the confident knowledge of your *true value*. If we cannot take our sexuality for granted, our style shouldn't either. Our style is about who we are and the kinds of relationships we have. If we shouldn't give ourselves sexually to just anyone, our style must facilitate this. This quality, that is, the refinement that protects our sexuality from the eyes and minds of just anybody, is called *modesty*.

Try not to conjure up the image of a character from *Little House on the Prairie*! Modesty isn't retro. It isn't weird or even self-denying. It is a positive paradigm for fashion choices; not a strain of fashion removed from the mainstream.

It blends. It's real and works for real women and promotes our material well being as well as (and even more importantly) our dignity.[1] It can be fashion-forward and will work in anyone's personal style – even the trendiest.

Sometimes modesty isn't appreciated until it's completely dismissed. Lots of people are wondering why our girls feel so physically inadequate, vulnerable, and on display. They shouldn't wonder too long: it's painfully obvious. Marilyn Monroe pinned it down when she said (two years before she died), "I sometimes feel as if I'm too exposed; I've given myself away, the whole part of me, every part, and there's nothing left that's private, just me alone."[2]

Modesty is a quality that helps us to respect ourselves, respect others, and help others to respect us. It also helps to simplify our lives by allowing us to fulfill our *whole* person on our own terms.

not just any woman

On top of it all, you are profoundly different from any other woman. You have specific tangible and intangible attributes that set a tone for how you present yourself to the world. This affects personal style, and in turn your unique demands for fashion. You are not just *any* woman.

style, not fashion

And so we turn to the fashion world. As a friend of mine once said, "There's the fashion world, and then there's the real world." The two have always had a love-hate relationship, each not knowing what to make of the other. It's best to spend some time peeling away the layers of the fashion world so we can see how it applies to the real one.

That same woman told me that if she ever met a fashion designer, she'd probably curtsey. Well, that kind of sums it up, doesn't it? The world has ranked all fashion authority somewhere between the archangels and Moses. It's kind of obscene. There's a long history to this that's tied up with the population's desire to mimic the aristocracy, and the aristocracy's desire to distinguish itself from the rank and file. Business historian Dwight E. Robinson observed way back in the 1950s that it seems "better for the lady of fashion to look like a freak than to be mistaken for her grocer's wife dolled up in a cheap version of something she herself sported a year or two ago."[3] That, in a nutshell, describes the human vice which has traditionally driven fashion in all times and in all cultures.

haute stuff

Haute couture (the high fashion we really place up there) was originally the design and production of handmade clothing for a great number of well-heeled clients, especially before World War II. Nowadays, it involves only a tiny number of buyers, and as in times past only the most exclusive of designers sell to them at their houses, without those pesky retailers in between. This fashion is presented semi-annually in Paris by designers who have been chosen by the *Chambre Syndicale de la Couture Parisienne* and is that flamboyant spectacle which produces all the strong feelings out there toward the industry. Truthfully, these shows have become more about art and publicity than a real woman's specifications. (That goes without saying!) But the serious *haute couture* does provide the highest quality, most breathtaking handmade ensembles out there in the fashion universe. Not surprisingly, it serves a shrinking clientele of less than two thousand women, as one item of clothing can run into the tens of thousands of dollars.[4] This fashion world is not the real world's fashion.

> *I always think the best way to dress is when the person notices you first and the dress after.*
>
> OSCAR DE LA RENTA

The next level of fashion is much more profitable for fashion houses and has a range from the exclusive designer name "collections" to their spin-off or diffusion lines. *Prêt-a-porter* (French for "ready-to-wear") clothing claims an international set of names that includes some designers who are known for their *haute couture*. (Some fashion sources will refer to the highest levels of *prêt-a-porter* as *haute couture*.) Although its most exclusive items are not technically "mass" produced, they are also not as elusive as Parisian *haute couture*. Most *prêt-a-porter* is firmly identified with the brand name of its respective designer and became popular with the younger consumers of the 1960s, when *haute couture* was considered to be a bit stuffy and unreasonably expensive.

The most successful fashion designers may work for the best fashion houses but often become known for their own lines. You can imagine the fast-paced movement of these guys (mostly) amongst the houses, as talent, egos, and combustible temperments are never in short supply. (This, and a little greed, also explains why fashion houses continually buy each other up – or out – like banks.) As designer names have become icons throughout our global society, even the poorest of rural Thailand can recognize the logos of some of the most pervasive brands.

fashion designer fact sheet

Once you discuss such things as *haute couture* and *prêt-a-porter* fashion, all those iconic names begin to follow like vocabulary words in a high school French class. Below is a guide to fifteen famous designers, some of whom founded fashion houses. I have chosen them because their names have consistently buzzed along in the history of later-twentieth and early twenty-first century fashion. Even many who try to ignore the fashion industry could easily have heard any one of these names. This list is not intended to represent the complete or current listing of *haute couture* fashion houses or *prêt-a-porter* lines. You will recognize most names from contemporary fashion magazines. [5]

CALVIN KLEIN
Founded: 1968 by Calvin Klein
Home: New York, *prêt-a-porter*
Best known for: Minimal, urban fashion using natural fabrics; blue jeans ("designer") of the 1980s and '90s; also known for several controversial marketing techniques.

CHANEL
Pronounced: SHA nell
Founded: 1913 by Gabrielle (CoCo) Chanel
Home: Paris, contemporary *haute couture*
Best known for: Its mother, Coco, who brought practicality to women's fashion and softened men's suiting for women's attire; also known for the "Chanel suit" and the popularization of the little black dress; Karl Lagerfeld revived the house in the 1980s.

CHRISTIAN DIOR
Pronounced: KRIS tee ahn Dee OR
Founded: 1946 by Christian Dior
Home: Paris, contemporary *haute couture*
Best known for: The "New Look" of the late 1940s; Dior was also the first to earn royalties in "licensing" (1948).

CHRISTIAN LACROIX
Pronounced: KRIS tee ahn La CWAH
Founded: 1987 by Christian Lacroix
Home: Paris, contemporary *haute couture*
Best known for: Opulent, extravagant evening and wedding dresses; sometimes called "baroque;" also known for his early work at Hermés.

DONNA KARAN

Founded: 1985 by Donna Karan; DKNY (diffusion line) in 1988

Home: New York, *prêt-a-porter*

Best known for: Comfortable career wear in somber colors; also known as an innovator for "bridge fashion" sold in department stores.

GIORGIO ARMANI

Pronounced: Jor GEE oh Ahr MAH nee

Founded: 1975 by Giorgio Armani as Giorgio Armani SpA

Home: Milan, *prêt-a-porter*

Best known for: Relaxed and modernized suits for men and women; considered a "trail blazer" for designers such as Donna Karan and Calvin Klein; also famous for its legendary brand placement in the movie *American Gigolo*.

GIVENCHY

Pronounced: GEE vahn SHEE

Founded: 1952 by Hubert Givenchy

Home: Paris, contemporary *haute couture*

Best known for: Creations for Audrey Hepburn; also known for glamorous evening wear.

GUCCI

Pronounced: GOO chee

Founded: 1921 by Guccio Gucci

Home: Florence, Italy, *prêt-a-porter*

Best known for: Shoes and bags, especially the iconic bamboo handle handbag; also known for his son Aldo's creation, the interlocking double-g logo; name is synonymous with "upscale" items not related to fashion.

JEAN-PAUL GAULTIER

Pronounced: Shawn Poll Go-tee-ay

Founded: 1976 by Jean-Paul Gaultier

Home: Paris, contemporary *haute couture*

Best known for: Sexual ambiguity in fashion and outrageous costuming for entertainers; known as *enfant terrible* in his town; also famous for his conical shaped bustier for pop star Madonna and underwear as outerwear.

OSCAR DE LA RENTA

Pronounced: Oskar de la RENta

Founded: 1965 by Oscar de La Renta

Home: Originally from the Dominican Republic and was first North American designer to be taken into Parisian *haute couture* (House of Lanvin and Balenciaga); New York, *prêt-a-porter*

Best known for: Feminine and elegant apparel, particularly evening gowns fashioned from the best materials and in an exciting array of colors and textures; also known for dressing the First Ladies and many in entertainment.

PIERRE CARDIN

Pronounced: Pee AIR Kar DEH

Founded: 1950 by Pierre Cardin

Home: Paris (was expelled from the *Chambre Syndicale*); first to show *prêt-a-porter* in 1959

Best known for: 1960s futuristic looks, unisex styles, and innovative use of materials; over-licensing during the 1970s and 1980s made him a study in how to cheapen a brand.

RALPH LAUREN
Pronounced: Ralf LAW ren
Founded: 1967 as Polo by Ralph Lauren (formerly Ralph Lifshitz)
Home: New York, *prêt-a-porter*
Best known for: Status dressing for the 1970s and '80s; also known for successful "lifestyle" merchandising; first to use ads which tell a story.

VALENTINO
Pronounced: Vah len TEE no
Founded: 1960 by Valentino Garavani
Home: Rome, *prêt-a-porter*
Best known for: Extravagant designs, feminine silhouettes, and his "Valentino Red;" known as "Master of the Dress."

VERSACE
Pronounced: Ver SAHCH ay
Founded: 1978 by Gianni Versace
Home: Milan, Italy, *prêt-a-porter*
Best known for: Innovative fabrics, bold colors, sexual allure, and ostentation; also known for designs by Gianni's younger sister, Donatella, and her association with popular musicians.

YVES SAINT LAURENT
Pronounced: EEV Sahn Lo Rahn
Founded: 1962 by Yves Saint Laurent
Home: Paris, *haute couture*; now part of the Gucci group
Best known for: His early work as head of Christian Dior; an influence of fine art, unorthodox combinations of color, and man-tailored styles for women; also known for introducing his pant suit "le smoking" (tuxedo).

back to earth

Most women (those in the real world) buy mass-produced clothing (often called "ready-to-wear," "off-the-rack," or "off-the-peg"). This clothing is manufactured into standardized sizes of varying price and quality, and sold at all levels of retail.[6] Although the styles are not comparable to *haute couture* ensembles, ready-to-wear is influenced by them to a certain degree. (They are influenced more so by the higher levels of *prêt-a-porter* because of their greater visibility.) It's a trickle down kind of fashion, although there is also a trickling up as "bottom-up" or "bubbling up" inspiration is a major theme in the fashion world.[7] It's almost like the cycles of precipitation: Evaporation from the lakes makes clouds, and the clouds rain down something. In fashion, the *something* that rains (or reigns) down may or may not help the vegetation. This mass-produced fashion is the fashion over which you have an influence with your tastes as a woman and your behavior as a consumer.

> *Everything a woman wears sends a message.*
>
> JOHN T. MALLOY

I enjoy tracking the fashion world. This is why when I open a current issue of some fashion magazines I can become a little baffled by some of the extremes that ruin the wonder of it all. For example, a few years ago I read an article in *Vogue* in which the editor had labelled a new collection of *haute couture* as "misogynous." (Sadly enough, I discovered the meaning of this word only after I began reading fashion commentaries.) The outfits – costumes really – were things I honestly could never describe to anyone under eighteen years of age.

Outrageous displays like these are common, and they inspire one to think that there is a serious disconnection between some fashion producers and normal consumers like you and me. The fashion designer Christian Dior once said that "no fashion is a success unless it is used as a form of seduction." What I'd like to know is exactly who is being seduced, what they are being seduced to do, and why they need to be seduced in the first place. I understand that fashion needs passion, and Mr. Dior was probably just trying to convey his love for the art. (I like to give the benefit of the doubt.) But if there is a conscious decision on the part of the makers of fashion to do anything like seduction, I want to know how this could be good for my career or relationships. I am, after all, the one wearing the clothes.

clear as a belle

In a perfect world, fashion would serve women. Fashion would celebrate a woman's dignity by respecting her sexuality with uplifting clothes, accentuating her attributes with beauty, and affirming her individuality with a greater amount of appropriate choices. Alas, this is not a perfect world, and some runways seem to sport fashions which wear the women rather than the other way around. So, we each have to become more reflective and more selective in our fashion choices.

God has given you minds, dear girls, as well as bodies.

ELIZABETH CADY STANTON

Personal style is a language. It communicates our attitudes, aspirations, life experiences, and sense of self worth. We can tell an employer that we respect the workplace in our impeccably clean and tasteful outfit or that we couldn't care any less in a pair of ripped jeans. We can say to our loved ones "I care about you" with our most attractive face or be in their faces with that "crazy lady in the attic" look. (You know, the one in the mirror first thing in the morning!)

No matter what angle you take, your style says a lot about who you are, where you are now, and where you are headed.

your style should lead to your face

If style is a language, then good grammar means clear and concise communication with the way your clothes, accessories, and makeup lead to your face. Your face, especially your eyes, communicates the important things about you: *your* dignity, *your* intelligence, *your* attitudes, *your* talents, *your* feelings, *your* beliefs, *your* reactions, *your* loves, and *your* dreams. Your eyes are the windows to your soul. Those who look at you should be focused on this area without impediments or distractions because clear, direct communication helps to cultivate mutually respectful relationships. Your face should be the *focal point* of your style.

A lot of fashion on the market does not lead to the face. We can all picture the blouse that is two parts flesh and one part fabric (focal point: breasts), and I've been feeling pelted by belly buttons for the last half decade (focal point: belly button). One reason these fashions don't work for a woman is that they move the focal point down to places other than the face and eyes. Let's face it: we've been taught in recent years that we should demand to be taken as more than "great set of breasts" or "a skirt." Of course, the average woman of the past always knew that she was infinitely greater than the sum of her parts (each part being wonderfully awesome), but now she can affirm and celebrate it in both her personal and professional life.

> ***Am I imagining this, or are people now looking into my eyes more often?***
>
> **FASHION CONSULTING CLIENT**

a funny thing happened on the way to the clothing rack

a little history

We couldn't always affirm and celebrate our womanhood with fashion. Let's put fashion into its place for a moment. If you really want a good laugh, read a history of fashion.[8] It has a way of helping us look at the current trends with a detached and informed perspective. For example, my colleague Jeannette Kendall and I love to peruse a certain book from her days at FIT in NYC. We'll get to belly-laughing at how seriously she took the fashions of the 1970s and how we both wouldn't be caught at a dog fight in some of these things.

Despite the almost fairytale-like creations of Charles Frederick Worth, the first fashion designer in the fullest sense, there wasn't that much affirmation or celebration happening in the late nineteenth century. After all, women were too busy sitting up straight to keep their corsets from piercing their lungs. Sure, many of these dresses were breathtaking in their craftsmanship and beauty, but very uncomfortable throngs of women were tying up their abdominal organs in whale bone and padding their breasts and buttocks according to someone's tyrannical S-shape ideal. (To be fair, the ideal may have been promulgated by Worth's designs, but they started with women themselves.) That gets you thinking when you see the same S-shape on those Hollywood profiles which tout enhanced and lifted breasts atop painfully slim waists and cupped buttocks.

Sometime between then and now a lot of change took place not only in the fashion world but also in the mind of the consumer. (Remember, they tend to work together: fashions are either rejected as duds or accepted to become trends by the consumer.) We all know that Paul Poiret and CoCo Chanel came along with their smart designs and liberated the last of the Victorians to a life of elegant, comfortable, and *realistic* dressing. (Never, however, place these two names together as allies.) Chanel was a powerhouse of insight to the practical considerations of a woman's to-do list (which was rarely factored into women's fashion). As a matter of fact, the bra as we know it now (more or less) wasn't a staple of a woman's wardrobe until the late nineteenth century. Even still, it didn't become a widespread phenomenon until the early part of the next century, after a fourteen-year-old New Yorker named Mary Phelps Jacobs fashioned two hankies together. (Can't you just picture her rolling her eyes at all those primitive undergarments?) She sold her patent to Warner Brothers Corset Company for $1,500, and the rest is history.

The 1920s came roaring in with revolutionary fashion due in part to the postwar experience of the urban working woman (work in places other than factories) and the exuberant economics of the decade. My grandmother from Brooklyn scandalously shortened her hem, cut her hair, and went to work against the wishes of her immigrant mother. She was a phenomenon of her own time without really understanding it. The silhouette of her dress loosened, straightening out to an athletic shape, and it lost nearly all prewar embellishment. This is the era we can thank for extinguishing the floor-length skirt and admonish for its attempts at androgyny.

> *The strict bodily standards set by the supermodels and top Hollywood stars dictate that no woman is supposed to weigh more than her lipstick.*
>
> DAVE BARRY

Not long after this, Hollywood began to influence fashion designs and marketing. The introduction of trousers, fashionable hairstyling, glamorous accessories, and all that jazz was wafted onto the public with the mystique of a voodoo spell. (Remember Katherine Hepburn and her sassy pants?) To this day we can find celebrity pages in the midst of fashion magazines, and a reader can see who was wearing what with whom and where. (Although now, admittedly, *mystique* is often not the appropriate descriptor.)

World War II erupted and a somber minimalism invaded women's closets. This, of course, was due mostly to the constraints of wartime, but also to the duties many women were facing while their menfolk were off fighting. Fabric colors faded, styles militarized, and the handbag enlarged to meet the needs of a woman with a lot on her mind. Eventually, the winds of war subsided, and Paris began to ride the softer breezes.

In 1947, Christian Dior gave an extravagant answer to the dowdiness of the war years. What became known as the *New Look*, a sumptuously feminine ensemble which revolutionized not only that year's fashion scene but the entire fashion market for years to come, won its status as the ideal in the imaginations of American women from all walks of life. The silhouette of the moment was an hourglass created by a prominent bosom and a plethora of fabric in the skirt, and it reflected an ideal of woman that was feminine and sophisticated if not very modern by our standards today. (It really wasn't a *new* look, if you want to get technical.) The American consumer was charmed by this image in a way that was fueled by a more materialistic approach to traditional women's roles and an ever-expanding media. The *New Look*, however, met its demise only after it met its extremes: sweater girls consigned their pointed brassieres, the red lipstick faded, hemlines migrated north, and the stage was set for the 1960s.

The beginning of the 1960s saw the likes of Audrey and Jackie, but by the end Mary Quant's mini-skirt had successfully infiltrated even elementary schools. As with all other trends in fashion, the tastes and beliefs of the consumer were such that even radical fashion could become accepted as mainstream – at least incrementally. We all know of the social changes of the 1960s, particularly the shifts in views of the role of women and the meaning of sexuality. If fashion is a language, it's going to communicate what's happening in the mind of the wearer.

A few fashion observers – especially the former consumers of 1970s fashion – like to claim that the 1970s were just kind of a "rotting of the 1960s," but that's a bit unfair. The 1970s brought out some beautiful silhouettes, a kind of functional simplicity, and strong egalitarian themes. Folk art revived (it had a bit of a run during the 1920s) then waned as the disco scene glittered on the runways.

So along came the 1980s with its bigger hair but *dress-for-success* attitude, and it again reflected the politics, economics, and general social scene of the times. In fact, James Laver, a well known fashion historian, painstakingly detailed the recurring cycles of fashion in response to social change, suggesting that there is even a link between fashion and architecture.[9] (That's a fun theory to reflect on.)

As a tidy example, many fashion historians often blame the huge shoulder pads, extravagant accessories, and bold colors of 1980s fashion on the relative health of the economy. More recently, workout apparel could only have been introduced if consumers had a little extra time on their hands to actually *work out* and a little extra cash in their pockets to invest in such a specialized wardrobe. Nowadays, you can see workout apparel even when people aren't actually exercising. That, incidentally, is thanks to the economics, politics, and social scene of the 1990s and early twenty-first century. But we'll revisit the ups and downs of casual style later.

Having said all that about politics, economics, and social landscape, it's actually not quite that cut and dry. (Sorry to mislead you.) There are two deeper principles of fashion that also have remained intact since humans began to fashion wooly mammoth furs together:

1. FASHION IS NOT THE PRODUCT OF REASON. Four inch heels make no sense for anyone's feet. However, we all know that there is just *something* about legs that end with spikes.

2. THAT "SOMETHING" IN FASHION IS A CONNOTATION WHICH DEVELOPS FROM A CULTURE'S AESTHETICS, MORES, AND MOOD. Just to keep us all on our toes, the something of now will be the something *else* of tomorrow. James Laver's explanation for this is now famous: "The same dress is indecent ten years before its time; daring one year before its time; chic (contemporarily seductive) in its time; dowdy five years after its time; hideous twenty years after its time; amusing thirty years after its time; romantic one hundred years after its time; beautiful one hundred and fifty years after its time."[10]

So you see? Fashion is not an exact science. I can talk about great, practical fashion for women, but I know that there will *always* be freaks on both the cutting edge of fashion and scattered behind it (sometimes like casualties on a battlefield). More importantly, the great, practical fashion of the moment will one day be considered the freak.

SEMINAR FAQ
getting used to it

QUESTION: Isn't fashion a lot about becoming accustomed to a look? If we all see something often, even if it is radical, don't we just get used to it so that it doesn't seem so radical anymore?

ANSWER: Yes. We humans do grow accustomed to things. That's why fashion changes so often. Fashion of the moment is replaced by a new fashion for the next moment once anyone becomes bored.

For example, most of us (not *all* of us) will get used to seeing bare belly buttons to a certain extent. But fashion ensures that by the time this happens, the style will change so that belly buttons aren't incorporated in exactly the same way. Nipple enhancers, deeply cut cleavage, cut-out strappy back styles, and painted on jeans are not designed for us to "get used to," but give a little shock value to a look (sometimes called "shifting erogenous zones" by people who are concerned with this subject). Essentially, those fashions exist as focal points to compete with your face and are not created by fashion designers as part of a vast conspiracy to get everyone naked. They'd be out of a job if that ever happened!

It's true that knees, or calves, or even ankles were once thought sexually provocative, but we've gotten used to seeing them. In the whole scheme of things, however, ankles are only artificially provocative. They have little to do with our sexuality. (One can make anything provocative by playing prudery against baseness.) True, some women's skirt fashion has a lot of upper thigh exposure today, but the shock value has never *really* worn off after over thirty years of thighs, thighs and more thighs. Just listen to men talk. If they aren't commenting on a passer-by's exposed upper thighs, the thighs are probably unattractive. (Or the guys are gentlemen.) Once they begin to talk about unattractive upper thighs, then it's a really sad situation. Guarding your privacy prevents a lot of mistreatment and misunderstanding. Whether a woman is naturally good-looking or not, a lack of modesty can reduce her to an object rather than a person.

your moment in history

So here's where you come in: Nowadays, the consumer determines with her purchasing power which fashions become trends. (Remember, that wasn't always the case.) You are the consumer. You have the power to reject or accept things on the market. You have the power to determine what becomes a trend.

In her book, *The End of Fashion*, Teri Agins suggests that from the late 1980s onward the fashion market had to respond to the demands of the consumer to survive. No longer do fashion houses hold absolute power to dictate what's fashionable. (They will always, of course, try. That's why they are there.) The new consumer demands practical and comfortable clothing, and the market, to a certain extent, has responded to this.[11] That's a relief.

But it doesn't stop there. You are more than a consumer. Remember, you are primarily a woman with all that this means. Demand what you need from fashion. Approach the market with *you* in mind by picking and choosing pieces that are acceptable to *you*.

Fortunately, the current market also has an extremely vast array of options. You not only have a great number of items from which to choose, but you have room to determine which colors to choose, where to hang your hemline, how to wear your hair (with or without a hat), or in what way to put it all together. In some ways, the market is an exciting place filled with options that can help you affirm and celebrate who you are. We have it so much better than our mothers, grandmothers, or great-grandmothers, who faced many dictates for fashion that were unreasonable, unhealthy, and often unflattering.

So, what do we do with this wonderful situation? We mess it up! Figuring out personally appropriate choices in the market seems to be the root of our fashion problems. The next three chapters will remedy that for you.

STYLE PROFILE #4
speak up!

There are two angles you must consider when studying your style:

What you *currently* convey with your style.

What you *wish* to convey with your style.

Reflect for a moment: *What is it you currently convey with your style? What story do you tell about your life, your attitudes, and your sense of self?* Think about it for a moment. Then, write what you think you currently communicate with your style below.

What I communicate with my style:

____

____

People have described my style as:

____

____

Secondly, consider what you *wish* to convey with your style. *Is it what you currently convey? What story do want to tell about your life, your attitudes, and your sense of self?* Think about it for a moment. Then, write what you wish to communicate with your style below.

What I wish to communicate with my style:

____

____

The greater the disparity between your two answers, the more important it is for you to focus on getting your style to work for you. That is the objective of this book.

On the other hand, if your answers to both questions are the same, you have one very critical issue behind you: communicating with your fashion what you want to communicate.

CHAPTER TWO

the elements of style
body type

what a simple solution!

Almost everyone has some little trick or time-tested solution to an everyday problem. My mother-in-law swears by a hard-to-get cleaning agent for her kitchen, bathroom, and laundry, and one of my friends uses an herbal remedy to reduce her chocolate cravings in the morning. (She lost thirty pounds from that one little change in her diet!) Once when I asked my husband what his field of accounting really involved, he said, "The only thing you really need to know is that debits are on the left and credits are on the right. That'll get you through."

I invent nothing. I rediscover.

AUGUSTE RODIN

The credits and debits of your style are based upon your *elements of style*. Once you know these – how they work specifically for you – you'll have the look you want. It's such a simple secret of the trade!

Obviously, there's a lot more to accounting than where to enter things into the ledger, and if you don't develop the discipline to stick with the *Generally Accepted Accounting Principles*, your business venture is in for ruin or you for criminal indictment!

Fortunately, the *elements of style* really work as simply as they sound. Knowing yours will mean the difference between successful style and style that's, frankly, *criminal.*

I just met a girl named Maria

Remember Maria? Remember the changes?

Well, just about every improvement in Maria's presentation can be traced to her *elements of style:*

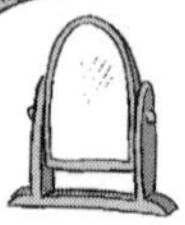

1. **BODY TYPE** (streamlined and neat silhouette)
2. **FASHION PERSONALITY** (consistent, current, and refined styling, personal and professional confidence, niche in the fashion world, and that *something*)
3. **COLOR PALETTE** (healthy glow because garment colors flatter)

Maria's peace and joy come from the knowledge that she's communicating what she wants without having to spend a fortune.

This chapter and the next two are loaded with work for you. I suggest you read them while you are able to get to the clothing you own now. That's right: you will be closet-cleaning in the sections entitled *Fashion Moment of Truth.*

You will need (for this chapter and the next two):

1. a pencil
2. a flexible measuring tape like the kind used for sewing (inches)
3. a full-sized mirror
4. this season's wardrobe – all of it!
5. looking ahead to chapter 4, you will have to gather together a large sample of the colors orange and pink. Other colors may be needed, depending upon the results you find in that chapter.

So, roll up your sleeves, turn on the lights, and get ready to change your life!

four great shapes: the first element of style – body type

At a recent event in Chicago, a participant pulled me aside and confided that knowing her body type has made all the difference in her wardrobe. "People are always asking me if I've lost weight. It's so much fun to know that it's only a matter of understanding how to combine color, where to place print, and which way to drape lines. It's great!"

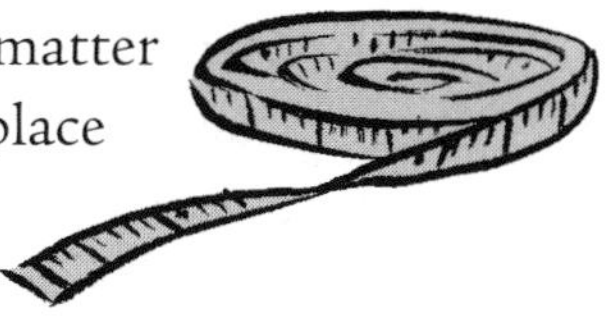

What she mastered was the art of creating an optical illusion of proportion. She hadn't lost any weight, and she hadn't made any huge fashion investments. Suddenly her shape and size weren't issues for her style in the same way they had been before. What a relief it was!

It's a cliché to say that women come in all shapes and sizes. That's certainly a given in this book. It's really not a given in the fashion industry, however. Garments are constructed with a perfectly proportioned body as the guiding standard. There may be plenty of garments in plus sizes, but that only addresses the issue of size. The first element of style has more to do with shape than with size: body type.

Three-tenths of a good appearance is due to nature; seven-tenths to dress.

CHINESE PROVERB

Body type is how all of a woman's parts come together and where she tends to gain weight, rather than an overall amount of body fat. So, even a woman who is a "perfect" size can have plenty of problems finding a garment to fit correctly. She may have even come to accept this as a part of life and just expects that her skirts will pull uncomfortably across her buttocks while her blouses gape ridiculously from her chest.

Fashion consultants generally define four body types. Most use the following shapes to illustrate them: Pear, Heart, Box, and Hourglass.

pear

The pear shape body type is characterized by a proportionately larger bottom in relation to bust and shoulders. A woman with a pear shape may have very large buttocks, very wide hips, or only sloping shoulders which give the illusion of large hips. She could be a size 2, a size 12, or a size 22. Again, this has little to do with overall size and weight, but rather simple proportion. That goes for the other three body types as well.

heart

The heart shape body type is the opposite of the pear shape body type. It is characterized by a proportionately larger top. A woman with a heart shape may have very large breasts or wide shoulders. Generally, she has very small hips and thin legs.

box

The box shape body type is characterized by a similar size for top, middle, and bottom. So, top and bottom are in proportion, but the middle does not draw in to create that curved, proportioned look. A woman who describes herself as "thick-waisted" may have this body type and will complain of "no figure" or a very boyish one. Often, she will have a shorter, thicker neck and a square jaw line.

hourglass

The hourglass shape body type is characterized by proportion. The top and bottom are relatively similar in size, and the waist has a significantly smaller measurement. It's important to note that most women have pear shaped body types, so the hourglass proportions are not necessarily more natural. This shape happens to be the preferred fashion of the moment. There have been other times in history which placed a higher aesthetical value on one of the other shapes (box in the 1920s, heart in the 1950s), and many cultures view a woman's ideal shape differently. Today the garment industry uses dress forms with hourglass proportions. These proportions have become a standard for which many women with other body types long but can never successfully achieve. We cannot diet to change a shape; dieting only helps us to lose weight.

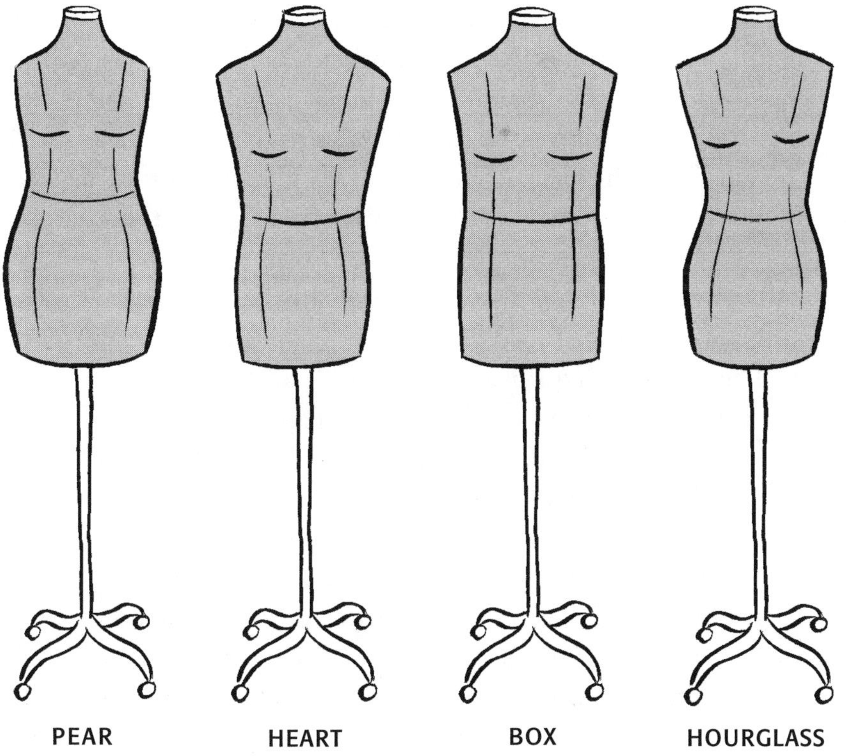

In fact, we each gain or lose weight according to our body type. A woman with a pear shape will gain in her hips but lose on top, while a woman with a box body type will typically add weight to her waist.

Body type usually never changes unless a woman is:

- in any stage of pregnancy
- postpartum
- breast feeding
- menopausal

So, for example, in the early part of pregnancy or during the few months after having a baby, a woman with an hourglass figure can find herself with box-like measurements. Another woman with an hourglass body type may temporarily have a heart shape. Some women find that their weight-gaining patterns change radically with the onset of menopause, and many women who are far past menopause may find that their body types have become exaggerated over time.

> *There is no excellent beauty that hath not some strangeness in the proportion.*
>
> FRANCIS BACON

After I gave birth to my twins, I foolishly believed that I had simultaneously changed into all four body types at one time. (Even after all my training!) Admittedly, my thinking may have been due to wacky hormones, but it sure did give me a scare.

Normally, I have a borderline hourglass-box body type. After my other pregnancies, I would just become a more exaggerated box with perhaps a brief flirtation as a heart. This time, however, my first visit to a dressing room put my imagination into overdrive.

It started with a sweater. I looked so top heavy that I didn't recognize myself: "Sure, I'm a heart for a while. That makes sense." While turning to retrieve another sweater, I spotted my bottom: "Good heavens! Where did all *that* come from? I guess I'm a pear . . . too. No wait! There's that familiar belly. What's happened to me?"

Later (but not too much later, thank goodness) I recognized that I had not changed body types, but that the body type I always had went up in size. All of me was bigger, but my waistline kept pace and was still in the same proportion.

OBJECTIVE: determine your body type and learn the related strategies so that you can design a wardrobe that creates the illusion of proportion.

STYLE PROFILE #5

go figure

Find out which body type you have. Numbers never lie, so to get yours find a flexible measuring tape in inches. It is best to do this in your underwear, but if you are fully clothed, which I suspect you are, be sure to remove anything really bulky like a jacket or sweater. Do this procedure standing up and in front of a mirror.

1. Using the inches side, begin by measuring your bust. Hold the tape with both hands and loop around your back, meeting again in front so that you can see the numbers. Ensure that the tape doesn't twist or slip and do not pull tightly. (The tape should remain parallel to the floor.) Note the measurement at the largest point on your breasts. Write the number below:

   Bust measurement: ______ inches

2. Next, wrap the tape around your waist. A good place to measure is the fleshy space between the bottom of your rib cage and the top of your hip bone where women traditionally wear a belt. The tape should be snug but not tight and should remain parallel to the floor. Note the measurement.

   Waist measurement: ______ inches

3. Finally, wrap the tape around the largest part of your buttocks. For some, the largest point may be slightly below the buttocks. Again, ensure that the tape remains parallel to the floor.

Hip measurement: ______ inches

surgeon? magician? genius?

Okay, so you know the numbers. So what?

Well, before you identify your body type, keep in mind that you are not doing this activity simply to confirm your suspicions and wallow in your self-pity. I am not sadistic: there is a method to this madness.

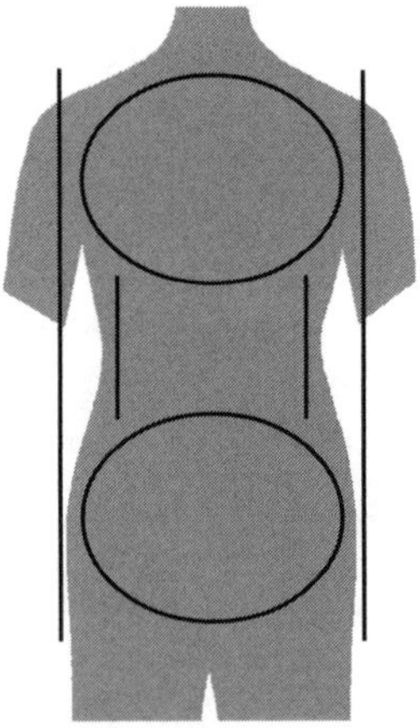

You are going to use color, line, print, pattern, and texture in your wardrobe to create the optical illusion of proportion. An optical illusion is only the *appearance* of an object or area that is receding, disappearing, moving, enlarging, or appearing from nowhere.

Proportion in a woman's figure creates a silhouette that is actually rather unremarkable. No particular part of the body is noticeable and lines are even and balanced. This proportion is just another way to make your face the focal point.

Women with an hourglass shape have proportion. Women with other body types will just have to work a little magic. Fashion gurus and other visual artists use these basic strategies for creating optical illusions.

1. **COLOR:** Dark colors recede or slenderize; light colors add the appearance of greater size or weight.

2. **LINE:** Vertical and diagonal lines slenderize; horizontal lines add the appearance of greater size or weight.
3. **PRINT:** Any print adds the appearance of greater size because it tricks the eye into seeing movement; the larger the print, the greater the appearance of size.
4. **TEXTURE:** The thicker the fabric or the richer the texture, the more it adds to the appearance of greater size or weight. Fabrics with a shine will also add the appearance of greater size or weight.

So, for each body type, you can manipulate the combinations of color, lines, prints, and textures to achieve the overall appearance of proportion. Now, let's figure out what your body type is.

figure it out!

Look at the three measurements and compare the numbers to each other. Read through these directions step by step. Do not skip down to the body type you think you have. *Note: You are only one body type. If you have a pear shape or heart shape body type, you do not also have a box or hourglass body type even if the numbers seem to work that way.*

- If your hip measurement is two or more inches greater than your bust measurement, you have a pear shape body type. Turn to page 49 for strategies.
- If your bust measurement is two or more inches greater than your hip measurement, you have a heart shape body type. Turn to page 57 for strategies.
- If your bust and hip measurements are within two inches (even 1 and 7/8 inches!) of each other then you either have a box or hourglass body type. Read on . . .
- If your hips are eight inches or more *greater* than your waist, you have an hourglass body type. Turn to page 70 for strategies.

- If your hips are less than eight inches greater than your waist, you have a box body type. Turn to page 64 for strategies.

Here are some hypothetical measurements:

- Bust = 36, Waist = 30, Hips = 39: She has a pear shape body type.
- Bust = 39, Waist = 31, Hips = 41: She has a pear shape body type too.
- Bust = 40, Waist = 32, Hips = 38: She has a heart shape body type. True, she has only a six inch difference between waist and hips, but her bust measurement in relation to her hip measurement is the determining ratio. Since she probably has a protruding tummy that needs no numbers to prove itself, she may want to choose some strategies to address that as well.
- Bust = 42, Waist = 38, Hips = 42: She has a box shape body type.
- Bust = 42, Waist = 34, Hips = 42: She has an hourglass shape body type.
- How about this one? Bust = 32, Waist = 22, Hips = 33: She has an hourglass shape body type.

be a genius! strategies for the four great shapes

You're going to love this part. You will find magic in these paragraphs, and you will be impressed by the genius of its simplicity. I've incorporated information not only on fabric and color, but also fit, style, cut, and bits of underwear. For simplicity sake, I've also included strategies for choosing a swimsuit, even though I cover that topic in more detail a little later in this chapter. You need not research any other body type but your own, unless, of course, you want to enlighten other women.

One little note of caution: Fashions come, and fashions go. You may be repelled by a suggestion, only to be excited about it the very next season. This list is perennial and is intended to work like a menu rather than a prescription.

strategies for working with the pear body type

GOAL FOR PEAR SHAPE: The challenge for you is to create the optical illusion of proportion by slenderizing the appearance of your bottom and moving an observer's eye upwards toward your face.

use of color for pear shape

Use color to create the illusion of proportion. Dark colors streamline, and light colors emphasize. Wear darker colors on the bottom (skirts, pants, shorts, etc.) and lighter colors on top. For example, you could wear a white top and a pair of navy pants.

use of line, print, and pattern for pear shape

Prints and plaids enlarge. In fact, the larger the print, the larger the appearance of what it's covering. Completely avoid prints and plaids on the bottom. Wear them on top. A floral-pattern blouse, plaid jacket, or ski sweater would be options for you. (*See figure 1.*)

1.

DO

Diagonal and vertical lines streamline. Horizontal lines widen. Avoid diagonal and vertical lines on top. (*See figures 2–4.*)

Remember that lines are also created with seams or details such as piping. The same rules apply to these as well. (*See figures 5–6.*)

2.

DON'T

3.
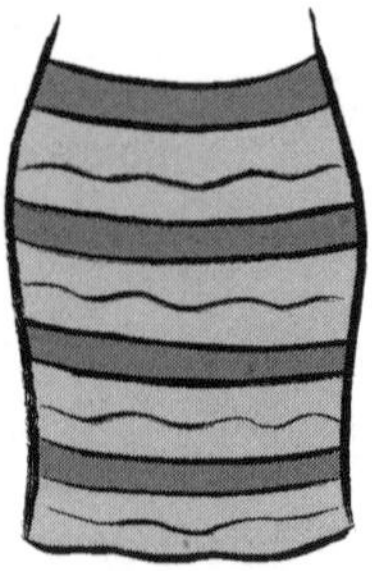
DON'T

use of fabric and texture for pear shape

Fabrics with thicker naps enlarge. Avoid corduroys, velvets, and boucles on the bottom. Wear them on top with confidence.

Shiny fabrics add the appearance of greater size. Use these fabrics for your tops only.

Vests made from thicker fabrics and bright colors are options for adding weight to your top. Also, shrugs, shawls, and ponchos help with overall proportion. Do not choose ponchos if you wear a plus size.

4.
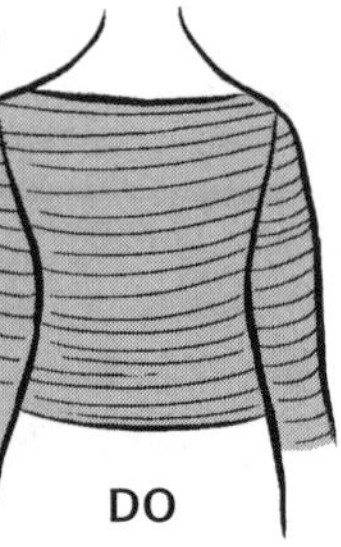
DO

5.

DON'T

6.
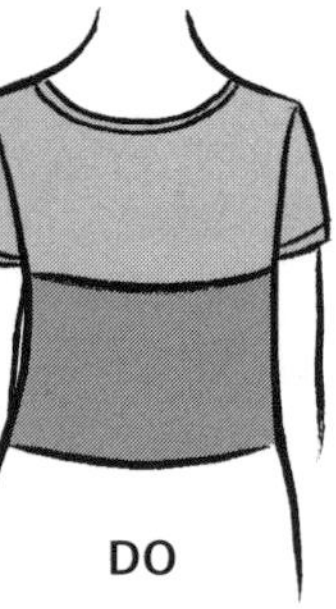
DO

7.
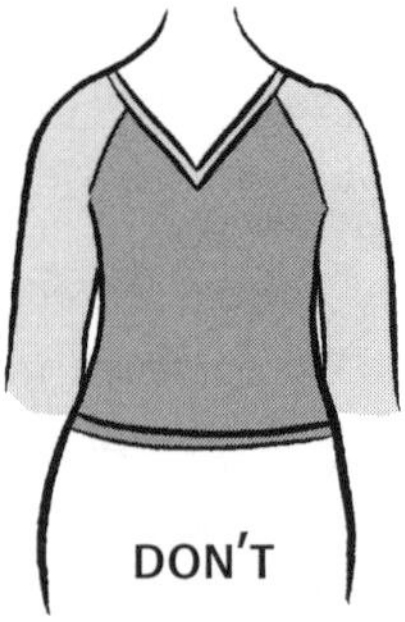
DON'T

tops for pear shape

Avoid sloping shoulders (raglan sleeves) or any kind of droopiness. Also, avoid the diagonal lines created by v-necks. (*See figures 7–9.*)

8.
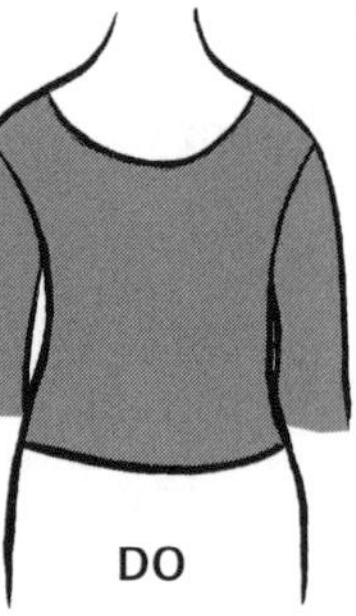
DO

9.

DON'T

10.

NOTCHED

11.

WINGED

12.
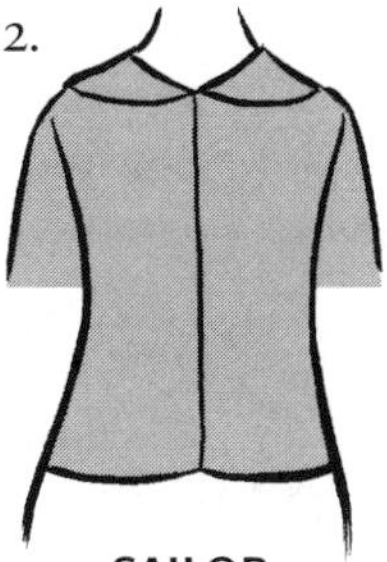
SAILOR

13.

BATEAU

14.
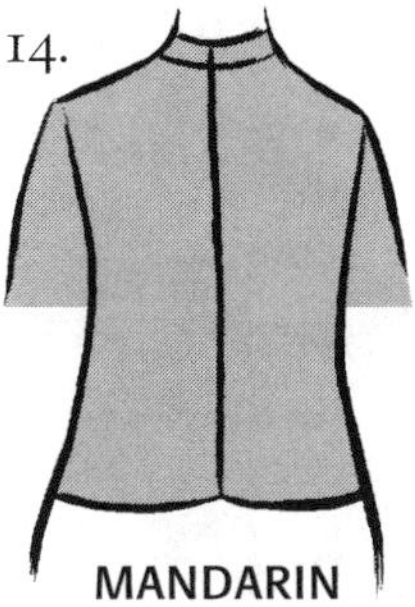
MANDARIN

15.

PORTRAIT

16.

JEWEL

17.
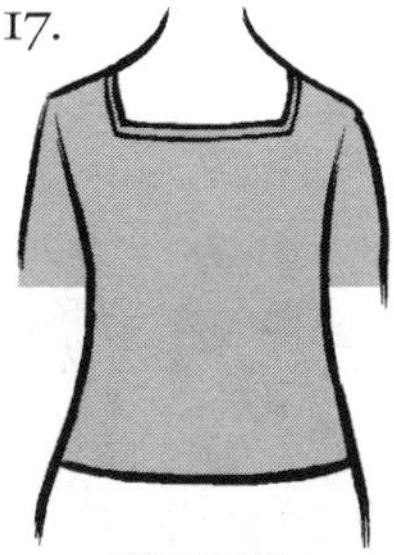
SQUARE

Blouses which provide structure are excellent for you as well. Choose tops with collars, jewel necklines, bateau necklines, mandarin or "Nehru," and portrait necklines. (*See figures 10–17.*)

Add shoulder pads (not mattresses!) to your garments. This will lift the eye upward and add proportion.

Wear a well-made and slightly padded bra. A racer-back bra keeps the straps from falling off sloping shoulders. (*See figure 18.*)

Allow your top to ride slightly over your bottom while wearing jeans. (*See figures 19–20.*)

18.
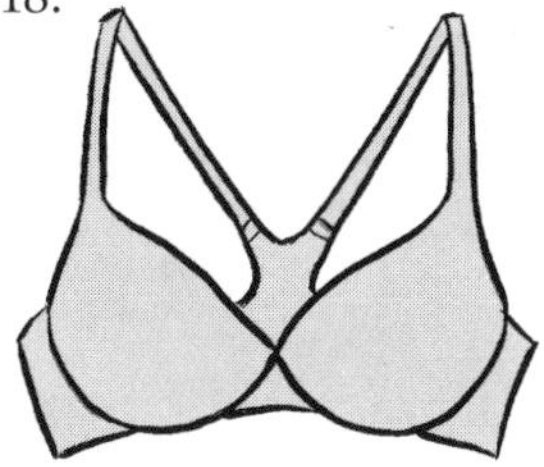

19.

DO

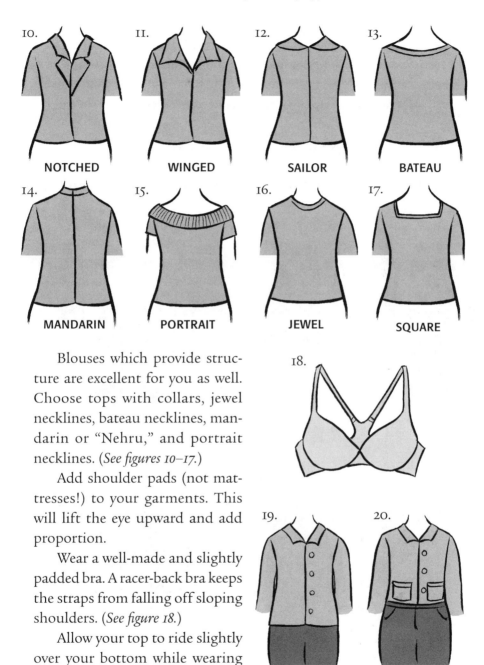

20.

DON'T

skirts for pear shape

Choose pencil (straight), gored, very subtle A-line (allows ease of movement for plus size women, but must be balanced with structure on top), or wrap skirts. By the way, secure wrap skirts so that they don't come apart on you while sitting. This can be a problem for women with pear shape body types. (*See figures 21–26.*)

Avoid the prairie, wide A-line, dirndl, culotte/gaucho, large-pleated, or yoke skirt, especially if you wear a plus size. (*See figures 27–31.*)

DO

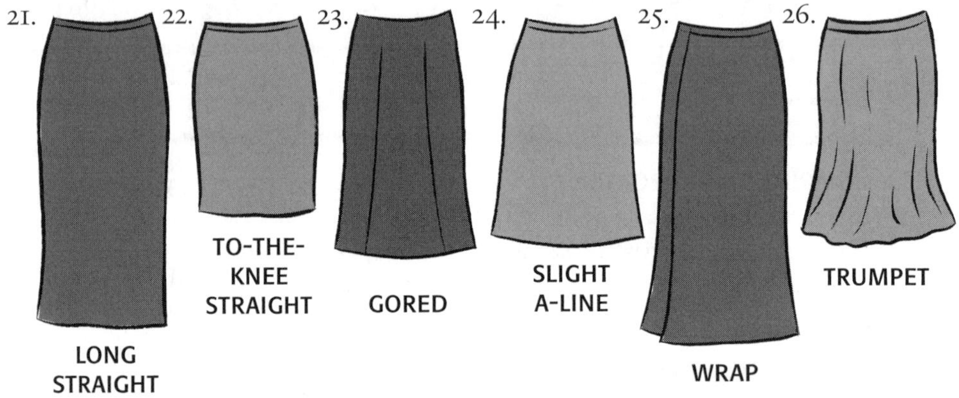

DON'T

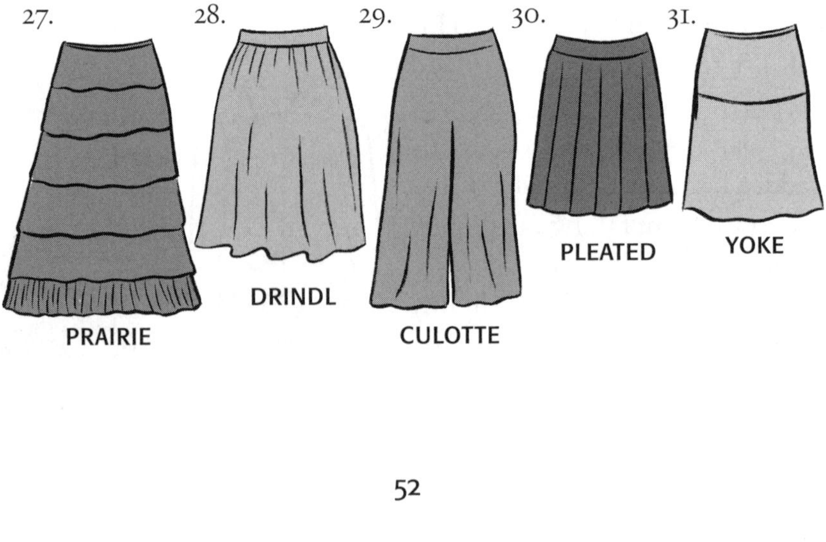

32.

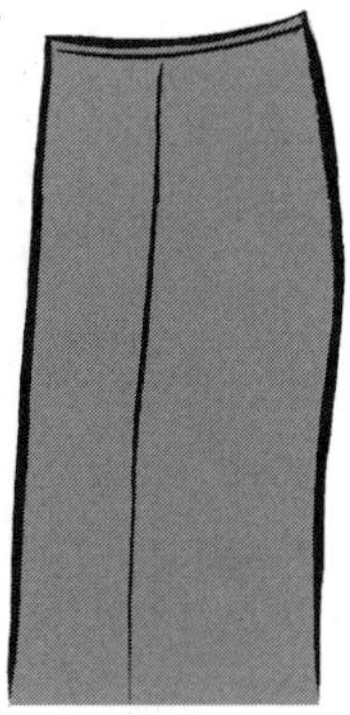

33.

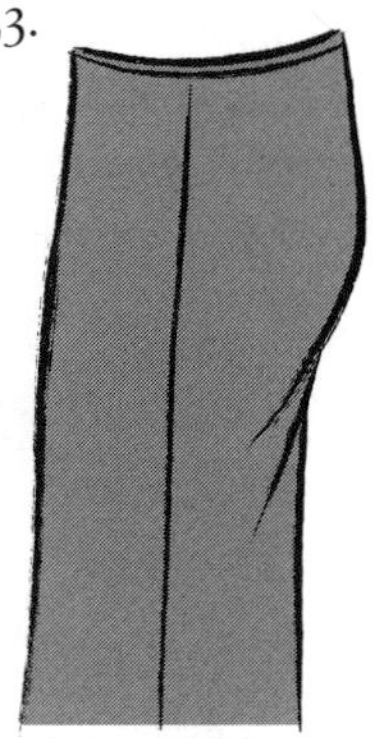

DO DON'T

34.

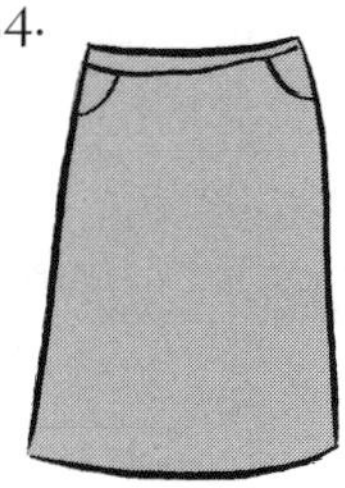

35.

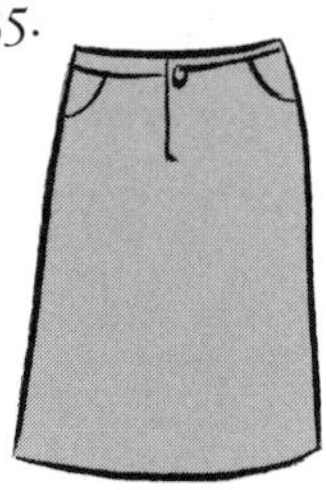

DO DON'T

36.

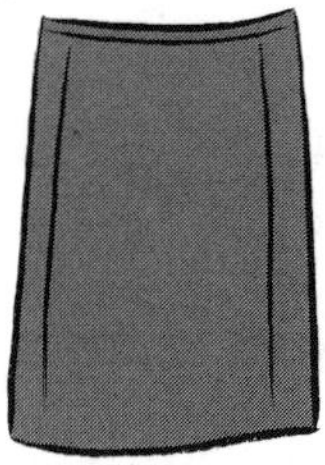

37.

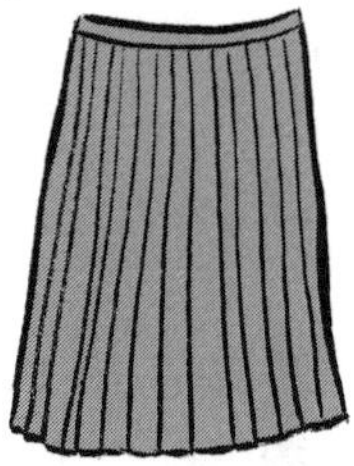

DO DON'T

Make sure that no skirt "cups" under your buttocks. Your silhouette should be even, with no remarkable projections. (*See figures 32–33.*)

Avoid fly fronts, especially on skirts. (*See figures 34–35.*)

Avoid pleats in your skirts because the extra fabric adds weight. (*See figures 36–37.*)

dresses for pear shape

Dresses are difficult to choose because if the bottom fits, the top is probably too large. (This is why suits are such an excellent option.) Choose a coat dress or a shirt dress in a woven fabric, because of the structure on top. (*See figures 38–39.*)

Choose a sheath dress to fit your bottom, but alter the top to fit if necessary. (*See figure 40.*)

38.

39.

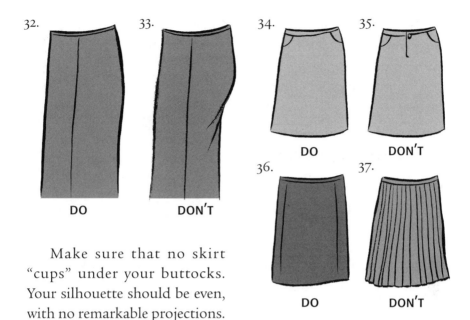

DO DON'T

Choose an empire style dress, but ensure that it is fitted along the bottom. (*See figure 41.*)

Completely avoid fitted knit dresses.

40.

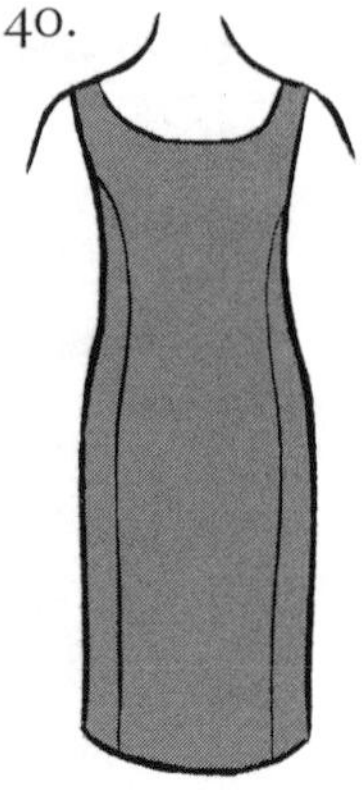

DO

41.

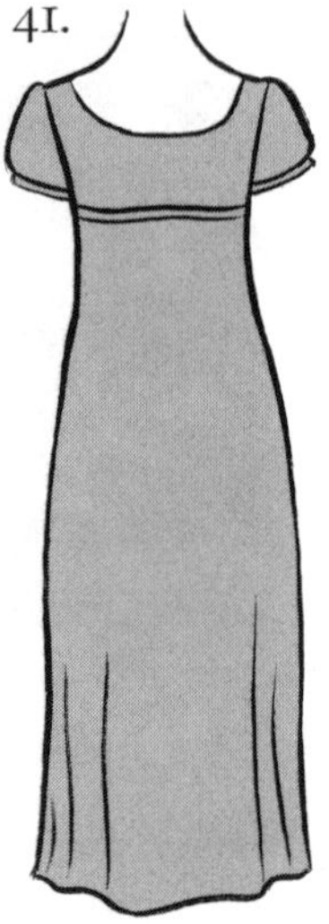

DO

trousers for pear shape

Trousers pose the greatest challenges for you. Once finished with this section, read p. 93 on choosing jeans.

Choose bottoms with flat fronts. The best style has no fly front and uses a side zipper. A slight low ride is best. Avoid extremely low-riding trousers – they run a horizontal line across your hips. (*See figures 42–44.*)

42.

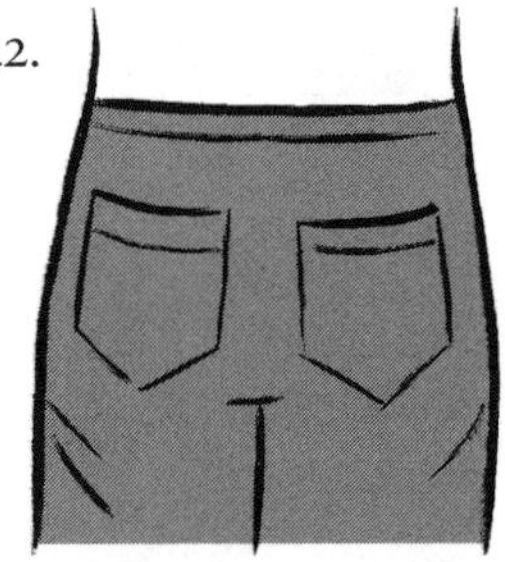

SLIGHTLY LOW
DO

43.

HIGH
DON'T

44.

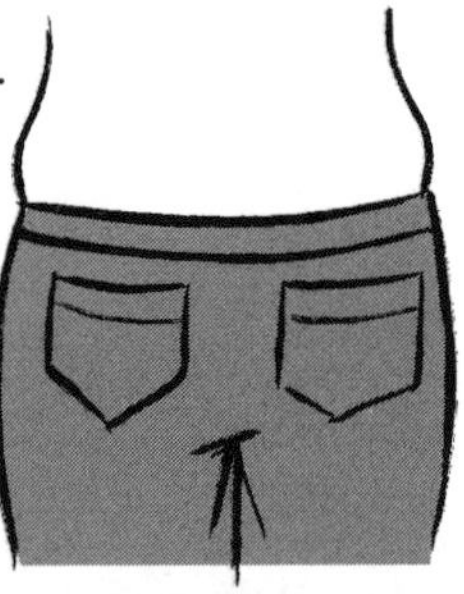

EXTREMELY LOW
DON'T

Avoid pleats in your trousers. (*See figures 45–46.*)

For trousers, choose straight-leg or anything with a slight flare such as boot-leg. (*See figures 47–48.*)

Choose well-fitting cropped pants. (*See figure 49.*)

Avoid palazzo, "elephant" bell bottoms, or very tapered legs. (*See figures 50–52.*)

Avoid bottoms made of fabrics that wrinkle. Creases at the bend of the leg create widening horizontal lines. (*See figures 53–54.*)

Check that jeans do not gather around the crotch. Back pockets should be an average size. Pockets that are too small tend to make the buttocks look bigger. (See p. 95 for more information.)

Be mighty particular when choosing shorts. Choose flat front shorts which fit perfectly and land along the thinnest part of your thigh. If you have a plus-size pear shape, you may have to decide to avoid shorts completely. Opt for skirts, Capri pants, and cropped pants instead.

Try a well-fitting body shaper for outfits that really need it. Also, hosiery with control-top action is excellent. (Much hosiery is made with cotton panels in the crotch. This makes panties unnecessary.)

Ensure that your purse swings above your hips, not at or below your hips.

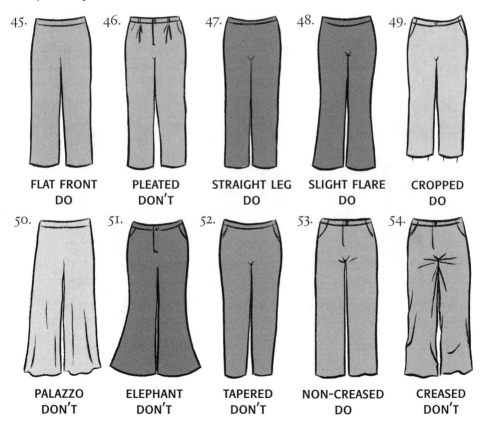

45.
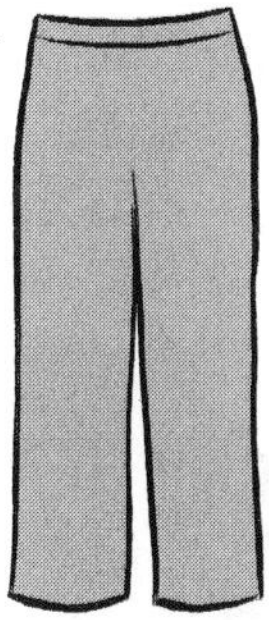
FLAT FRONT
DO

46.
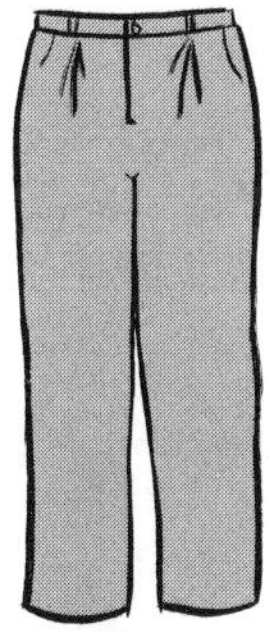
PLEATED
DON'T

47.
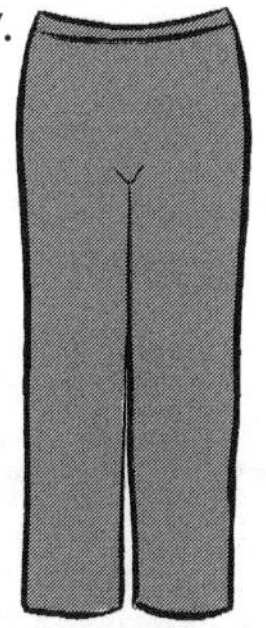
STRAIGHT LEG
DO

48.
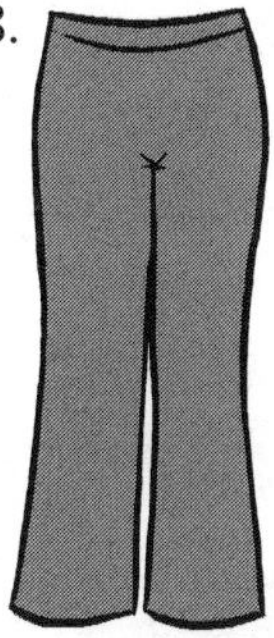
SLIGHT FLARE
DO

49.
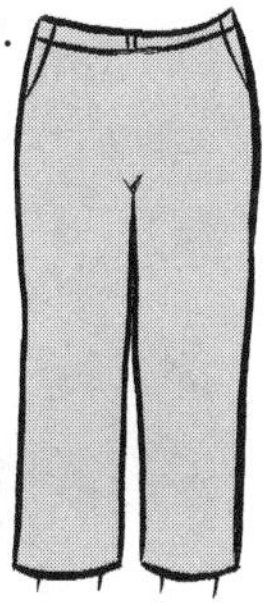
CROPPED
DO

50.
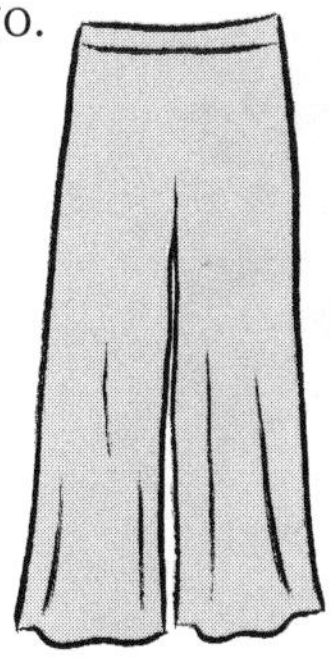
PALAZZO
DON'T

51.
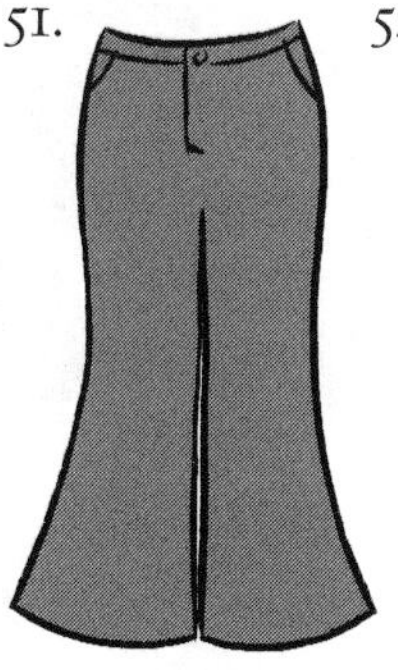
ELEPHANT
DON'T

52.
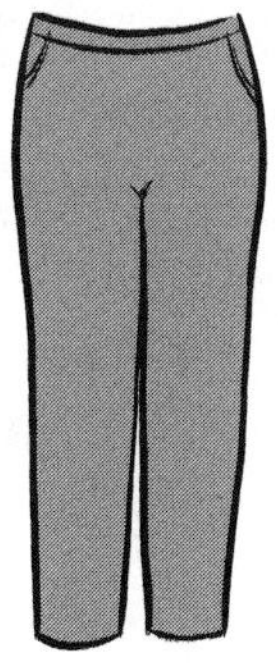
TAPERED
DON'T

53.
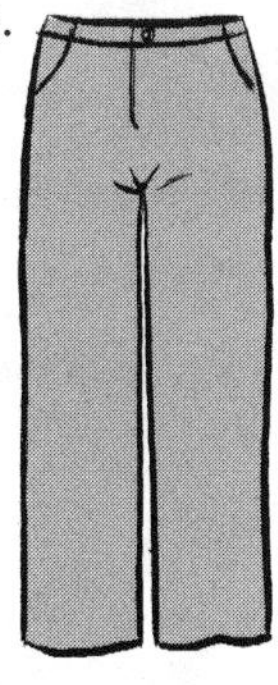
NON-CREASED
DO

54.
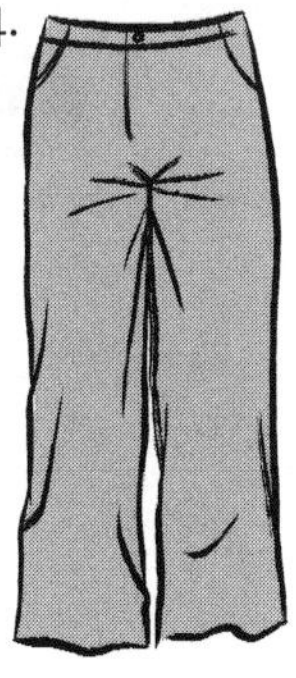
CREASED
DON'T

coats for pear shape

Check that your winter coat is in good shape and doesn't pull downward or have overly large pockets. Sloppy coats are awful for you. (*See figures 55–56.*)

55.

DO

56.

DON'T

swimsuits for pear shape

Be extra vigilant when trying on swimsuits. Spend time checking them over to ensure that the fit around the bottom is perfect. Choose a suit with embellishment at the top and a darker color toward the bottom. Avoid ruffles and wide skirts at the bottom. Sarong covers are a good option for you because they provide a diagonal line across your largest area. (*See figures 57–59.*)

57.
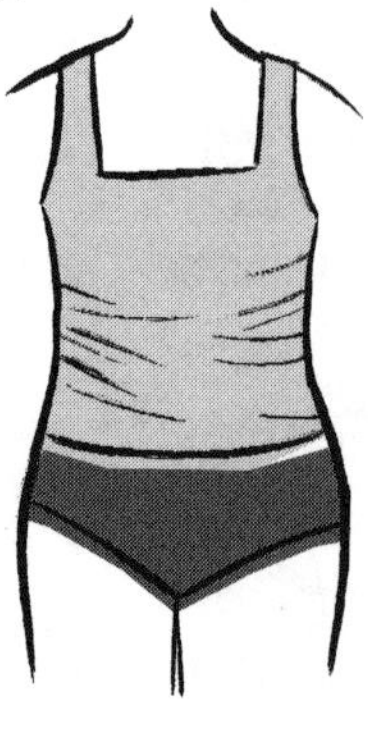
DO

58.

DON'T

59.
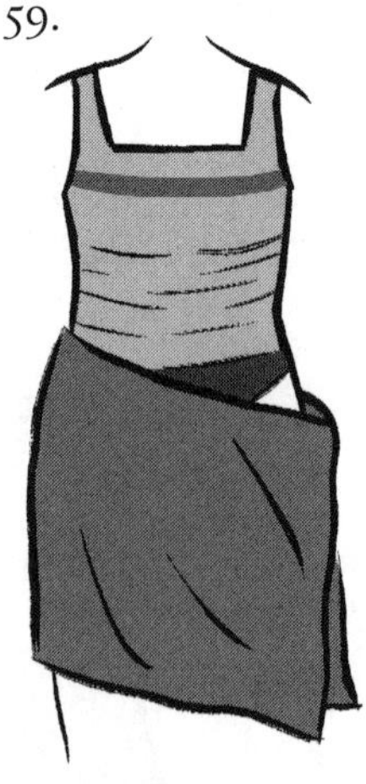
SARONG COVER
DO

strategies for working with the heart body type

GOAL FOR HEART SHAPE: The challenge for you is to slenderize the appearance of your top, creating the overall appearance of proportion and moving an observer's eye upward toward your face.

use of color for heart shape

Use color to create the illusion of proportion. Dark colors streamline and light colors emphasize. Wear darker colors on the top (shirts, blouses, sweaters, etc.) and lighter colors on the bottom. For example, you could wear a black top and a pair of white pants. (*See figure 1.*)

1.

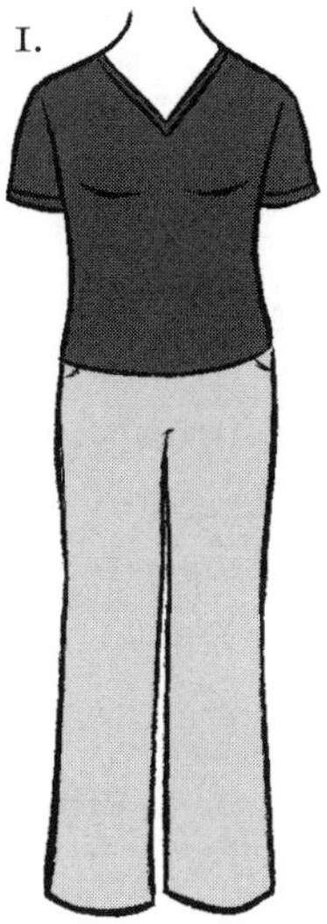

DO

2.

DO

use of line, print and pattern for heart shape

Prints and plaids enlarge. In fact, the larger the print, the larger the appearance of what it's covering. Completely avoid prints and plaids on the top. Avoid large pattern blouses or plaid jackets. Choose printed or plaid bottoms. (*See figure 2.*)

Diagonal and vertical lines slenderize. Horizontal lines widen. Avoid horizontal lines on top. They can be used for bottoms. (*See figures 3–4.*)

3.

DO

4.

DON'T

Remember that lines are also created with seams or details such as piping. The same rules apply. (*See figures 5–6.*)

use of fabric and texture for heart shape

Fabrics with thicker naps enlarge. Avoid corduroys, velvets, and boucles on the top. Wear them on the bottom with confidence.

Any fabric with a shine will add the appearance of weight. Try these fabrics for your bottoms only.

Avoid large pockets on top. Large pockets are flattering toward the bottom. (*See figures 7–8.*)

Go for a fitted (but not tight) look on top. Avoid bulky or oversized tops like chunky knit sweaters or fleece jackets.

5.

DO

6.

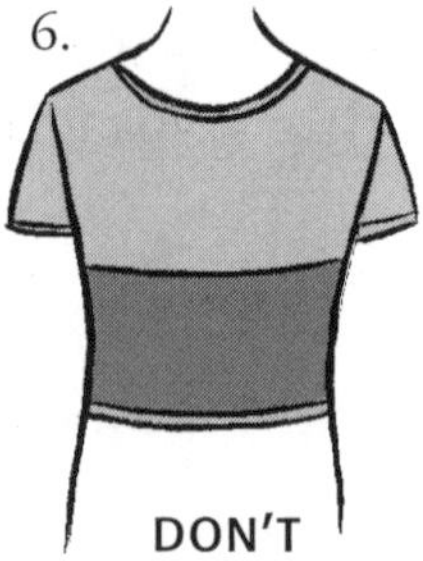

DON'T

7.

DO

8.

DON'T

9.

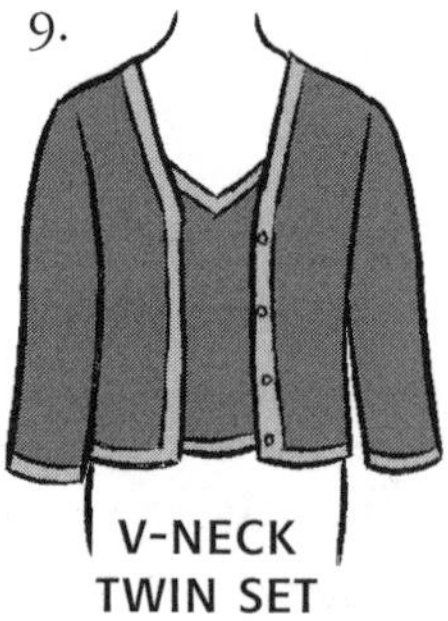

V-NECK TWIN SET DO

10.

QUILTED JACKET DON'T

11.

RAGLAN SLEEVES DO

12.

WRAP TOP DO

13.

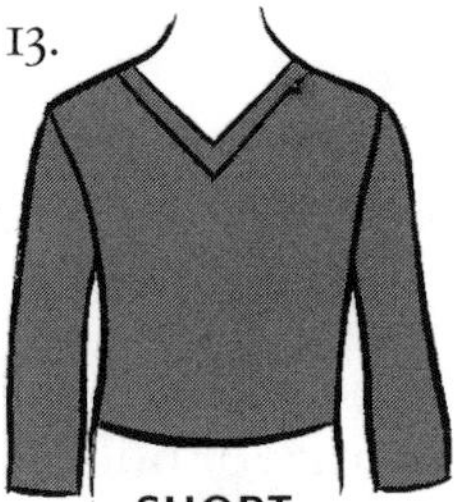

SHORT
V-NECK
DO

14.

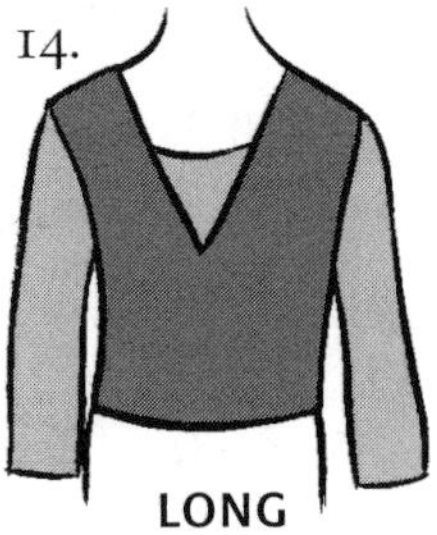

LONG
V-NECK
DO

tops for heart shape

Choose tops with diagonal or vertical lines such as raglan sleeve styles, wrap (surplice) tops, twin sets, and v-necks tops. (*See figures 9–14.*)

Avoid baring cleavage in any top and secure wrap blouses. These tops provide competing focal points with your face.

Avoid tops with horizontal lines such as bateau neck tops, strapless styles, spaghetti strap styles, shawl neck tops, halter styles, and wide scoop neck tops. (*See figures 15–17.*)

Wear a well-made bra that gives you support. A minimizer may be necessary. (See p. 80)

15.

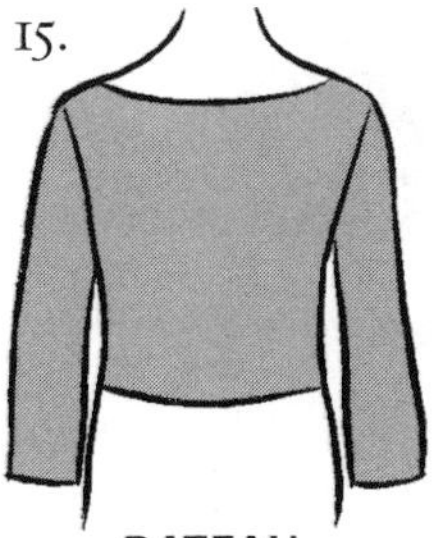

BATEAU
NECK
DON'T

16.

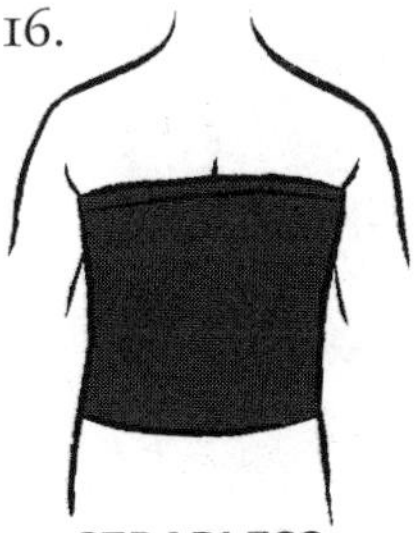

STRAPLESS
DON'T

17.

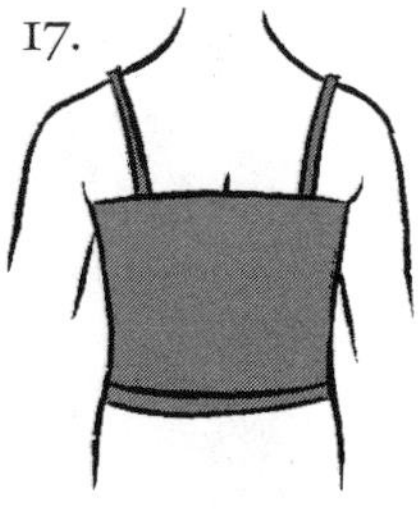

SPAGHETTI
STRAP
DON'T

skirts for heart shape

Choose A-line, dirndl, large pleated, trumpet, gaucho, and full skirts in general. This is the area where you want to add the appearance of fullness. (*See figures 18–22.*)

Avoid thin pencil skirts, wrap skirts, or broomstick skirts, especially with tops that have a lot of structure or bulk. (*See figures 23–25.*)

DO

18.

A-LINE

19.

DRINDL

20.

TRUMPET

21.

LARGE-PLEATED

22.

FULL

DON'T

23.

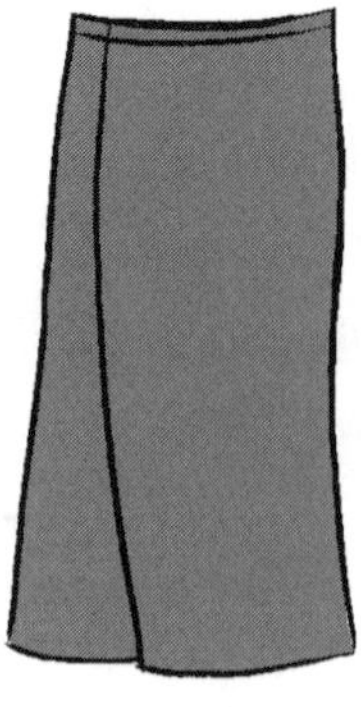

WRAP

24.

PENCIL

25.

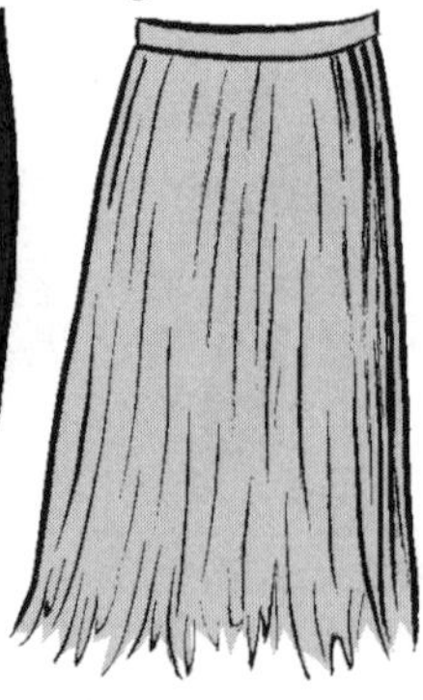

BROOMSTICK

dresses for heart shape

Choose wrap/surplice dresses, peplum style dresses, sheath dresses, and any kind of dress with a full skirt. (*See figures 26–29.*)

Avoid empire (horizontal line toward top) with fitted bottom, strapless, spaghetti strap (strong horizontal lines, too much flesh), and coat dresses. (*See figures 30–31.*)

27.

FULL
DO

26.

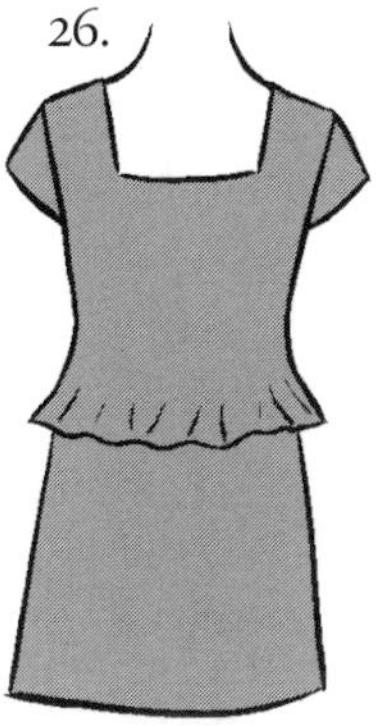

PEPLUM
DO

28.

WRAP
DO

29.

SHIRT DRESS
WITH FULL SKIRT
DO

30.

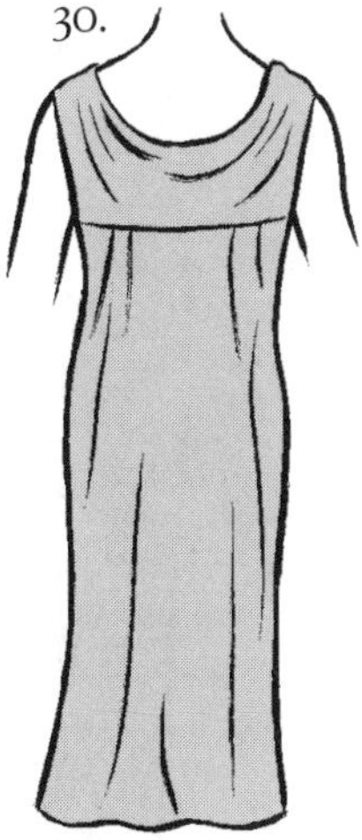

EMPIRE WITH
FITTED BOTTOM
DON'T

31.

COAT DRESS
DON'T

trousers for heart shape

Choose trousers with pleats. (*See figure 32.*)

Choose straight-leg trousers, full-leg trousers, gauchos, and palazzo pants. (*See figure 33.*)

Choose trousers with slight bell bottoms or flared legs such as boot legs. (*See figure 34.*)

Avoid very tapered-leg trousers. (*See figure 35.*)

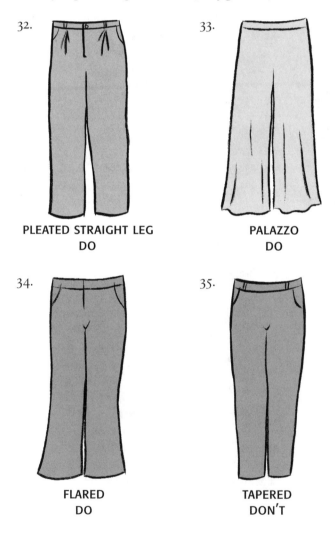

32.

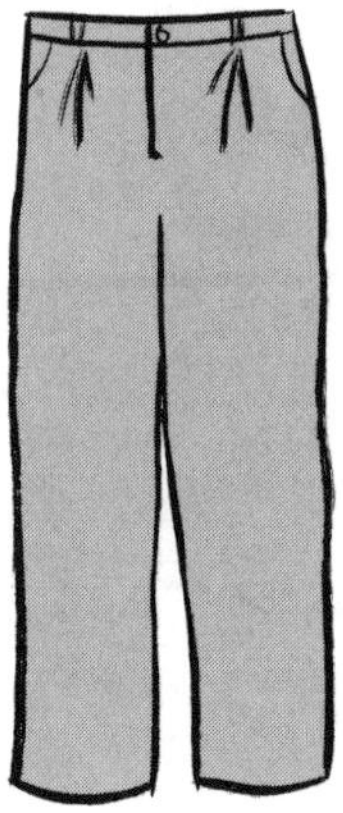

PLEATED STRAIGHT LEG
DO

33.

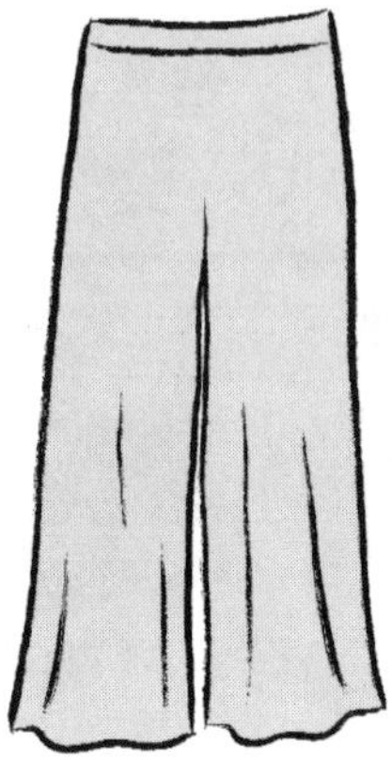

PALAZZO
DO

34.

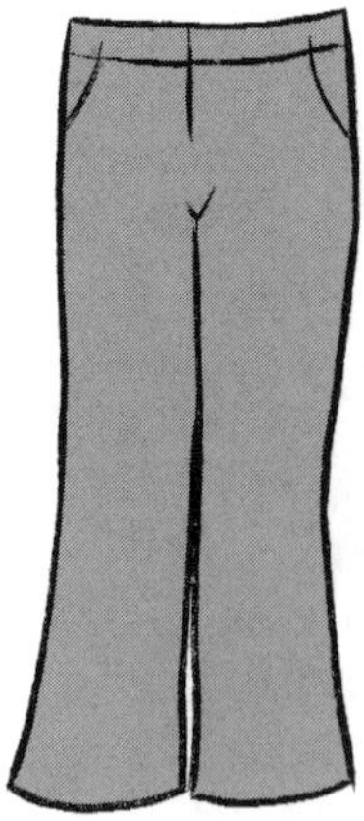

FLARED
DO

35.

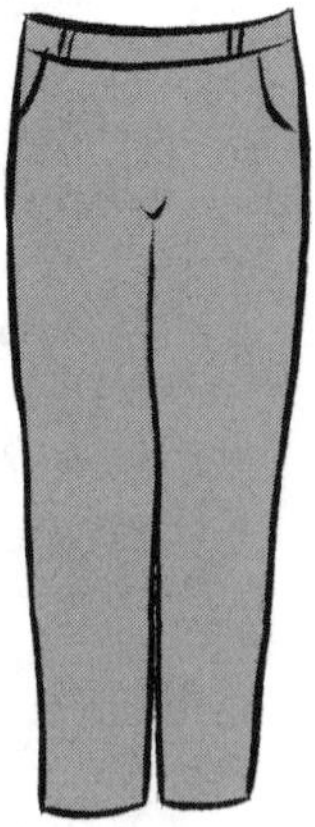

TAPERED
DON'T

coats for heart shape

Check that your winter coat is in good shape. Avoid bulky embellishments or excessive fabric on the top. Avoid double-breasted styles. Large pockets toward the hips will enhance proportion. A swing coat is an excellent option. (*See figures 36–37.*)

36.

DO

37.

DON'T

swimsuits for heart shape

Be extra vigilant when trying on swimsuits. Spend time checking them over to ensure that the fit around the top is perfect. Choose a suit with embellishment at the bottom (ruffles, flouncy skirt, or accessories, etc.) Or, try a suit with a dark color at the top and a lighter color on the bottom. (*See figures 38–40.*)

38.

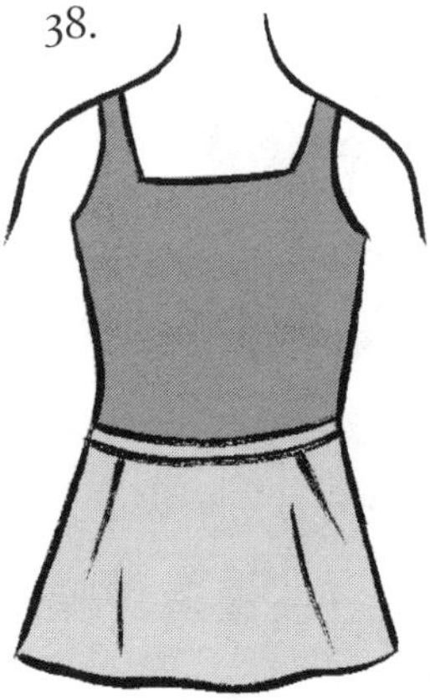

DO

39.

DO

40.

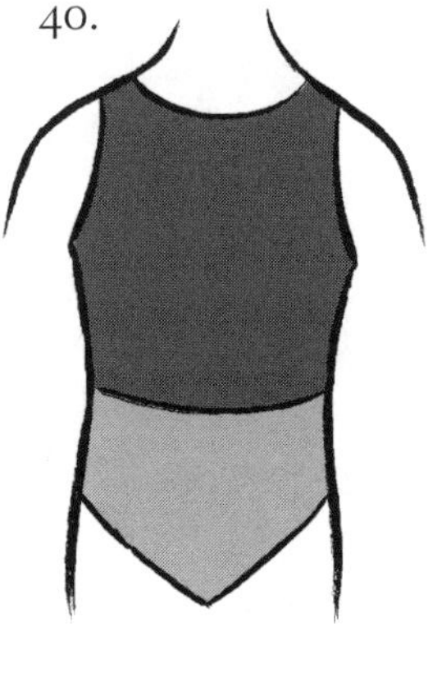

DO

strategies for working with the box body type

GOAL FOR BOX SHAPE: Your challenge is to create the optical illusion of an indentation at the waist, or a more curved silhouette. You want to trick the eye to skip over the waist. This will help to move the focal point to your face.

1.

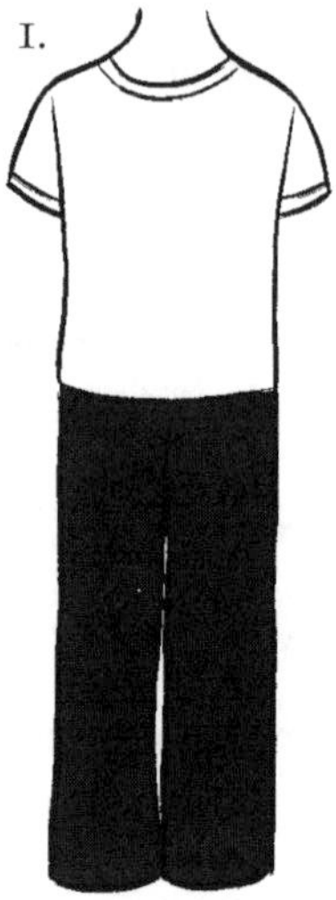

DO

2.

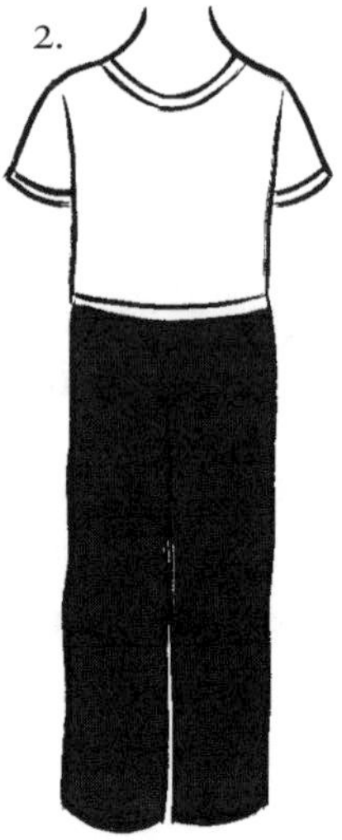

DON'T

use of color for box shape

Avoid creating a focal point at your waist. A focal point is created by the sharp line where two contrasting colors meet. Lower the color contrast to below your waist. Or choose monochromatic dressing (one color or shades of one color from top to bottom). This will streamline your overall appearance. (*See figures 1–3.*)

3.

DO

use of line print and pattern for box shape

Avoid a horizontal line at your waist with a belt. Choose styles that do not include belts. (*See figures 4–5.*)

Avoid printed patterns that create a horizontal line at the waist. Choose styles that place print at either your top or bottom. (*See figures 6–7.*)

4.

DO

5.

DON'T

6.

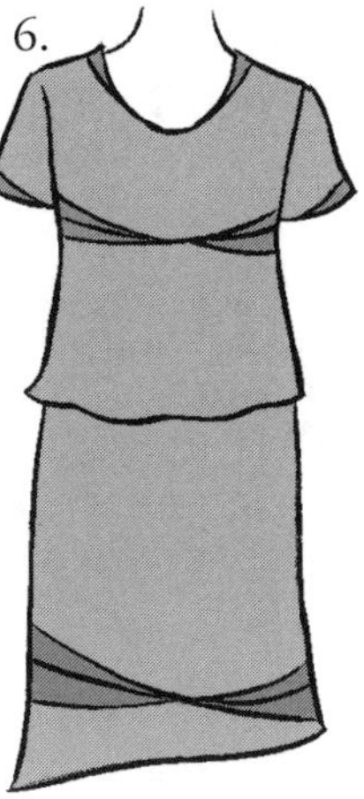

DO

7.

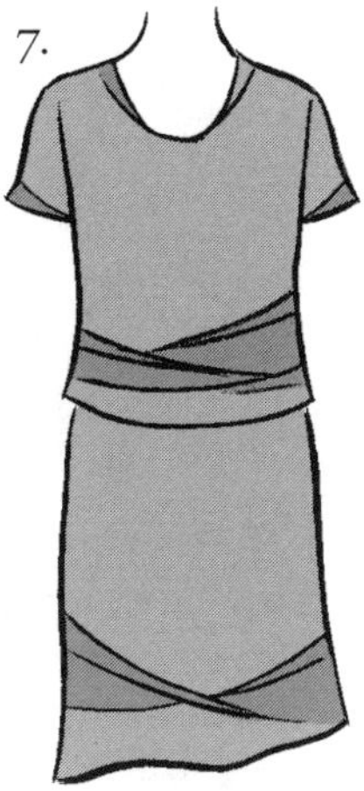

DON'T

use of fabric and texture for box shape

8.

DO

9.

DON'T

Fabrics with thicker naps enlarge. Avoid echoing the box-like dimensions of your torso with boxy tops. Avoid bulky jackets and sweaters that end near your waist. (*See figures 8–9.*)

tops for box shape

Avoid horizontal lines which echo the width of your waist. Choose tops that fall well below your waist and are styled to give you a curve at the waist. Choose surplice/wrap blouses that fall below your waist, fitted knits, western style, man-tailored shirts (without shirt tails), Basque-style shirts, and longer-waisted jackets that provide a bit of a curve. (*See figures 10–13.*)

Padded bras and subtle shoulder pads are also a plus for you. These will help give you a little curve and help the eye flow upwards toward your face.

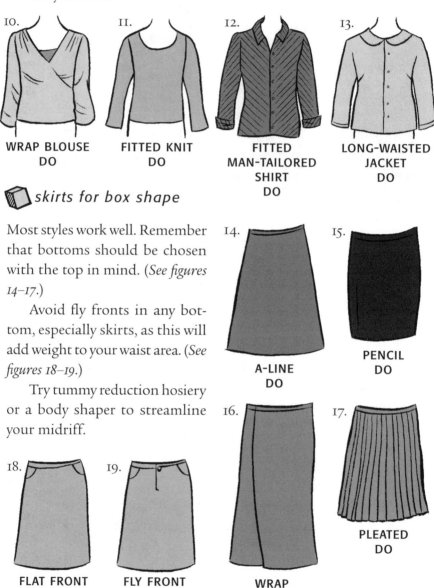

10.
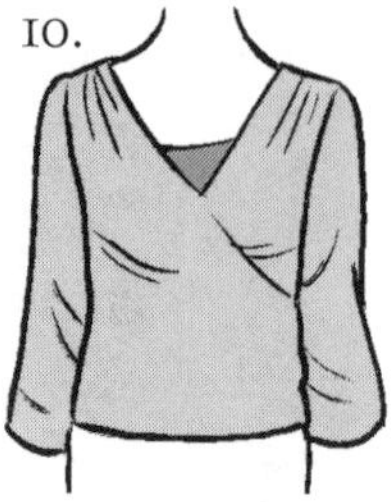
WRAP BLOUSE
DO

11.
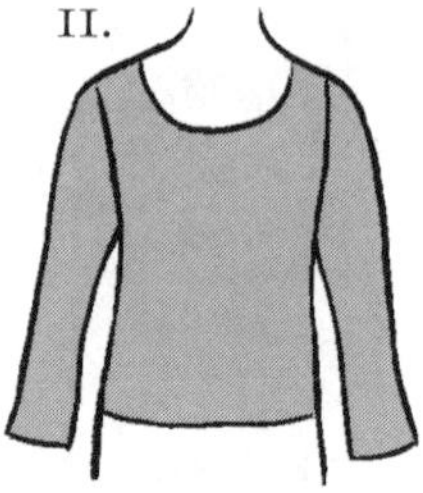
FITTED KNIT
DO

12.
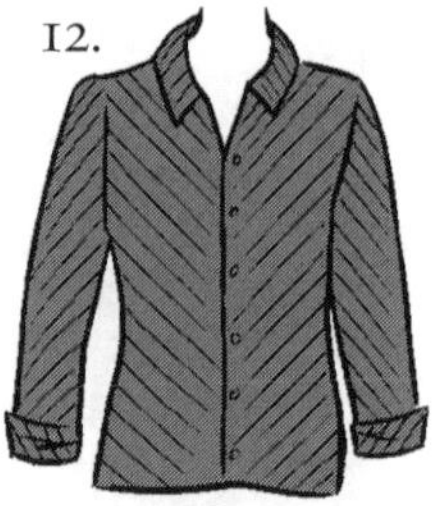
FITTED MAN-TAILORED SHIRT
DO

13.
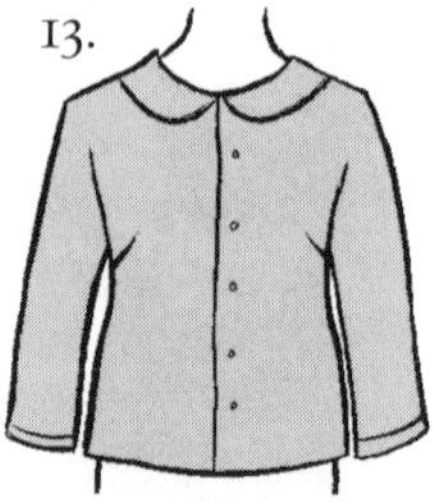
LONG-WAISTED JACKET
DO

skirts for box shape

Most styles work well. Remember that bottoms should be chosen with the top in mind. (*See figures 14–17.*)

Avoid fly fronts in any bottom, especially skirts, as this will add weight to your waist area. (*See figures 18–19.*)

Try tummy reduction hosiery or a body shaper to streamline your midriff.

14.
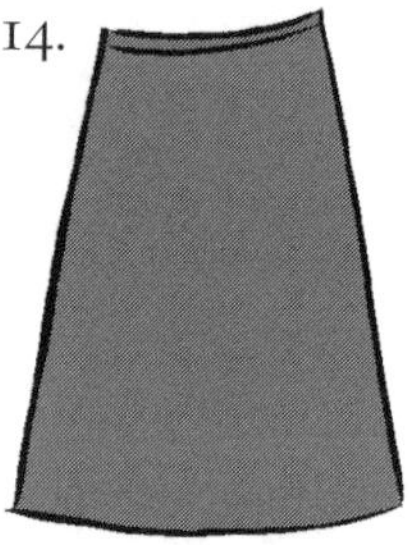
A-LINE
DO

15.

PENCIL
DO

16.
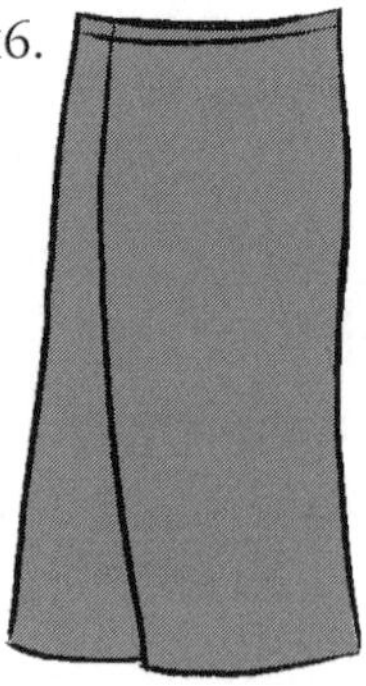
WRAP
DO

17.

PLEATED
DO

18.
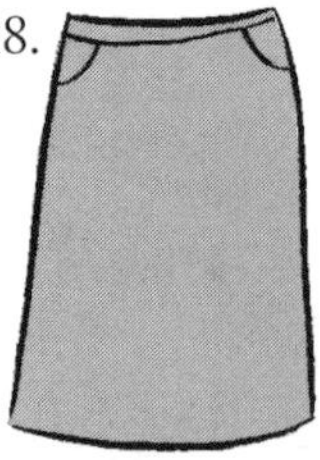
FLAT FRONT
DO

19.
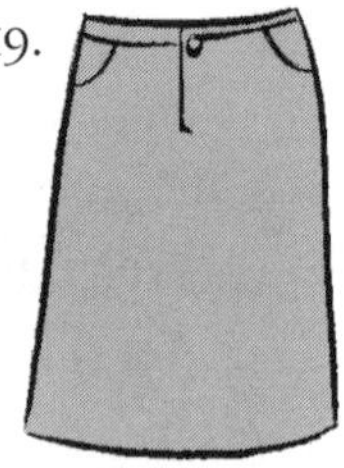
FLY FRONT
DON'T

dresses and suits for box shape

Monochromatic dressing is a plus for you, especially in the form of traditional suiting using longer jackets and tunic styles. (*See figures 20–22.*)

Choose empire, sheath, wrap, or bias-cut styles. (*See figures 23–25.*)

20.

TUNIC PANT SUIT
DO

21.

TUNIC SKIRT SUIT
DO

22.

TRADITIONAL SUIT
DO

23.

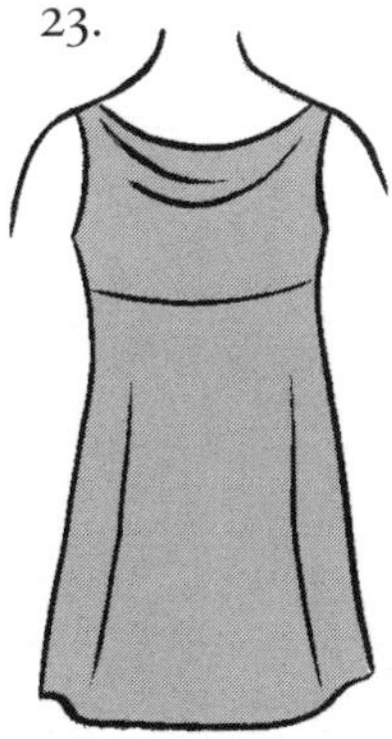

EMPIRE
DO

24.

SHEATH
DO

25.

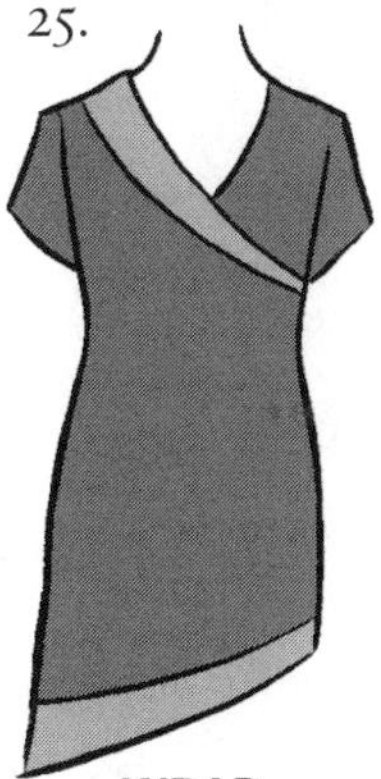

WRAP
DO

trousers for box shape

Avoid trousers with pleats or pockets. Go for a clean line in front with flat-front trousers. (*See figures 26–27.*)

Choose flared, full, or straight-leg trousers. Avoid tapered-leg trousers. (*See figures 28–31.*)

Avoid low-sitting trousers. Choose a natural waist. The hem of your top should hang below the top of your trousers. (*See figures 32–33.*)

26.
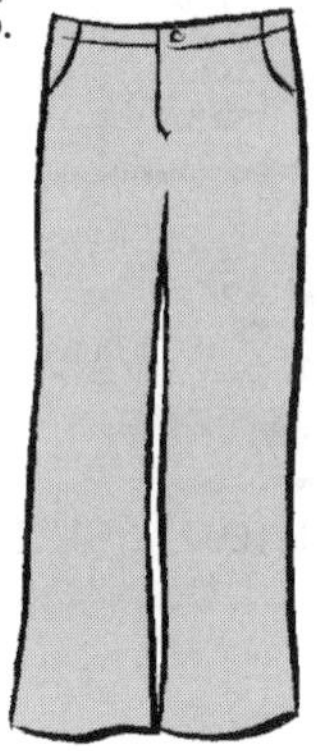
FLAT FRONT
DO

27.
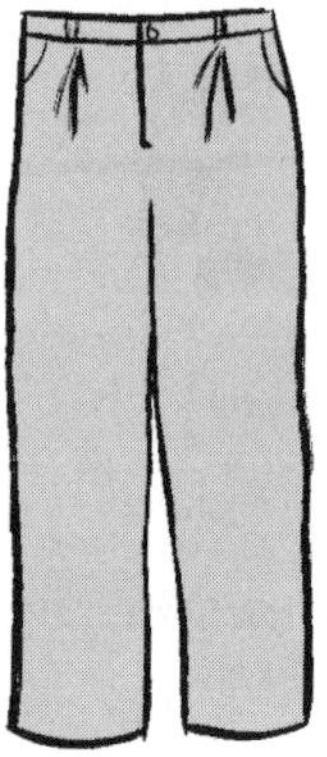
PLEATED
DON'T

28.
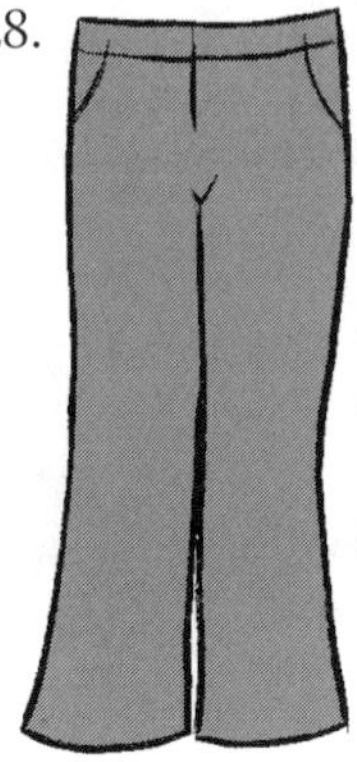
FLARED
DO

29.
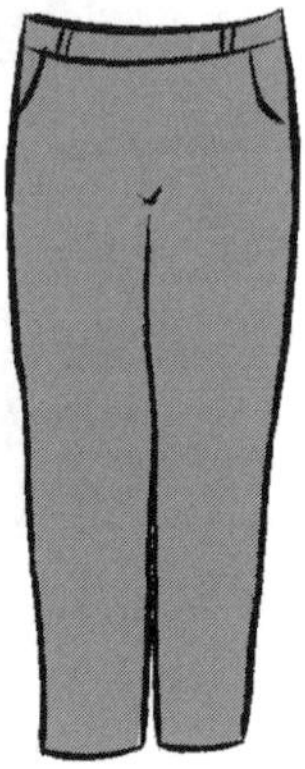
TAPERED
DON'T

30.
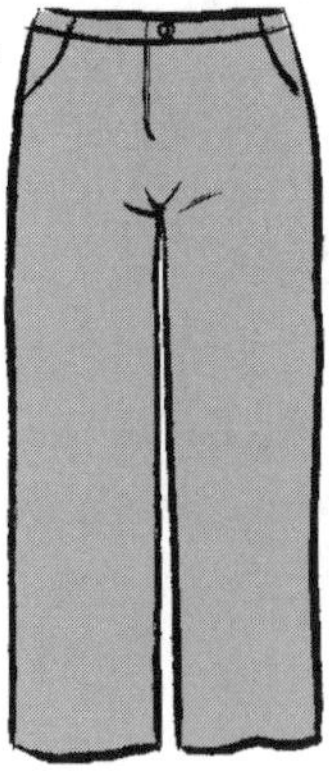
FULL
DO

31.
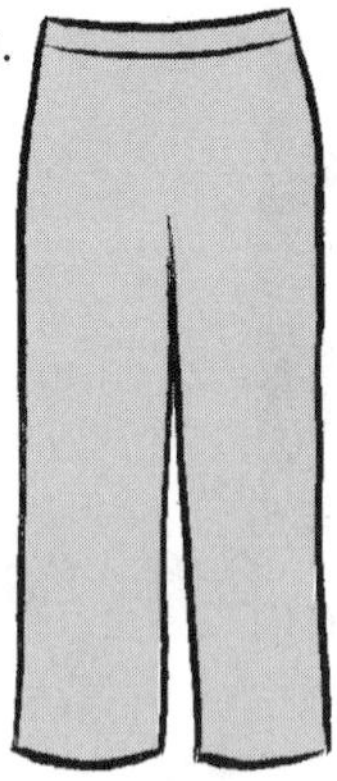
STRAIGHT LEG
DO

32.

NATURAL WAIST
DO

33.
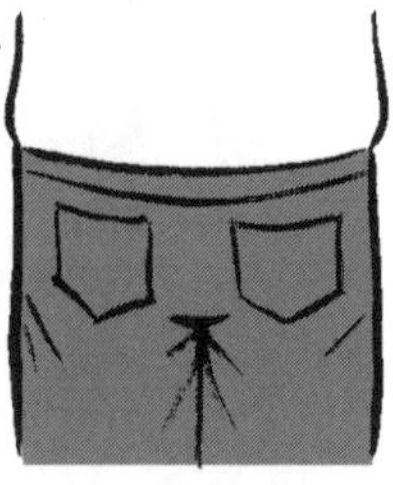
LOW WAIST
DON'T

coats for box shape

Avoid coats which echo the box-like dimensions of your torso. Choose streamlined coats that fall below your waistline. (*See figures 34–36.*)

34.

DON'T

35.

DO

36.

DO

swimsuits for box shape

Choose a swimsuit which minimizes your waistline. A monochromatic look from top to bottom is excellent, but also a very small print or texture can keep the eye dancing so that rolls aren't noticed as much. Avoid embellishment around the waistline and go for styles that cinch the fabric to one side of the torso, thus creating a diagonal line around the waist. If possible, find a swimsuit with a pattern of diagonal lines across the waist. Vertical seams and color blocking with dark sides are excellent. (*See figures 37–39.*)

37.

DO

38.

DO

39.

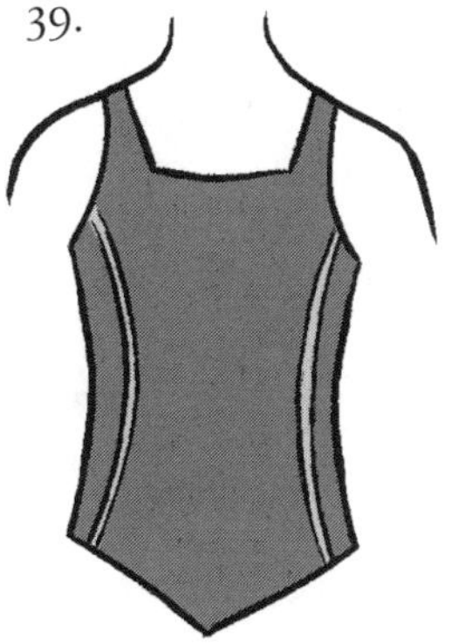

DO

strategies for maintaining the hour glass appearance

GOAL FOR HOUR GLASS SHAPE: Your challenge is to ensure that the clothing you choose doesn't knock-off your natural proportion. The garment industry creates clothing specifically for the hourglass, so most of the guidelines have to do with *not overdoing* or *not exaggerating.*

use of color for hour glass shape

Avoid cutting your appearance in half with a strong focal point at your waist. This is especially critical if you have borderline-box measurements. A focal point is created with a sharp line or is a point where two contrasting colors meet. Choose to pull down the color contrast to below your waist. Or, choose monochromatic dressing (one color or shades of one color from top to bottom). This will streamline your overall appearance. (*See figures 1–2.*)

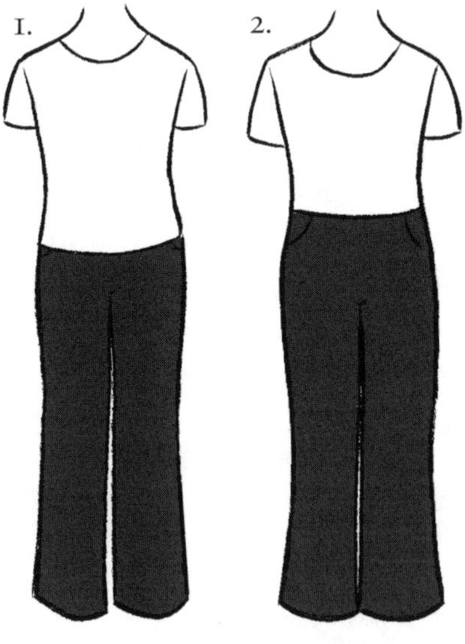

1. DO

2. DON'T

use of line print and pattern for hour glass shape

Avoid too many horizontal lines. This is especially important if you wear a plus size. (*See figures 3–4.*)

Avoid very busy patterns. Choose flattering patterns only. (*See figure 5.*)

3.
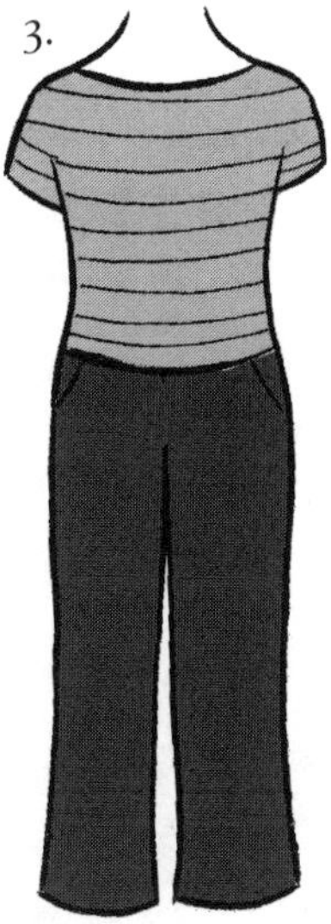
DO

4.
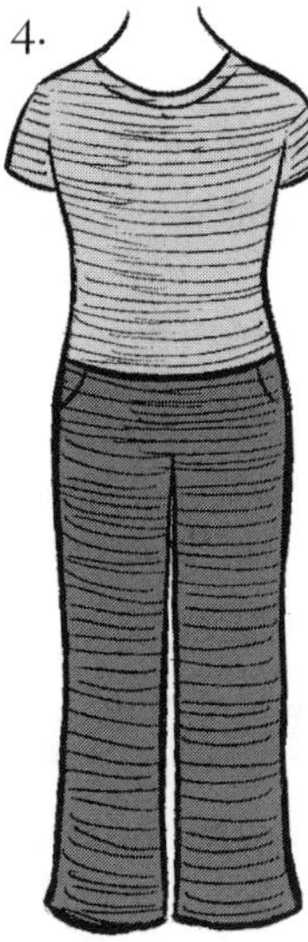
DON'T

5.

DO

use of fabric and texture for hour glass shape

Fabrics with thicker naps enlarge. Avoid adding weight to your look with too much fabric in one area. *(See figures 6–7.)*

6.

DO

7.

DON'T

tops for hour glass shape

Most styles will work well for you. Avoid extremely exaggerated styles. *(See figures 8–9.)*

8.
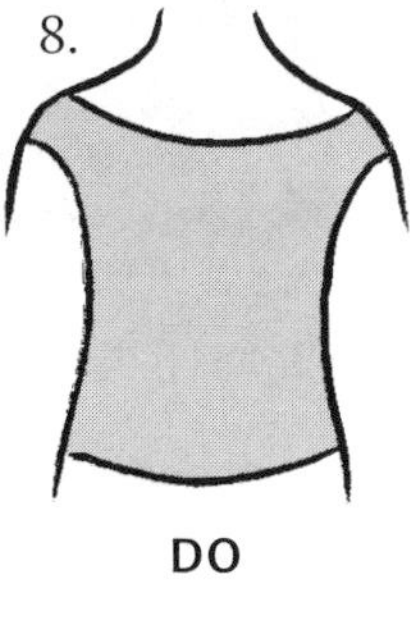
DO

9.
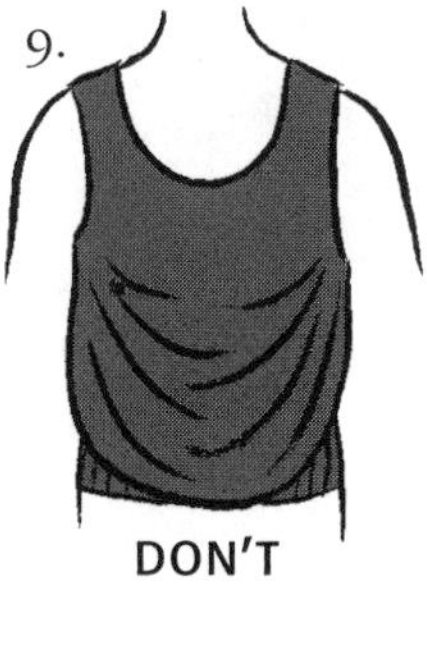
DON'T

skirts for hour glass shape

Most styles work well. Remember that bottoms should be chosen with the top in mind. Check this chapter for tips on fit. (*See figures 10–13.*)

Avoid adding weight to your midriff and bottom with an oversized dirndle or large pleated skirts. (*See figures 14–15.*)

Avoid a fly-front in a skirt as this will add weight to your waist area. (*See figures 16–17.*)

10.

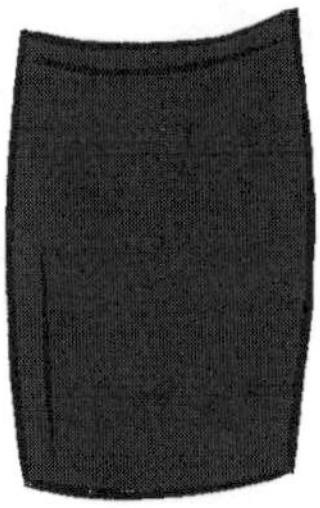

PENCIL
DO

11.

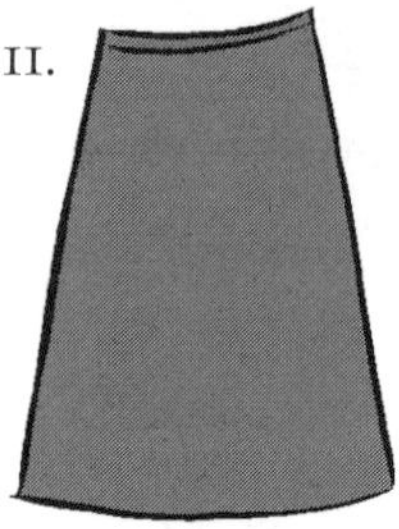

A-LINE
DO

12.

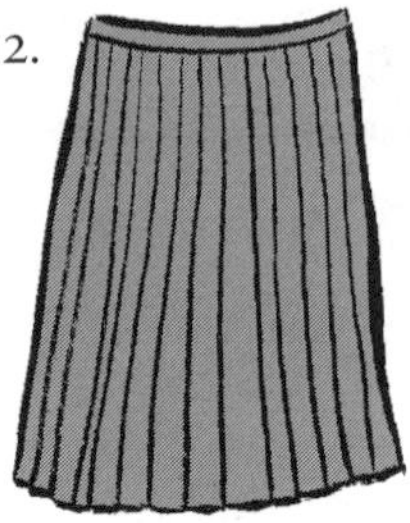

PLEATED
DO

13.

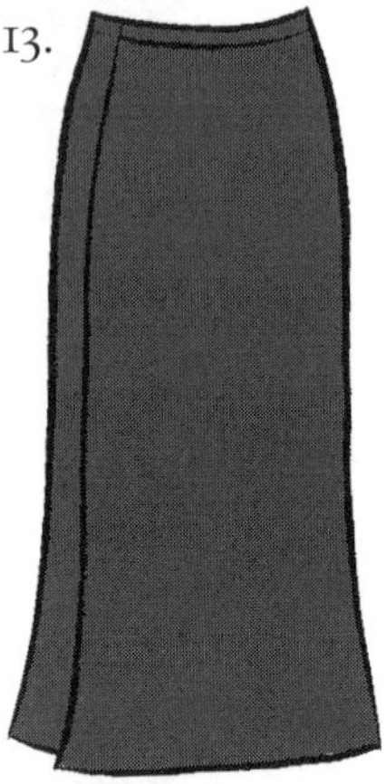

WRAP
DO

14.

DIRNDL
DO WITH CAUTION

15.

LARGE PLEATED
DO WITH CAUTION

16.

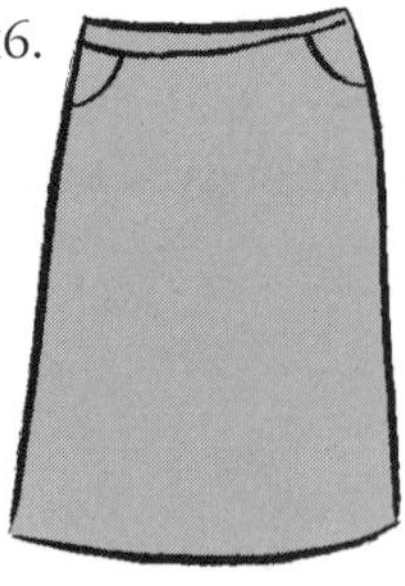

DO

17.

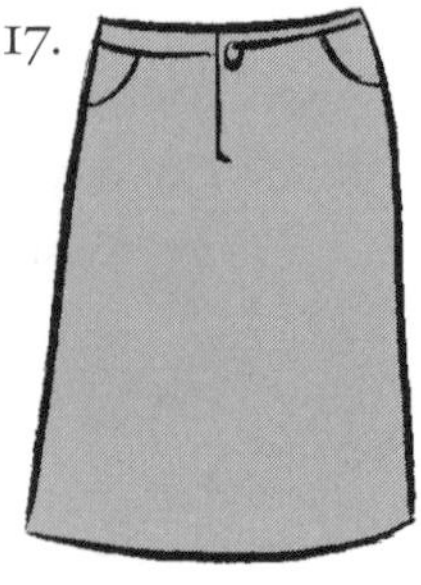

DON'T

dresses for hour glass shape

Most dress styles work for you. Any style which is fitted will work best. (*See figures 18–22.*)

18.

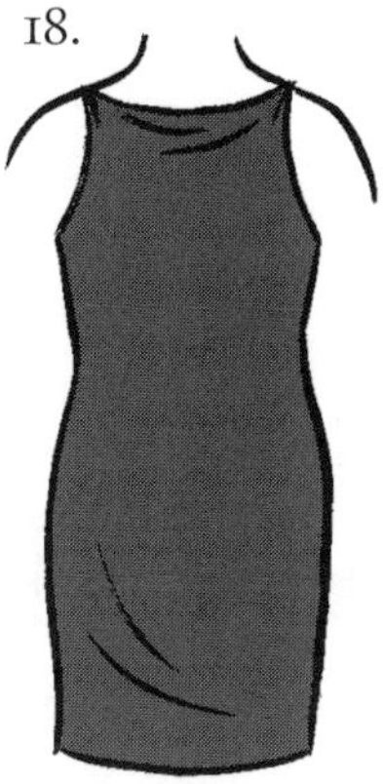

DO

19.

DON'T

20.

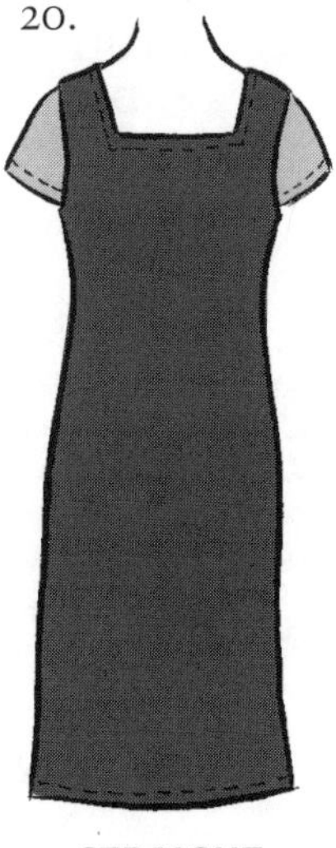

STRAIGHT AND FITTED DO

21.

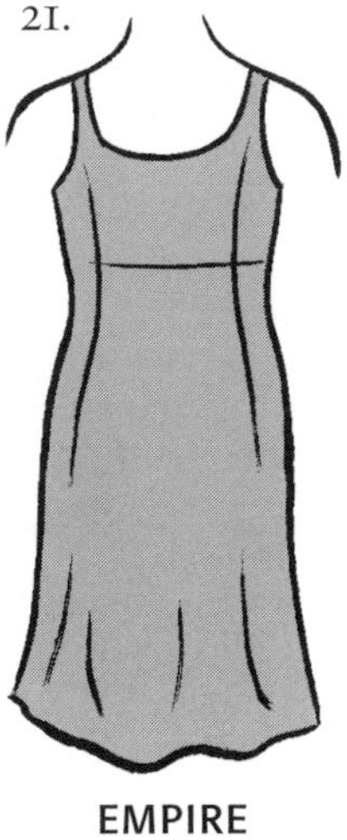

EMPIRE DO

22.

A-LINE DO

trousers for hour glass shape

Avoid trousers with pleats or pockets if you wear a plus size. Go for a clean line in front with flat front trousers. (*See figure 23.*)

Choose flared, full, tapered, "skinny" (if you do not wear a plus-size), or straight-leg trousers. (*See figures 24–25.*)

23.

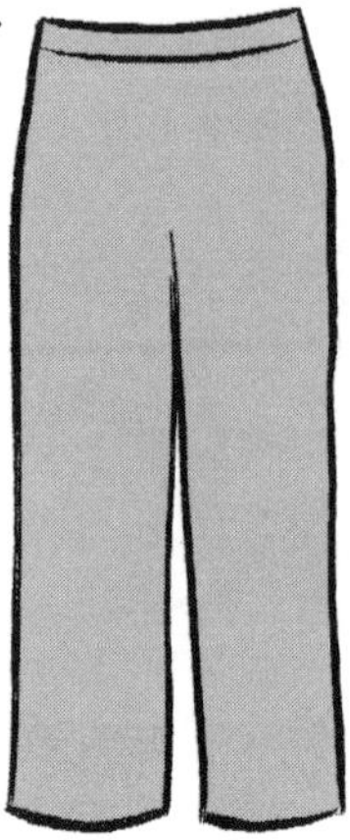

FLAT FRONT
DO

24.

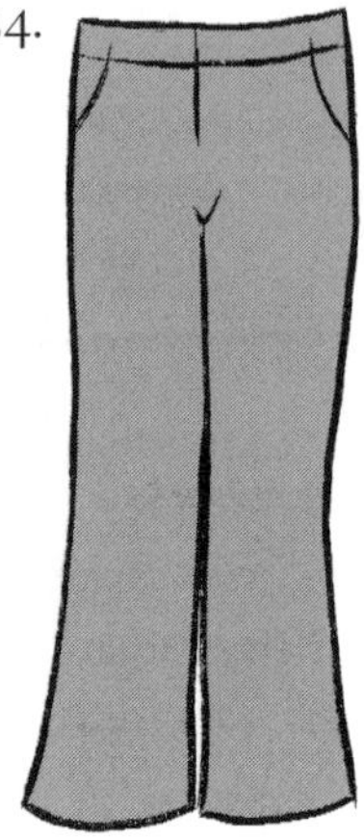

FLARED
DO

25.

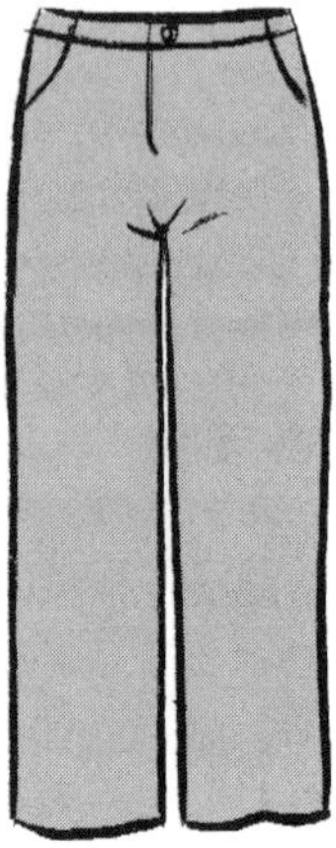

FULL
DO

Avoid very low-sitting trousers that allow no privacy. Allow the waist line to fall along your natural waist or slightly below it. (*See figures 26–27.*)

26.

SLIGHTLY LOW
DO

27.

EXTREMELY LOW
DON'T

coats for hour glass shape

Avoid coats which add bulkiness to any one part of your body. Choose streamlined coats at any length. (*See figures 28–29.*)

28.

DO

29.

DON'T

swimsuits for hour glass shape

Many swim suit styles work. The most flattering styles are one-piece suits which maintain a curve at your waist. (*See figures 30–32.*)

30.

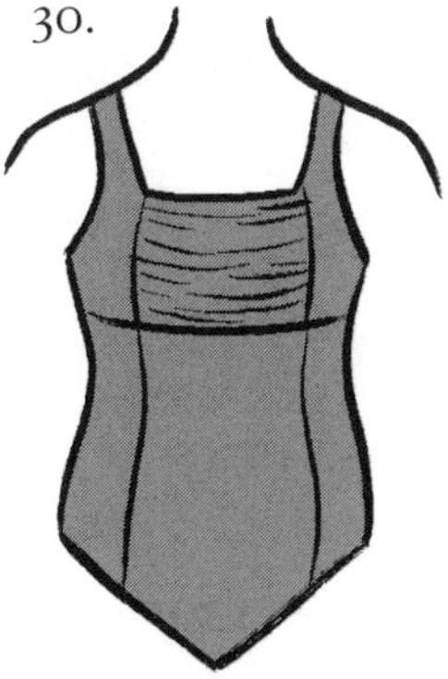

DO

31.

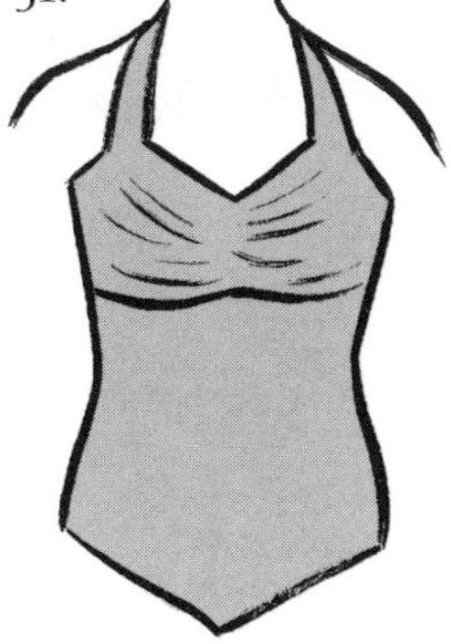

DO

32.

DO

SEMINAR FAQ
styles and body types

QUESTION: Doesn't adhering to these guidelines restrict each of us to only certain styles of clothing? How limiting! I hate to be pinned down.

ANSWER: I guess the answer is yes, you are limited to a certain number of styles using these guidelines. But wow! What a large number of styles! If you are feeling a little left out in the cold, it could be that you have your heart set on a style, and you don't want to let go. (Check the next chapter for why this is the case.) Step back and look at yourself in the style. Is it *really* flattering? If it works against the guidelines for your body type, then it's not.

Experiment with some alternatives. Study the recommendations to see if there is any way you can marry a favorite style to them. (Also, don't forget to extrapolate from the recommendations; if it says wide collars, then a "Peter Pan" collar is okay, even though it's not listed.) You will end up loving the results because you will have the best of both worlds: a favorite style in a flattering combination!

DON'T (HEART)

Here's an example: You say you love detailing on your tops but you have a heart shape body type. How about choosing a style that places detailing along the abdomen rather than over the breasts?

DO (HEART)

fundamental principles: fit and undergarments

All the points about fit for each body type provide a great opportunity to cover the standards for garment fit and, of course, undergarments. Let's begin with fit and work our way down.

are you wearing your sister's clothing, or couldn't you afford an alteration?

There are some standards to follow in the area of fit:

- All your garments should fit you correctly. They shouldn't be so tight that every curve of your body is accentuated. In other words, your shadow shouldn't look as if you're wearing nothing at all. On the other hand, loose clothing adds bulk to your overall appearance. Be sure to wear the right size in all your ensembles.
- A neckline should be checked for gaping. It shouldn't dip and reveal when you bend forward.
- Full-length sleeves should end at the wrist, right between that knubby little wrist bone and the beginning of your palm.
- Full-length pants should end at the top of the heel of a medium-height shoe.
- Skirts shouldn't cup around the buttocks – even if it is the current fashion.
- Skirt length is determined by fashion personality, leg condition, and height. Longer skirts shorten a person's appearance, but can be wonderful for camouflaging leg problems.
- Jackets should allow ease of movement. Your arms should be able to swing in full circles without straining seams.
- Skirts should never ride high up the thigh when sitting. A just-above-the-knee length is the most flattering and can be adjusted to an acceptable length while sitting.

yeah, you know Marge – she's the one with the panty lines

The poetry you want in motion is probably not the extra movement under your garments. You want your undergarments to control these and provide a nice clean line to your look.

- Don't go nuts with slips. You only need one when the fabric of your skirt or dress is sheer.
- Don't load on tons of undergarments around your buttocks. Try hosiery with a built-in panel. It eliminates the need for panties and extinguishes panty lines completely.
- Try a body shaper or girdle that goes to the mid thigh for any knit garment that calls for it. Knit is a hard material to wear successfully if you have a pear shape or wear a plus size, but others may be able to get a successful look.
- Many of the complaints about discomfort or incompatibility with certain garments are rooted in our taking panties for granted. Try a panty that has a regular cut to the leg openings and provides a waistband that sits at the highest point on your torso right before it peeps up over the waistband of your trousers. (It should never peep above the waistband of your trousers.)
- Avoid patterns on your panties. Flesh-tone is the best color choice, and it's a requirement under white trousers because your undergarments should be undetectable.
- A thong may extinguish the panty line, but there are complaints about discomfort amongst those who have experimented. In any event, a thong should never be part of a fashion either by appearance under a sheer fabric or by peeking above a waistband.
- Always check yourself in a full-length mirror – front, back, and both sides – before you leave the house.

Body-shaping undergarments aren't what they used to be. (Skeptics will just have to try some new ones to see.) Usually, you can pick your area and find a corresponding body-shaper. My one caution is that if you have a problem with circulation or varicose veins, check with your physician before you decide to invest in body-shapers. They usually begin at around thirty dollars per item and can go way up from there.

Also, to extend the life of these undergarments, follow washing instructions loyally. Body-shapers usually have to hang dry because heat from the dryer can ruin their strength.

happiness is a bra that fits

I distinctly remember the moment – I think it was sometime in my thirties – when I realized I needed a "serious" bra. (I guess this is in contrast to a silly or funny one.) Anyway, once I put the thing on it seemed that my outlook on life changed. I not only looked like a woman at my still slight size, but I had a general sense of optimism: life was kind, people were good, and global warming ceased completely. That's what new-found comfort can do.

directory of bras

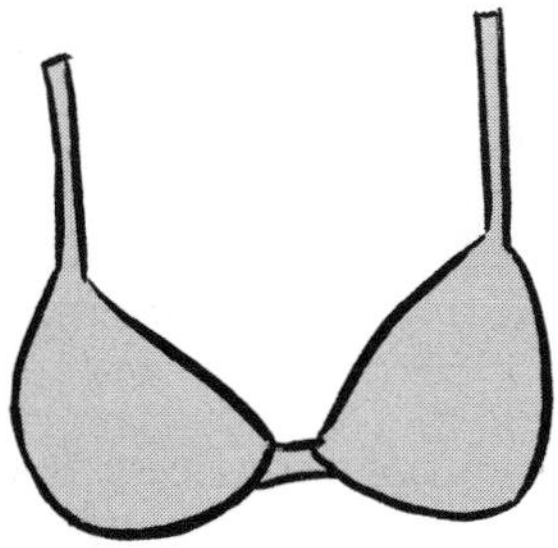

DEMI-BRA

Wide set straps and low cut; provides lift. Good for wearing under button-up tops; avoid under knit tops.

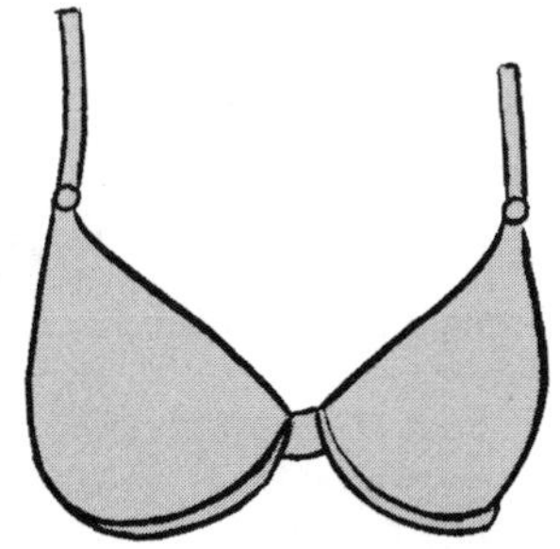

UNDERWIRE

Contains flexible wire under the cups to lift and support. (Some brands will set off metal detectors!)

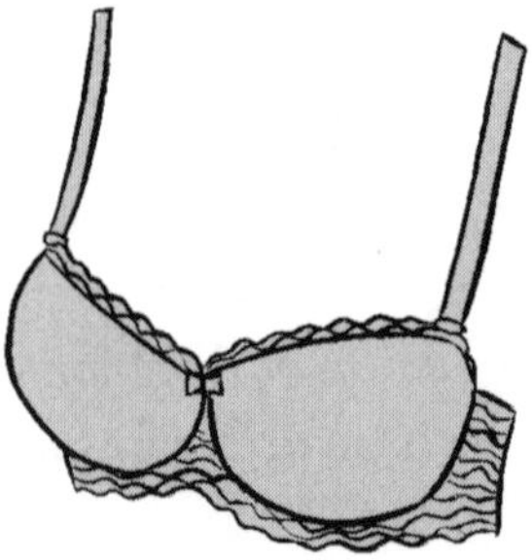

CONVERTIBLE

Has detachable straps which work as strapless, racerback, or halter style.

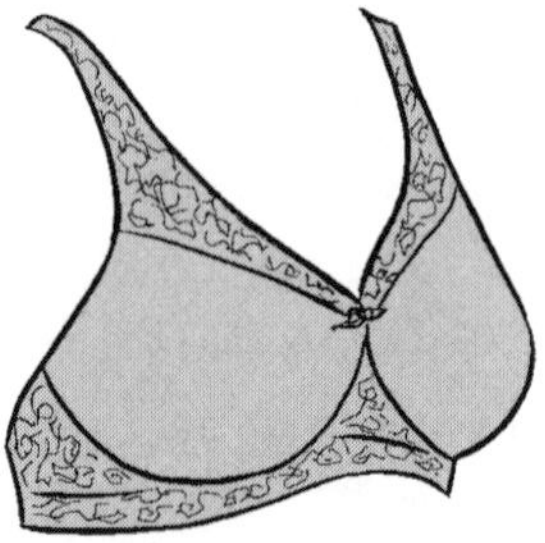

MINIMIZER

Minimizes breasts with strong microfiber material.

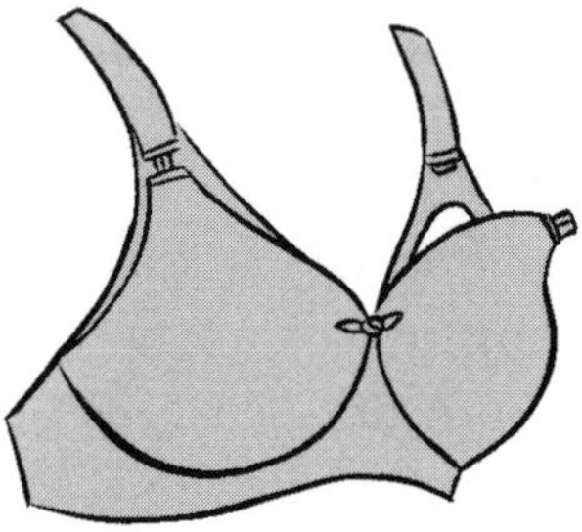

NURSING BRA

Fronts detach to expose nipple for nursing.

A typical wardrobe requires three flesh tone bras (of preferred kind) and one convertible bra.

Inventory and check the condition of each bra that you own:

- Look for holes created by your fingers toward the back clasps, and discard anything that is irreparable.
- Check that the cup is not bunched or stretched out of shape.
- Ensure that straps are still doing their duty. If a strap is stretched out or if it leaves red marks (it probably always did, and you just put up with it) discard it.

Try on the bras you decide to keep:

- Check that the straps don't slide off your shoulders, by circling your arms or mimicking common movements. Racer-back bras are a good option if you have sloping shoulders.
- If the bra continually shifts around during any kind of physical activity, it's too large for you and should be replaced.
- Check the patch of fabric between the cups by pushing down with your finger. It shouldn't bounce back like a spring board. If it does, the bra is too small.
- Also, check that your breasts aren't bulging over the sides or tops of cups. If they are then your bra is too small.

what to do with a bra

You need a bra if your garment does not have one built-in. Bra-less fads come and go and should be ignored. A good bra is *always* a good investment.

Also, nipples should not peek through, even for personal casual wear. Nipple-related fads come and go, but nipples compete with your face as a focal point even if you have extremely small breasts. (It's just the way nipples work. People look at them.) Choose a bra which gives complete and smooth coverage of your nipples or use adhesive-backed nipple covers.

Most women know that you only wear a bra *under* a top. It is never *part* of a look, only a *foundation* to a look. Sometimes, when one of my toddlers gets a hold of my bra, she puts it on her head. This doesn't work. Showing your bra through your garment doesn't work. Exposing your bra straps doesn't work. Remember, the brassier falls into the *under*garment category.

Properly put on a bra by first bending forward. Slip your arms through the straps. Hook up under the shoulder blades while still bent. Stand up after you have hooked it up and before you get a head rush. You should feel some support, but absolutely no constraint. The bra should be comfortable and almost unnoticeable.

Take care of your bras by washing as the instructions direct. Hang them to dry because the polyester fibers can be ruined by heat of the dryer.

Buy a bra by adhering to the following:

- Choose a flesh-tone color to wear under white garments. These bras are best to wear under anything.
- Wear a camisole or silk tank over the bra for sheer tops.
- Avoid lacy cups for all garments except sweaters or tops in dark colors and thick fabrics.
- Avoid demi-bras under knit tops.
- Choose padded cups if you need to help things along.
- Try on any bra you decide to buy. Do not take your size for granted. It may change with age, weight fluctuation, water retention, lactation, or pregnancy. Also, manufacturers may differ in sizes.
- Be prepared to replace your bras regularly. The typical lifespan of a bra is less than two years.

how to determine bra size

There are several ways to measure for bras. This method is the easiest and most common. (You may do this in an unpadded bra.)

1. Measure right under your breasts and around your entire rib cage with a flexible measuring tape. Pull snugly to get an accurate number (in inches). Add five to odd numbers and six to even numbers. This is the band size.
2. Measure breasts with flexible measuring tape. Place tape over largest part snugly.

3. Subtract underbust measurement (band size) from bust measurement. This will determine cup size.
4. If the difference between those two measurements is:

   0 – you will need an AA cup
   1 – you will need a A cup
   2 – you will need a B cup
   3 – you will need a C cup
   4 – you will need a D cup
   5 – you will need a DD (E) cup
   6 – you will need a DDD (F) cup
   7 – you will need a G cup

So, if your underbust measurement is 31 and your bust measurement is 38, the math goes like this: 31+5=36 and 38-36=2. The bra you would want to buy is a size 36B.

There are other ways to measure for a bra, and you may have to adjust a little for each brand, but this method is not only the easiest, it's the most compatible with the bra manufacturers.

sizing up for style

fit the fashion to you

You might be thinking that as a fashion enthusiast I would recommend getting to an ideal weight to make your outfits look good. Good advice; bad reasoning. You should strive for your ideal weight for *you*. And contrary to what we may have been influenced to think, an ideal weight is the weight at which you are healthiest and feel your best. Your style should serve your body. Your body shouldn't serve any style.

If I have to tie in weight to fashion, then I must say that moderation will do wonders. Eat nutritional foods, drink more water, reduce your intake of fats and sugars, and exercise. I often tell busy women that exercise can mean climbing stairs whenever possible, parking far and walking, and running around the house while cleaning. Many of us just can't afford to join a health club or find the time to go running for an hour, so we have to get creative.

Aside from making lifestyle changes, a few adjustments to your wardrobe design (above and beyond sticking with the strategies for creating an optical illusion of proportion) will instantly slenderize your overall appearance.

- Choose a monochromatic look using dark neutrals. (See chapters six and seven.)
- Avoid prints in garments.
- Maintain a strong vertical line in your styling.
- Avoid any horizontal lines in your styling.
- De-clutter your look by choosing only the most streamlined styles for coats, outerwear, and bags with structure – no lumpiness! (See chapter eight.)
- Choose accessories and hairstyles that draw the eye toward your face.
- Maintain structure around your face with collars and accessories.
- Choose smart undergarments. (See page 77.)
- Wear makeup.

Dressing to slenderize a figure is such a popular issue in fashion that I've incorporated tips and strategies into just about every section of this book. It permeates many decisions in fashion.

As all of us know, weight problems can affect our emotional well being. This, in turn affects our self-concept and our sense of style. It is a treat for me to know that I have helped a woman enhance her sense of style. It is sheer joy when I know that I've helped one improve her self-esteem. It happened once at an inner-city high school in a Midwest city.

During a seminar, right after the segment on body types, I realized that this gal, who was probably about forty pounds overweight, sat hidden behind a mane of oily hair hoping and praying that no one would look back at her. She obviously wasn't enjoying herself.

It was also obvious that she lacked any self-esteem and was probably forced to come to my workshop on fashion. I felt for her, and went out of my way to make her feel a little bit more comfortable by cracking my corny jokes and affirming everyone's uniquely beautiful features whenever I got a chance.

I searched my mind for a subtle way to show her that caring for her body is just as important as caring for a body that is a size 6. So I slowly shifted into the weight gear and explained that no matter what your size, your body is your body *now* and needs to be dressed. You need to look beautiful on the outside because you are beautiful on the inside. You have something to offer the world, so use your fashion as part of that offering. Slowly, she brushed aside her veil of hair.

A girl in the front asked a question I occasionally get at my workshops: "What if you know you can lose weight? Why not just wait and save some money?"

I answered her as I have time and time again: Your body needs clothing *now*. There isn't some sort of weird inverse relationship between your weight and your worth where if one goes up the other must go down! You are just as deserving now as you are when you are twenty pounds lighter. And some people carry a lot of weight because that is just the way their body works: if you are healthy and can function well at your current weight, then you are at a healthy weight now.

I ended by also explaining that until one is dressed well, fueling confidence and appeal, one can not really make a logical, right-headed decision – like the decision to lose weight.

Suddenly, the girl in the back smiled. And she was beautiful.

For the next hour or so, this same girl raised her hand to ask a question, spoke out in her small group activity, and generally looked like a person with a lighter heart – if not body.

Remember, style isn't about dieting to have the Twiggy look. It isn't about the pursuit to mirror freaks of nature. It's about working with who you are, where you are, right now.

points for petites

You wear a petite size if you find that clothing in the regular misses sizes is usually too long in the arms and legs. Generally, women under 5 feet, 4 inches need to visit the petite racks and will find most sizes. The goal for you is avoid looking like you're swimming in your clothing. On a good day, your style can elongate your appearance. Try these ideas out for size.

- Be sure to buy only petite size clothing as it is sized to fit your shorter arm, leg, or torso lengths.
- Avoid cuffed pants. The horizontal lines will cut off the length of your legs.
- If you want to look taller, select 1-inch heels or greater even for casual wear. Heels give you lift and lengthen your look.
- Tailor when necessary. Your trouser cuffs should hit the top of your shoe heels, and your sleeves should reach the area between the knobby bone in your wrist and the beginning of your palm.
- Do not cut your appearance in half by creating a horizontal line at your midriff with either contrasting colors or a belt.
- Monochromatic dressing adds the appearance of height.
- Avoid longer skirts. Long skirts shorten your appearance.
- Do not choose accessories that overwhelm your size.

this mirror doesn't show my best features

Often, it's not the overall proportion that poses a problem for style, but one little part of the physique that seems to be too large, too long, or too droopy. Usually, women find that asking for advice on these problem areas takes more humility than the average human can drum up.

On the other hand, this is a neat little place to make a very important point about your God-given features. Everyone has something they'd like to change: eyes, nose, mouth, hair, toe – you name it. Although a very easy but costly solution these days is to submit to a major medical procedure, there may be room to put a whole new spin on it.

For example, if your forehead is "too high," think again that maybe it's only a little quirky and perhaps even something that could become signature. There may be ways to minimize the feature, but after that it's all a matter of how you spin it. It could be your distinguishing mark for style.

Just look at some of the fashion icons we know and love. Jackie Kennedy didn't have a perfect face but there are museum exhibits featuring all things *Jackie* style. Cher didn't have a perfectly proportioned face before all that surgery, but the world still went nuts for her. And Sophia Loren used to comment on all the irregularities of her face and still managed to become a beauty of international fame. It's all in how you spin it.

Audrey Hepburn was one who had such appealing style – even amidst the likes of Ann-Margaret and Marilyn Monroe – that a shorthand term for elegant style has become "That's so Audrey!" Rarely were her uneven teeth, thick eyebrows, and broad nose noticed, but Audrey once commented that she never thought she would be big in "pictures" with a face like hers. Audrey's advice to others: "Analyze yourself like an instrument. You have to be absolutely frank with yourself. Face your handicaps, don't try to hide them. Instead, develop something else."[1]

I've seen this "Audrey effect" a little closer to home. I once saw the 1981 wedding photo of a friend whom I had always considered to be absolutely put-together. The picture told a completely different story. My friend was actually very funny-looking. Who would have guessed? Nowadays, her layered-bob hair cut, carefully chosen clothes, and great amounts of mascara (emphasis on the eyes) de-emphasize her rather – God forgive me – strange looking face. She had learned over time that attention needed to be turned away from her uneven facial features, large ears, and crooked teeth and turned toward her thick hair, large blue eyes, and petite size. What a little self-knowledge can do! (So many of us laugh at our wedding pictures because with age we learn a lot about style.)

As for those body parts which seem to upset the balance of your overall figure, a little fabric cut in the right way can go a long way! Not too long after giving birth to my Gracie, I was hovering beside my children in the pool wearing a very carefully chosen swimsuit. It had a square neckline and a subtle and slimming pattern in a one piece style. It was flattering, and I didn't feel the least bit self-conscious in it.

Suddenly, a bevy of bikinied moms called out to me that I looked great. "Why don't you wear a bikini with that fabulous shape?" one asked.

"Because then you certainly would *not* say that I had a fabulous shape," I answered. No one had a clue as to how much flesh was under there, and no one had a right to know.

Again, the same rules apply regarding color, line, print, and texture. Here is a summary of tricks and strategies to streamline the appearance of these areas.

DON'T

DO

THICK NECKS OR DOUBLE CHINS

- Avoid very long hairstyles.
- Avoid chandelier earrings.
- Completely avoid choker and bib necklaces.
- Keep structure around your face in your collar. Avoid droopy necklines.

- Turtlenecks or mock turtlenecks are very good if you tend to have a double chin but also a long neck. A wide, short neck is not flattered by a turtleneck.
- Try a scarf softly draped inside a blouse neckline.

THICK UPPER ARMS

- For summer apparel choose either short sleeves that fall almost to the elbow or choose three-quarter-length sleeves. Avoid cuffs on either of these styles. A horizontal line created by either cuffs or a short sleeve will widen the appearance of an arm.
- Avoid sleeveless blouses or blouses with capped sleeves.
- Choose bell sleeves in both three-quarter or full-length styles.
- Avoid tight knits that cling to your arms.
- Choose loose fitting sleeves in general.
- Avoid large prints on your sleeves.

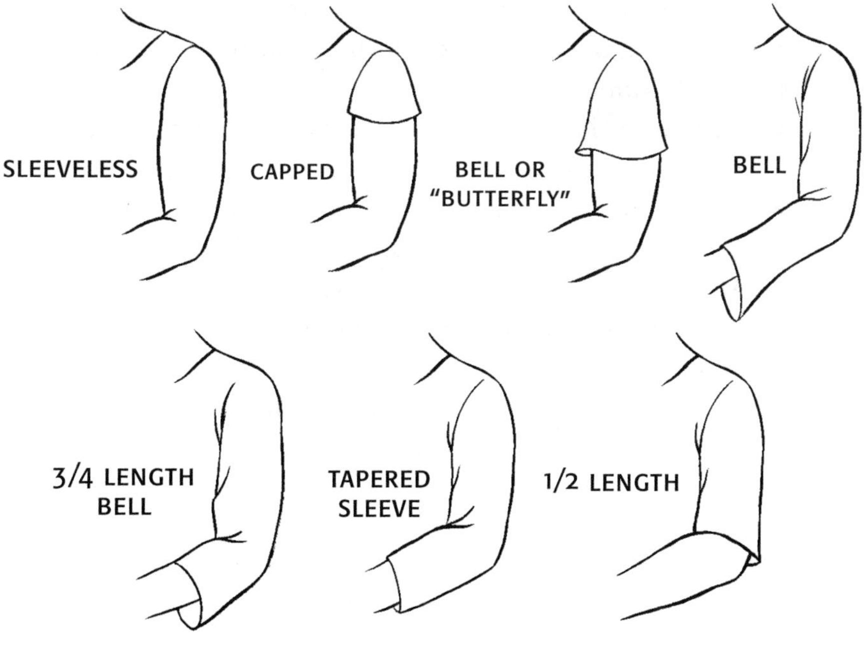

LARGE THIGHS

- Avoid skirts that expose any part of your thigh. Skirts which hang slightly above, at, or below the knee are all great options. They place the horizontal line along the thinnest part of your leg.

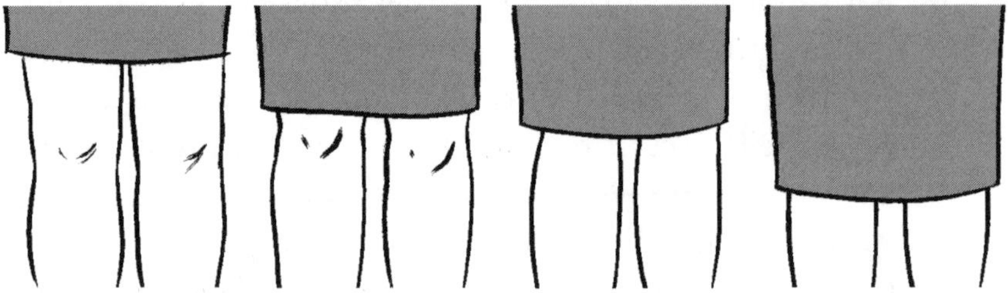

- Straight skirts or slightly A-line skirts are flattering
- Avoid knit bottoms, especially if you wear a plus size.
- Avoid prints in your skirts or pants.
- Choose capri pants or skirts instead of shorts unless the shorts fall in a way that your problem area is completely covered.
- If you must wear jeans, ensure that they do not fit too tightly or gather at the crotch. A "relaxed" fit is best.
- Avoid fabrics for trousers and skirts that tend to wrinkle. Horizontal creases create horizontal lines and therefore widen that area.
- Avoid ruffles along the bottom of your swimsuit.
- Wear a sarong wrap over your swimsuit.

LARGE OR DIMPLED KNEES

- Choose capri pants or skirts instead of shorts.
- Wear your skirt to just below your knee or longer. Avoid wearing your hemline at the middle of your knee as this horizontal line will add weight.
- A skirt with a flounce that dips to just below the knee provides a little variety.

DO

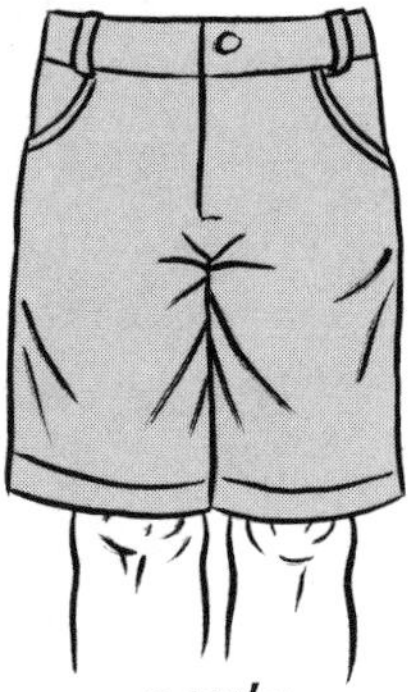

DON'T

THICK CALVES

- Avoid placing a horizontal line at the calf with the hemline of a skirt or capri pant.
- Try cropped trousers instead of capri pants. Place the horizontal line at your ankle or slightly above it.
- Try a skirt that hangs almost to the ankle if you are not concerned with appearing taller.

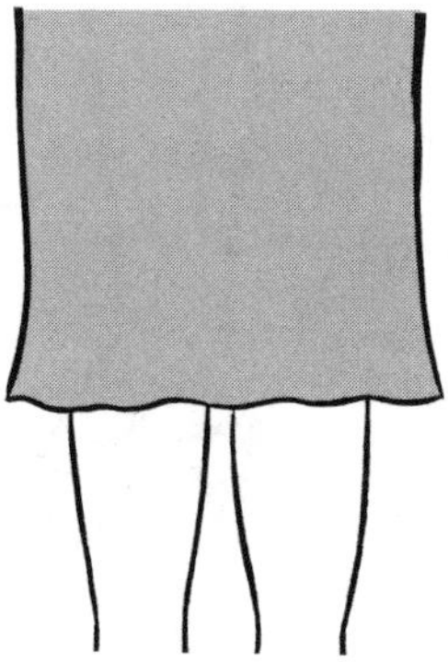

TO THE CALF
DON'T

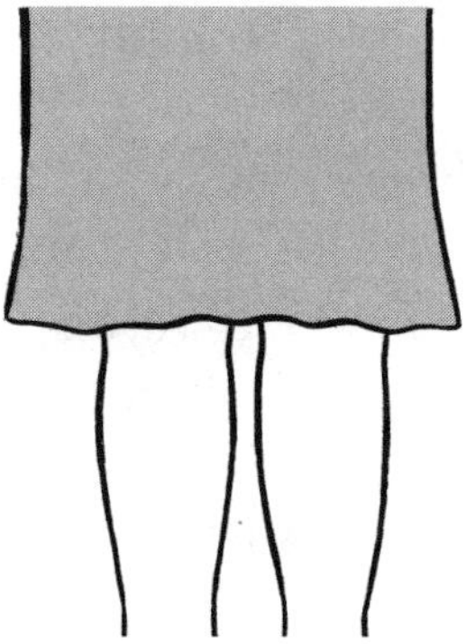

SLIGHTLY BELOW
THE KNEE
DO

- Choose darker hosiery for wintertime and carefully coordinate your shoes.
- Wear solid-color shoes with little or no embellishment.
- Choose fashion boots, especially high ones (avoid booties).
- Avoid ankle bracelets.
- Avoid embellished hemlines or bordered skirts.
- Avoid flats, low boots, or chunky heels with skirts. Try medium and high heels in thin styles.

THICK ANKLES

- Avoid placing the horizontal line at your ankles. Choose full-length trousers rather than cropped trousers.
- Wear a to-the-knee skirt rather than a skirt that falls to your ankles.
- Choose darker hosiery for wintertime.
- Wear solid color shoes with little or no embellishment.
- Choose fashion boots, especially form-fitting, high-heeled ones.
- Avoid ankle bracelets.
- Avoid shoes with ankle straps.
- Choose medium to high heel heights.
- Choose a medium thickness for heels. Extremely thin heels or chunky heels will emphasize thick ankles.

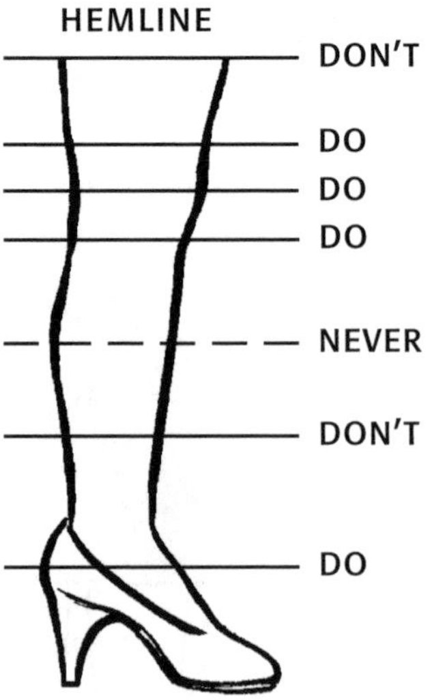

PROTRUDING TUMMY

- Read all of the points for the box body type. A woman with any other body type can also have a protruding tummy.

jean therapy: how to choose a pair of jeans

Now I'm going to throw in a little bonus section on that all-too-ubiquitous pair of jeans. Dungarees, blue jeans, or denims – whatever you call them – are a wonderfully functional addition to our fashion universe. While they may not be over-rated in my book, they are, very unfortunately, overused.

In this funny culture of ours, the blue jean can by itself signify things about the wearer such as socioeconomic status or age. That's the ironic power of these seemingly egalitarian trousers, and some groups of people are very particular about the kinds of jeans its members wear or how they fit. I think it used to be a lot more apparent, and for kicks I like to reflect upon how my choice for jeans has changed throughout the years.

Age 0–3: The pretend blue jeans. (I didn't exactly choose these.) The fabric is soft and dotted with Pooh-bears and Piglets. The fit is loose and bubbly.

Age 4–12: Sears brand bell-bottom jeans. Any self-respecting kid growing up in the seventies would never have limited him or herself to just *blue* jeans. The same kid never noticed the fit.

Age 13–17: Jordache or Calvin Klein brand jeans. The tighter the better. My friends and I would have to lie on our beds to pull the jeans up over our rears, then suck in our tummies to zip up. If I was really prepared, I'd have a comb sticking out of a rear pocket.

Age 18: A brief parting with the blue jean. I had to go preppie that year.

College: Faded Levis. For a few years they needed to have holes in the knees, and it was a matter of pride to look poverty stricken. They were fitted but not too tight.

Single life: Dark blue straight-leg jeans with a leather belt. Wearing them with loafers was a fashion-must.

Middle age: Blue jeans are no longer a foundation for any of my wardrobes. I'm a little saddened by that, but only in the same way I'm saddened about not wearing a back pack any more. If I must, I wear dark denim jeans in either a slightly flared or boot leg cut. I like a fitted look without any tightness.

I suspect that if and when I make it to age ninety-five I will have found that this timeline is actually a circle. I will eventually return to soft, pretend blue jeans that fit loosely.

Blue jeans are a work-horse item in your *personal casual* wardrobe. There is no other place for them, no matter how often you see them in the office, at an evening gala, or even at a wedding. Last year, heaven help us, I even saw a woman wearing them at a funeral.

Here are my tips for choosing the right pair of jeans for you:

- Jeans should be a complementary item, not an anchor in your wardrobe.
- Decide if jeans are really for you. Do they communicate what you want about your style or circumstances in life? Be honest. It may be best to decide against having them. I remember consciously deciding while I was a senior in high school that I wanted to be accepted as a good student with a future. I actually went the entire year wearing only chinos and skirts; you know, the preppie thing. By the time I hit college, I went back to my faded Levis because in that setting jeans like that implied the same thing. Go figure.
- In deciding if jeans are for you, take into account whether or not they flatter your figure. Blue jeans hold the dubious honor of framing the buttocks like no other kind of bottom. (Yes, you can live without jeans.)

- If you decide to incorporate jeans into your wardrobe (read my chapter on wardrobe planning); begin by choosing the color. Black jeans imply a little more sophistication but can fade easily and are a pain to keep dying. Dark blue jeans are the safest bet for maintaining a crisp appearance, and medium-blue jeans are a nice second. No woman over twenty-one should wear faded jeans unless she is working in a barn or setting dry wall.
- Always wash jeans inside-out and hang to dry.
- If you are trying to create a signature look or highly fashion-forward uniform for yourself, choose bottoms other than jeans. Blue jeans are currently the uniform of the masses.
- If you have large buttocks, avoid small back pockets. Also avoid jeans with no back pockets.

POCKETLESS SMALL POCKET MEDIUM POCKET

- Check that your jeans don't wrinkle along the bend of the leg in front. This creates a horizontal line and can add the appearance of weight.
- If you have *really large* buttocks, wear jeans with blazers or jackets that cover your rear. Otherwise, don't wear them at all.
- Decide on studs or embroidery only after you find out about your fashion personality. (See the next chapter.) From time to time, ripped, faded, or "dirtied" jeans appear on the racks at clothing stores. Never buy them. You can dirty them yourself.

- Be choosy about size. Ignore the numbers and try on many. If you are tall, choose jeans labeled *tall* or *long*. If you are petite, choose jeans that are labeled *petite* or *short*.
- If you want to give the appearance of longer legs, choose a dark-color jean which hits the floor when you stand barefoot. Try a pair of sandals or shoes with a heel. If you do not have a box or pear body type, choose a top in a dark color that stops at your waist line.
- Choose a pant-leg according to the type of shoe you tend to wear the most. If you like boots, choose boot-leg. If you tend to wear loafers, tapered or straight-leg jeans look best. Any other trendy pant-leg such as bell bottom or "skinny" should be chosen with age appropriateness, body type, and fashion personality in mind.

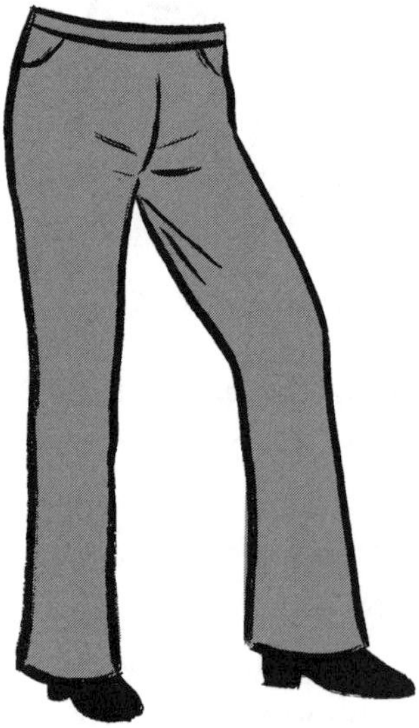

BOOT LEG
WITH BOOTS

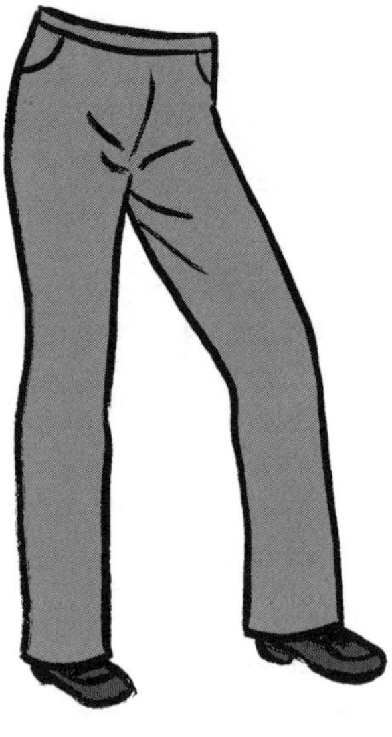

STRAIGHT LEG
WITH LOAFERS

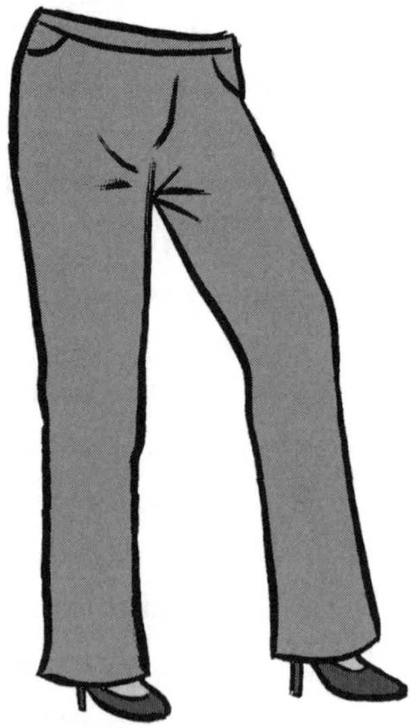

LONGER LEGS
WITH HEELS

- Avoid pleated jeans, hip huggers, or low-rise jeans if you have a pear shape body type. If you are a box, consider that your tops should fall well below the belt line of the jeans.
- While trying on a pair of jeans, ensure that there is no pull along your inner thighs. They also shouldn't "scoop up" your buttocks. The fly-front should sit flat and shouldn't bow out.
- Jeans should not be so baggy that they need a belt to hold them up. Try the next size down instead.

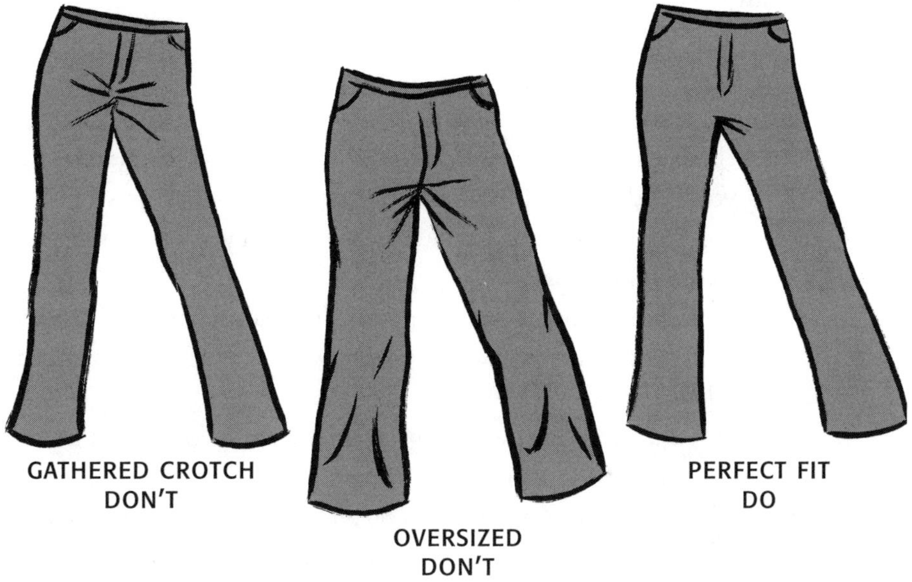

- Finally, don't get caught up in the designer label thing just for the sake of the label. In the area of shopping for jeans, the no-name or department store brands tend to wear just as long. The high price for designer labels is just for that: designer labels. No one should be reading things off your backside anyway. (And people do. Once while standing in line at the post office, the guy behind me pointed out that my Levis label said "M" and proceeded to explain to me why numbers aren't used for women's jeans. Thanks for the information, sir.)

waterproof fashion: how to choose a swimsuit

A little stressed just by the title? It's amazing how a strip of spandex can control our emotions so much. Just to set the record straight, imagine yourself only *swimming* in your swimsuit. For any other activity around the pool or beach, you can add a little wrap or cover. Swimsuits are no good for parading around in. Inevitably something sticks out without your permission.

So here are some guidelines:

- Budget for both the suit and the wrap or cover. If you want a little elegance, budget for a matching bag and towel as well.
- If you tend to use a pool and hot tub, have separate suits for each. The heat of the hot tub is harder on your suit and will shorten its lifespan.
- Don't skimp on the amount of money you spend. You need a well-made suit with a built-in bra and a perfect fit around the leg holes.
- Keep in mind your *elements of style*. You need your focal point at your face just as much as ever.
- Yes, color is still important – even with a tan. If you want a little zest, keep those wacky, trendy colors the secondary colors in your suit. (See chapter four.)
- Black or navy is a good universal color for streamlining.
- Strategies for proportion still apply here. Place embellishments, print, and stripes where you want to add the appearance of greater size to balance your entire look.
- Wear darker colors and vertical or diagonal lines where you want to slenderize.
- A small to medium print or texture in a one piece suit keeps the eye dancing over the rolls of flesh. This creates a wonderful optical illusion. (It does not work this way for street wear.)

- Square necklines are flattering for most body types.
- There is no happy medium in a bikini. You either look so sexually alluring that you cause a stir (Did you notice that your friend won't introduce you to her husband?) or so bad that you evoke pity. (The vast majority of us do not, shall we say, look the least bit appealing. But that's okay. The bikini is fashion that never really fits, and no one should ever feel the pressure to make it fit.) Also, remember how important your focal point is. Bikinis rob the face of the focal point whether you look good or bad. Bikinis should be completely avoided.
- Choose a two-piece so that the bottom half either covers your belly button or runs right under it. Too much flesh at the midriff adds weight. Some of the better retailers sell top and bottom pieces with the option of buying a matching bottom wrap. Wearing the wrap out of the pool helps to keep the focal point on your face.
- While trying on a swimsuit, lift your arms up above your head to see what happens.
- Check leg holes to ensure that you don't have to do any *unreasonable* hair removal. (But always do so when and where necessary.) A slightly high cut (high enough to create a diagonal line) is flattering for some. Avoid either too much of a horizontal line or too much flesh.
- Don't worry about looking sexy. Save that for your lingerie.

surgeon?

Just about any discussion on blue jeans and swimsuits leads to thoughts of cosmetic surgery in some crowds. It's hard to ignore the popularity of cosmetic surgery. I've been trying, but as I get older I find that I just can't. I hear it discussed on television, in fashion magazines, and even amongst my peers at the pool and soccer fields.

As procedures become less risky and more effective, ordinary folk are inquiring in ways they thought only the wealthy could.

Some of my very astute friends have suggested to me that perhaps the new socioeconomic line of demarcation (the line that was once determined by authenticity of stones for jewelry or furs for coats) will be the artificial youthfulness of sixty and seventy-something faces, chins, and buttocks (without the tell-tale scarring). That might be the case, but I'll say up front that society-climbing shouldn't dictate personal style, or – heaven forbid – medical procedures.

So, what are some guidelines to follow when deciding on cosmetic surgery? After all, this decision is highly personal and shouldn't fall prey to peer pressure. You should weigh the following:

1. Is there really a "problem?" Or are you looking for perfection? Determine whether you are fixating on something that really isn't a problem. In other words, if you were really busy, would you care?
2. Could the "problem" be disguised with some of the strategies discussed in this chapter? They are very inexpensive options.
3. What are the chances that the procedure will deliver the long-lasting and natural-looking results you expect? What exactly is involved with the procedure?
4. What are the risks? Can you afford it? Can others in your family afford for you to get the procedure? Can you afford the time recovering?
5. Finally – and this is the hardest part – is the choice to opt for the procedure rooted in something deeper than fixing one "problem"? If it's rooted in something deeper like self-esteem, a neurotic quest for perfection, or psychological revenge against an ex-husband, look those issues straight on

> and seek a more direct, pervasive solution to the real problem before spending thousands of dollars on a part of your body.

I am not opposed to cosmetic surgery. I can't think of a particular procedure that doesn't have any merit. I can even see some justifications to have the infamous breast augmentation – for some women. It depends upon all of the above.

My only reluctance to a full-throttle endorsement is that in opting for so much surgery, we are attacking the natural process of aging with unrealistic expectations for both our styles and our emotional well-being. No one is hot stuff at ninety. (Well, everyone is hot stuff at ninety but in a different way.) No one will live forever, and fatality rates today are the same as they were one thousand years ago: 100 percent!

In light of the fact that surgery is opted for at even younger ages, I must add one more bit of wisdom: Don't sweat it! Don't worry so much about your imperfections that you begin to loose confidence about dressing well.

Our quest for symmetry in our facial features, flawless skin, and perfectly shaped body parts could be called a perfection obsession. We all love perfection, but we soon forget that what isn't perfect about us adds interest and individuality. One of the many beautiful things about intimacy is that scars can be smoothed over and features re-aligned with each passing day. When we know this for ourselves, we feel accepted and loved, and we may even wonder why we thought we needed to change something in the first place. It can happen in love and in friendship. And we can make it happen for others.

FASHION MOMENT OF TRUTH

wardrobe analysis for body type

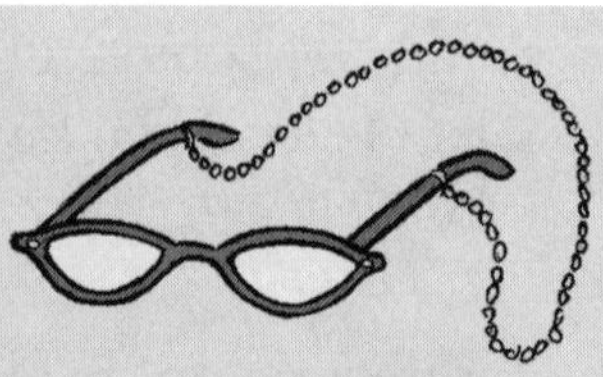

March straight to your closets, dressers, and shelves while this stuff is fresh in your mind. Beginning with this season's wardrobe, pull out all dresses, jumpers, tops, and bottoms. Lay them across the bed in the full light, or hang them around the room on hangers. The important thing is to get them in full view.

Grab a trusted, honest, and style-savvy friend to assist you with this activity if you suspect it will help. (You can help her with her wardrobe as well one day.) If you don't have a friend who meets those three qualifications, do this activity by yourself. Remember to get a babysitter if necessary.

Now, take a deep breath. Detach yourself from what you see. You just can't worry about who gave you what or where you wore something. *These* are just clothes. Nothing more.

Next, take each garment in your hands and reflect upon how well it works with your body type. Check it for color combinations, lines, prints and textures. *Remove anything which does not suit your body type.* Stick the items in bags so that you can't go back to reexamine them. *Promptly remove the bags!*

Need some ideas as to what to do with these items? Try any of these:

- Give them to a friend or family member.
- Donate them to a charity. There are many organizations who suit up needy women for career changes.
- Donate them to an organization such as Goodwill, the Salvation Army, or Amvets (among others).

- Consign them.
- Sell them at a flea market or on the Internet. That's called recycling.
- Have a rummage sale.

Avoid passing along these discarded items to folks with the same wardrobe maladies. Avoid passing along anything in disrepair. (It's okay to throw badly worn items into the garbage.)

Do not worry about how you will replace them. Never think in terms of "replacing" fashion mistakes. Also, use your discarding plan for items discarded during the next two *Fashion Moments of Truth*.

Finally, leave out this wardrobe and read through the next section. You'll return to these clothes in a short while.

If you can't leave out your wardrobe, place it away and return to it and the next chapter when you have a moment to continue analyzing.

CHAPTER THREE

the elements of style
fashion personality

this better not hurt

"I'm a really casual dresser," a very pretty woman once said to me. "I like to be as comfortable as possible."

"Tell me about it," I thought. Truthfully, she didn't need to say that. I could see by her pilled sweater and sweatpants that she was as serious about her comfort as an investor is about her portfolio.

"Yes, but what do you feel is your fashion personality?" I asked, kind of knowing the answer but wanting to get her to articulate some of the information I had just taught her.

Achieving a sense of style is not only a wonderful gift to yourself, it is a generous gesture to all those who see you.

AMY FINE COLLINS

"Casual, like." I said. I could hear a mild "duh" at the end of it, but maybe I was imagining.

Judy (let's just call her that) did have a fashion personality, but it wasn't "casual." Casual is a level or tone of dress. All fashion personalities have a casual level just as they each have a business, business casual, or evening form of dress. Judy was missing the point, but she did have a pretty clear idea of how she chooses fashion.

Although I'm a little too young to remember the days when blue jeans were revolutionary, I do have a vague recollection of the storm it brewed. Once, when I was in first grade, my parents had a teenage guest to our home who took off her shoes and sat on the floor instead of a chair. "Hippy," I thought, proud to know the lingua of socio-economics. Soon after, *everyone* was trying to be really, really casual. I could tell that my parents had a hard time with this, but to me it was just part of the landscape of the adult world.

Consequently, casual or "laid back" or (especially) "cool" is sort of virtuous. If you are casual, the wisdom goes, you are not pretentious, stuffy, or uptight. Now, no matter where I teach fashion, when I get to the segment on fashion personality, someone is there to remind me how important it is to be casual.

Relax! (I'm sure you already do in your clothes.) Knowing your fashion personality doesn't mean giving up comfort. It doesn't mean stereotyping. Fashion personality means knowing how to get fashion to fit you!

there's something about her glasses that reminds me of the Carter administration

It's usually at about this point in a seminar that someone asks if we think it's important to be "in style." Well, they've asked this everywhere except California.

By *in style* one usually means *up-to-date* or *current*. This is not to be confused with the personal style I discussed earlier.

My answer is *yes*! Without giving into fads, a woman can and should be concerned with maintaining a current appearance. It's important in many of the same ways that personal style is important. Additionally, a current appearance yields very clear benefits:

- A current style is psychologically refreshing. Everyone naturally seeks change, and clothing tends to satisfy this intrinsic yet mysterious desire. It's just pleasant to see the times reflected in a person's fashion. The only exception to this would be in times of economic distress or war. Even then an ethic can arise for fashion. So, for example, during World War II, evidence of rations and overall sacrifice for the war effort would be reflected in clothing.

- A current style promotes credibility, especially in the professional realm. It sends the message that the wearer understands the latest capabilities of her own profession and is capable herself. This is especially important in sales and marketing, business, medicine, science, manufacturing, technology, and most branches of education.
- In personal life, a current look can help a person appear to be informed and in-touch with what is happening in the world. Again, this can aid credibility in a person as a source of advice and inspiration.

So, what constitutes *the* look of the season? Fortunately, these days there are many looks for any single season, and they make up what fashion forecasters refer to as *trends*. There are trends in styles, themes, silhouettes, colors, accessories, and all those little items that scream *fad*.[1]

While it may be easy to identify what the trends are, tracing their roots can become a bit complicated. Sometimes a trend's inspiration comes from what's happening in politics or world events. Inspiration can also come from less lofty things such as a movement in music, art, pop culture, or the "mood of the streets." I have even heard one designer say that his inspiration for a shoe was from a napkin design in a small town café.

When several designers move in the same direction, a trend in design is born. The trend then gets the full red-carpet treatment and, before we know it, we see it on Hollywood celebrities, in movies and sitcoms and at charity balls and award nights. The publicity continues with photography spreads and written reviews in fashion magazines and on the Internet. If consumers purchase the items related to the trend, it sticks around for a while and becomes a true fashion trend or something referred to as "in style."

You'll learn more about how to fashion forecast when you consider shopping for wardrobe items. Your job now is to learn to distinguish the trends that work like *friends* for your wardrobe and the trends that are no better than short-lived *fads*.

The guidelines below are effective for evaluating particular items in the market.

FAD

- The item is generally unflattering for most women.
- The item has limited application. It can only be worn with a small number of things or only by itself and for limited occasions.
- The item is unreasonably uncomfortable even when it fits.

FRIEND

- The item is generally flattering for most women.
- The item has varied and multiple applications. It can be worn with many other things and for many different occasions.
- The item is comfortable to wear.

Just a few years back, animal prints were all the rage. You could see leopard spots, tiger stripes, or snake-skin patterns on everything from scarves and blouses, to trousers, purses, and shoes. Truthfully, the trend had all the features of a friend rather than a fad: It is generally flattering to most women because it can be translated into so many different colors; it can be worn with just about anything for any occasion; and it's been designed as part of many comfortable things.

But I had my reservations. It was way too ubiquitous. It got to the point where you could run into a drug store and find a children's plastic rain slicker in a hot pink snakeskin print. In a way, it was returning to its original cheap connotations. (Remember how radical it all seemed when it first came out? Well, radical except in Northeastern states that have names which begin with the word "New.") It was becoming equivalent to a lollipop flavor like fuzzy watermelon or radioactive lime.

My advice to women was to purchase it in moderation. It was a quick way to update, but you wouldn't want to invest too heavily or you'll date your wardrobe. (The well-dressed in those same states always knew this.)

I must be getting absent-minded. Whenever I complain that things aren't what they used to be, I always forget to include myself.

GEORGE BURNS

I was right. When I see an animal print top, bottom, or dress (oh no, not that!) I can tell you the year it was purchased. On the other hand, all things moderate survived and evolved into a classic look. Certain accessories still appear crisp and fashion forward in some animal prints, and designers are happy to come up with new and improved variations of the theme. This is a tidy example of how something that was all the rage and border-line faddish became a reliable classic in lower doses.

It is somewhat true that fashion trends are cyclic. I say *somewhat* because no trend ever returns exactly the way it was when it first appeared. Usually a look, termed "retro," will return, and retailers will depend on consumers visiting them for new and improved items rather than raiding the attic trunk. Most often, everyone can tell the difference between your grandmother's suede clutch and the clutch with the "something" of the moment.

Just to complicate the situation, keep in mind that different retro looks conjure up different feelings for different people. So, for some of my friends who dress circa 1969 and wish to vibe freedom and free love, people like me are just picking up on fond childhood memories, and people like my parents think of drop-outs.

I'm really fond of 1920s vintage (my house is an arts and crafts bungalow of the period), but those friends of mine who vibe and ooze think of vast right wing conspiracies. Once, when I showed my co-worker, Linda, a photo of my baby boy with his red bow tie, she said, "So, you are really into the fifties?"

Fifties? What? I thought all baby boys wore bow ties. That's what they're for, right?

But then I saw my father-in-law's 1959 high school graduation photo, complete with flattop and bow tie, and it all came together for me. Linda thought I was some sort of reactionary, longing for the days of Mrs. Cleaver.

Although things like this will happen no matter how well you plan, it's important to remember that by going partly retro in a wardrobe, a person conveys a little more than what most contemporary garments convey. Remember, fashion is a language.

it's ridiculous only in front of other people

Whenever I'm part of a discussion about trends and fads with a group of teenage girls, I often get the feeling that I just flew in from Venus (as opposed to Mars, of course). The trends with which I am familiar are vastly different from the trends they love and cherish. That's legitimate. Teenagers have different lifestyles, tastes, and – especially – physiques. We both need to communicate healthy attitudes about ourselves and others through our fashion; that's a given. But teens have other things to communicate such as their youth, idealism, and optimism, and these are different from some of the things I need to communicate such as, for example, professionalism. (See chapter ten for a discussion on fashion for youth.)

It's one thing for a teen to mimic the fashion of her mother or mother's friends. Before there even was a youth subculture, girls strove for the elegance of their mothers, often with wonderfully bonding rites of passage. It's quite another issue for grown women to copy the fashion of teens. Now, unfortunately, some strive for the carefree nature of some teen fashion, and it's usually the kind that is inappropriate even for teens. Often, a woman sees teen fashion as *the* fashion, for reasons that range from an undeveloped notion of style to a grasping for youth.

A woman's unhappiness is to rely on her youth. Youth must be replaced by mystery.

COCO CHANEL

This is an issue of age-appropriateness, and it usually creeps up in personal casual and business-casual wardrobe choices. The effects can be painfully counterproductive. The simplest solution for any woman to become more age appropriate in her fashion choices is to sit back and ponder her goals in life and how they should be communicated in her style. If they are the same goals as a fifteen year old girl, then the issue isn't fashion. It's something a lot deeper.

fashion personality is deep stuff

Let's return to fashion personality, the second *element of style.*

Unlike body type, fashion personality does not have handy numbers that speak for themselves. It's deeply psychological and requires, in the beginning, some reflection when purchasing any given garment or accessory. But it's also so much fun!

Knowing your fashion personality is important for three major reasons:

1. It fosters your self-confidence because you will wear things in which you will feel comfortable and capable.

2. It helps you to avoid purchases that end up in the back of your closet, saving you money.
3. It provides a consistent theme for your wardrobe. You save time in decision-making and always appear polished and complete.

I always sort of had a name for the style I wanted, but it seemed as if I would change according to the occasion for which I was dressing. For example, I would call myself "professional and classic" at work, but "refined" in the evening or on weekends. For my casual wear, one day I would describe myself as "informal and relaxed," while the next, "structured and preppie." What I was doing, however, was describing the *tone* of my dress for different occasions (kind of like Judy at the beginning of this chapter). This had only a little to do with deep-rooted, gut-level, *fashion personality*.

Generally, fashion consultants describe four. Of course, within these categories there are an infinite number of possible variations because no one can be pigeon-holed into any one label.

Here's the burning question: *Can you consciously choose your own fashion personality?* True, it's different from body type: no changing that because it's physiology. But fashion personality is *psychology*. You are who you are, and it's impossible to successfully and confidently function in a style that has nothing to do with you. So, the answer is *no*, unless you are an award-winning actress.

Fashion personality might change as you change, and it's fair to say that it can change many times in a lifetime. I know mine has.

OBJECTIVE: understand your fashion personality so you can select wardrobe items more conscientiously.

STYLE PROFILE #6

I've got personality

Find out yours! Choose the most appropriate answer for you. None may be perfect, but one is close. Don't think too hard.

1. When I get ready for a special occasion I tend to . . .
   a. keep it simple. Sometimes I apply a little makeup to improve my coloring.
   b. apply my makeup with a conservative use of colors, but always careful to look polished.
   c. apply my makeup to create a soft, delicate look.
   d. apply my makeup to achieve flair. I tend to use noticeable colors on my eyes and lips.

2. Generally I like to wear my hair . . .
   a. in a simple, no-fuss haircut; maybe a pony tail.
   b. in a timeless cut that can be stylish through any fashion trend.
   c. in curls, long and flowing or soft and current.
   d. in new and innovative styles that follow current trends. I am not afraid to try new things.

3. If I had my own clothing store, I would name it . . .
   a. *Navy Blues, Back to Basics*, or *Simple Style*
   b. *Classic Treasures, Sharp Image*, or *Lauren Taylor*
   c. *Victoria's Attic, Wistful Thinking*, or *Scarborough Faire*
   d. *All That Jazz, Chica's*, or *Never Limited*

4. For my photograph on the book jacket of my autobiography, I would choose to wear . . .

a. a pair of jeans or khakis and a knit top.
b. a straight skirt or crisp pants, a blouse with a collar, and a smart jacket.
c. something very pretty like a dress or skirt and soft sweater with matching pearls.
d. something that really shows that I am different.

5. When I shop . . .
   a. I find what I want in a catalogue pretty quickly. Otherwise, I'm efficient with large retailers.
   b. I expend a little extra effort to find quality. I have my favorite retailers and I'm willing to pay a bit more for the right look and the proper fit.
   c. I use both department stores and boutiques, although I have to feel inspired and uplifted. Spring is my favorite shopping season.
   d. I use a mix of shopping techniques, including a few visits to some off-beat places to put together a look that's different.

6. When I go out in the evening I like to create a look that is . . .
   a. simple, understated.
   b. elegant, tasteful.
   c. feminine, soft, and flowing.
   d. striking and fashion-forward. Something that makes me stand out from the crowd.

7. The theme I use when choosing accessories is . . .
   a. *Simplicity*: Do I have to wear accessories?

b. *Timelessness*: I like to wear jewelry (maybe even a scarf in a pinch) in classic themes.
c. *Romance*: It has to be pretty.
d. *One of a kind*: I'm willing to try new things.

8. An ideal winter coat for me . . .
   a. can zip into a duffel bag. It's sporty and has pockets.
   b. is tailored and made of wool.
   c. has fur or faux fur trim and a large hood. I like a soft silhouette.
   d. is in a strong color with novel details.

9. If I were stranded on a deserted island (in a moderate climate) with only a sewing machine and a lifetime supply of fabric, I would wish the fabric to be . . .
   a. a solid color; especially a neutral. A knit would be best.
   b. a solid or simple print in primary colors. Denim, Khaki, or a light-weight wool would be very acceptable.
   c. a beautiful print in a fluid fabric. Or, maybe cashmere or angora to stay warm. Can I get a bolt of lace too?
   d. any fabric, and I could use some island materials to accessorize.

10. For me, the ultimate compliment about *my style* would be . . .
   a. "She is so natural. She has a simplicity about her and an understated beauty."
   b. "She is a tasteful, well-groomed woman with an eye for quality and detail."

c. "She is feminine, pretty, and reminiscent of more chivalrous times."
d. "She is interesting, exciting, and wears things I could never look good in."

Tally the number of times you have chosen:

A: _____

B: _____

C: _____

D: _____

The letter that you have chosen the most corresponds with your fashion personality. Check below for this letter and find out what your fashion personality is.

Most likely, you have chosen one letter the majority of the time. If you end up tying for two (or very close to tying for two), turn to page 126. Maybe it's the case that you are a combination of two. It's rare for someone to tie for three or four fashion personalities. (Sometimes d's will tie up for a few.) If you have a pretty even split of three or four, continue reading all the guidelines below to see which describes you best.

The guidelines under each fashion personality are meant to help clarify what you probably already know — if only subconsciously. I also include helpful tips and suggestions. At the end of each of the four personalities, I include a list of "best bets." I only suggest these items to illustrate for you the most basic example of that fashion personality. From those, you can build up. These best bets are no-brainer outfits, and tend to be four-season items.

if you chose mostly A, you have a **relaxed** fashion personality.

You like simplicity and no fuss. You avoid too much structure, and you love to feel comfortable. Enjoy your carefree style, but avoid becoming recklessly carefree about the way you look.

Use these guidelines to enhance your style.

- Go for high quality knits which wash well. Reserve the sweats and gym-wear for the gym and try newer styles to update and revitalize.
- Avoid faded denim even for casual wear. Go for a little more structure and a darker blue if you decide to buy a denim skirt. Never try to pass these off as "business casual" unless they are dark-colored and structured.
- Buy wrinkle-free items when the option is there. If you hate ironing, be realistic with yourself and avoid buying fabrics that look like they've been through four generations after just a few washes.
- Wear makeup even when you don't feel like it (a little bit can still appear natural!).
- Check that your look is polished and clean in the professional setting. Clean up that business casual wardrobe.
- Avoid totally frumping out even when at home. There's a difference between having a relaxed style and being a slob.

- Examine your hairstyle. Is it working for your face and your style? Is it right for you? Is it time to *get* a style? Some love the short, maintenance-free style. This is a plus, but consider other factors such as face shape or hair texture.

- Personal casual best-bets: solid knit top in a fantastic color for you (see the next chapter), *coordinated* trousers, and comfortable loafers (besides sneakers or slippers).

My friend Peg has this personality. She's got a carefree pixie haircut, wears the same gold stud earrings just about every day, and is a real genius at mixing and matching knit separates that have the aura of comfort but the elegance of good fit and high quality. She's the type of woman who inspires someone of any other fashion personality to respect the simplicity of the relaxed.

Remember Judy, my casual friend? She also has a relaxed fashion personality. She appreciates very simple lines and few frills.

Judy, however, did what some do; she frumped out. (Each fashion personality has its own pitfall.) In fact, I would never have guessed that she was a very wealthy woman who "loved to shop," as she admitted to me. Sadly, most of her fashion purchases (which amounted to a vast fortune) were made with *only* comfort in mind. Let's face it: Comfort doesn't have to cost big bucks and shouldn't eclipse other considerations.

deeper thoughts

Now that you know you have a relaxed fashion personality, it's time to explore a little more about your style. Reflect on what kind of relaxed style you have. Is it earthy? Natural? Woodsy? Athletic? Whimsical? Youthful? Academic? Write your ideas below.

___

___

___

Return to page 126.

if you choose mostly B, you have a **classic** fashion personality.

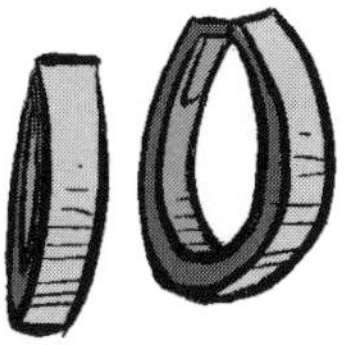

You desire structure in your wardrobe, and you appreciate timeless accessories, a slightly man-tailored appearance, and attention to details. Enjoy the continuing success of this look, but avoid becoming boring or pretentious.

Use these guidelines to enhance your style.

- Buy high quality garments made from wool, cotton, silk, and fine fibers (both natural and synthetic).
- Avoid faded denim even for casual wear. If denim doesn't make you feel elegant, don't bother with it.
- Iron when necessary.
- Wear makeup even when you don't feel like it. Update your look when necessary.
- Try the versatile man-tailored white or cream colored shirt (see the third *element of style* before you choose a color) as a basic item in your wardrobe. Layer it with turtle necks and/or blazers, add a belt, and try a scarf. You can get many different looks with this one, simple item.
- Check basic items such as blazers, skirts, and trousers to ensure that they are still in excellent shape. They may be in style, but also threadbare from excessive use.
- Check accessories such as scarves, jewelry, purses, belts, and shoes. Are they tired? Replace with slightly up-to-date versions of the same classic styles. Coordinating them will make you feel complete!
- Throw away any white or ivory hosiery. It went out with the Reagan era.

- Check your hairstyle. Is it time to update? Some classics love bobs, page boys, and styles with hair bands. These styles can be updated as well.
- Classic personal casual best-bets: man tailored blouse in white or cream, blazer and/or silk or cotton twinset in your best color, structured trousers in a versatile color, signature accessory (pearls, earrings, or watch) and loafers.

I know a classic named Carmen who always looks so put together no matter what she is doing or where she is going. Her characteristically classic forte is her ability to coordinate accessories such as scarves, necklaces, earrings, and even gloves and umbrellas. Her preference for high quality is evident in her woven tops and woolen trousers, but she's a far cry from stuffy. Instead she makes you feel classy just being with her.

The pitfall for the classic is really two-fold: boring or pretentious. Boring *and* pretentious can be really painful. Since I've picked on poor Judy, let's move on to a classic with some issues.

Maggie once suffered from this two-fold pitfall. During her closet-cleaning, I removed a total of sixteen knit tops with nautical gold-emblem detailing, four blazers with various other gold emblems, two pairs of gold flats, and a twenty-year-old tweed blazer. (She gave me permission to tell you about it!) She giggled as I pulled out each item, and admitted that she had no idea how much she had subconsciously imitated a fanatical country-clubber.

deeper thoughts

Now that you know you have a classic fashion personality, it's time to explore a little more about your style. Reflect on what kind of classic style you have. Is it urban? Country? Town and country? Euro? Old world? Preppie? Refined? Sophisticated? Cosmopolitan? Write your ideas below.

____

____

____

Return to page 126.

if you chose mostly C, you have a **romantic** fashion personality.

You love pretty details, a feminine aura, and softness. You truly enjoy the art of being a woman, and choosing beauty has never been a problem for you. Ensure that your look is never "girlish" and that your professional appearance is serious and "ready to work."

Use these guidelines to enhance your style.

- Assess your current wardrobe. Are there too many outdated floral prints and paisleys? Are the dress styles – although very pretty – a little too out of date? Try new patterns where and when appropriate.
- Try the sweater or "twin" set. (See p. 200) It can be romantic and is usually found in abundance. I recommend cotton, silk, or cashmere. Top with pearls, and you'll have a beautiful look.
- Continue your use of romantic detailing. Cameos, antique pins, chandelier earrings, pearls, or glass beads are wonderful fashions to explore.

- Throw away any white hosiery.
- If you are over forty or if you have a long face, shorten or shape the long hair style. Ensure that whatever you do flatters your face.
- Don't neglect your shoes. Keep them clean and up to date.
- Leave headbands and girlie hair pieces home and out of the office.
- Romantic, personal casual best-bets: flattering skirt, romantic sweater (bateau neck, shawl-collar, or twinset in cotton, silk knit, cashmere, or angora), coordinated shoes, and a signature accessory (pearls, pin, earrings, etc).

I'm really not kidding about the romantic always enjoying what is pretty. It's innate. My little sister is a great example. She wears solid colors in softer cuts and accessorizes with romantic pieces. What's really fun about her is that every visit to her home reveals to me a new bit of décor only a romantic could find. Everything from the rose-patterned lampshade to the needlepoint throw rug makes her abode a bit more comfy and leaves her signature. You know that this place is Elizabeth's.

The pitfall of the pure romantic is that she can get so carried away with the floral prints and ruffled detailing in her clothes that she ends up looking like a little girl. For example, Moira was a romantic and an at-home mom. She had been so for such a long time that her wardrobe consisted of only trousers, shorts, dresses, t-shirts, and sweaters. The romantic in her always ensured that she had a bit of elegant detailing with attractive patterns or accessories, so her casual wardrobe only needed a little updating. The issue came up whenever she had to dress up for a special occasion like a family event or a date with her husband. For these times, she'd pull out one of two obvious "stand-by" dresses. Each had a long and fluid skirt in a conventional floral print topped with a jewel-neck bodice adorned with lace.

Fortunately, poor Moira finally decided, after years of dressing this way, that the world suspected her fashion sense had ended sometime in 1987 and that during that year she must have joined a strange cult that preached: "Thou shalt wear flowers in thy dress-up clothes." This revelation compelled her to take advantage of some of the newer romantic styles of the fashion season.

Many women I know, especially those whose fashion heyday was in the 1980s (that would include me), traditionally believe that even their work wardrobe must include a floral print somewhere (usually a skirt, blouse, or vest). Romantics tend to carry this to extremes.

If floral prints are a way of expressing your personality, use current and *flattering* patterns (in low doses) rather than the ones that are simply the prettiest from a wallpaper point of view. It's nice to see Waverly at a home décor shop, but the accounting department can probably forgo this. (All three of your *elements of style* will help guide your selection.)

deeper thoughts

Now that you know you have a romantic fashion personality, it's time to explore a little more about your style. Reflect on what kind of romantic style you have. Is it country? Home spun? Old world? Bohemian? Vintage Hollywood? Victorian? Whimsical? Glamorous? Sophisticated? Write your ideas below.

___

___

___

Return to page 126.

if you chose mostly D, you have an **expressive** fashion personality.

You have panache and see fashion as an art form. Avoid hooking onto too many fads that lack the requisite longevity and tone down extremes in the workplace.

Use these guidelines to enhance your style.

- Assess your current wardrobe. Update if necessary and don't hesitate to discard faddish items for which you are awaiting a return. They will not come back in quite the same way they made their last appearance.
- Purchase only high-quality garments that have some versatility to them.
- Avoid an evening look for day. Always consider the purpose of your dress for each activity of your life.
- Throw away any white, pink, lime, red, yellow, green, cobalt, or orange hosiery. Did that cover it? You get the point.
- Stick with your natural hair color (or at least a close approximation to it). If it grays, color it your natural hair color before it was gray or add contrasting highlights to add interest.
- If you wear false nails, keep embellishments to a minimum for the workplace.
- Continually assess if any given garment is age-appropriate.
- Expressives tend to be fashion-forward. These clothes really stand out when they are too old so keep in mind those shorter expiration dates.
- Personal casual best-bets: one monochromatic outfit in your favorite dark neutral, a pair of coordinated shoes, and a signature accessory (bag, scarf, earrings, or watch).

Over the years I've known a few women who each had radically different expressive styles. One was all sophistication in her completely black ensembles and another used colors in ways that made her seem more exciting than an action film. One client placed her drama only in her accessories while another kept her accessories dramatically minimal. This breed is a lot of fun. They usually love their pitfalls. The challenge for them is to tone them down and avoid overdoing it.

A while ago, I had a wild and expressive friend who made every day things a big deal. Usually, her outfits would be the talk of the party . . . but for both good and bad reasons. For every wonderful fashion statement she made with glass beads or fur, she would make an embarrassing blunder with orange shoes or boas. Don't get me wrong: no one had a problem with the items *per se* . . . on Halloween. It was all a matter of when and where she wore them.

Okay, expressives: Think *apropos* when choosing your outfits. That will get you far in life.

deeper thoughts

Now that you know you have an expressive fashion personality, it's time to explore a little more about your style. Reflect on what kind of style you have. Is it sophisticated? Euro? Eastern? Exotic? Bohemian? Native? Glitzy? Jazzy? Theatrical? Chic? Write your ideas below.

____

____

____

Return to page 126.

what to do if you are a combination of fashion personalities

If you have tied for two or even three fashion personalities you may be a combination. You could be:

- relaxed with classic structure
- relaxed with romantic touches
- classic with relaxed simplicity
- classic with romantic detailing
- classic with a bit of drama
- romantic with relaxed tendencies
- romantic with classic structure
- expressive who borrows from everyone
- expressive with classic structure
- expressive with romantic themes.

Rarely will you see an expressive-relaxed combination, so the omission was intentional.

Decide your combination, but read the tips for both personalities. After a while, you will find that you tend to favor one over another, so stay open minded.

it's in the details

I'm betting that after all this explaining you have segmented every garment in the world into one of these four fashion personalities. Great! You're learning. But here's the curve: Fashion personality has more to do with how an ensemble is *put together* than with the pieces which make up any particular look. Of course, extremely obvious romantic and expressive pieces will only work for someone with those personalities, but even then there may be interesting ways to remake items for other personalities.

While teaching about fashion personality, my colleagues and I like to use a sheath dress to explain what I mean. Picture a wonderfully ordinary sleeveless black sheath. Here's how it can be modified to each fashion personality for a casual occasion on a warm day:

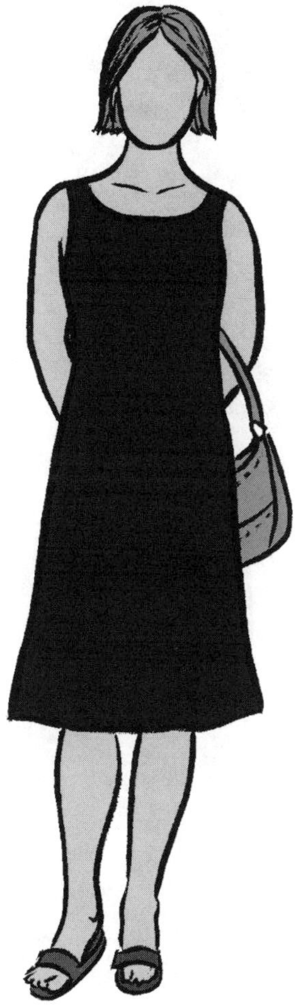

1. RELAXED: Don't accessorize at all. Slip into a pair of flat slides. Add a simple leather hobo bag.

2. CLASSIC: Accessorize with a simple necklace and matching earrings. Add a black pair of one-inch heel slides and a structured satchel handbag.

3. ROMANTIC: Wear an antique choker and a decorative hair comb. Step into a pair of maryjanes with a kitten heel and add a clutch or wristlet.

4. EXPRESSIVE: Tie a scarf in a magnificent color around the neck. Wear large hoop earrings and a pair of embellished shoes. Add an oversized bag.

That's the beauty of fashion personality! You add your own touches!

SEMINAR FAQ

shopping for fashion personality

QUESTION: How do you shop for your fashion personality? After all, most retailers don't spell out the fashion personalities to whom they are appealing.

ANSWER: The simplest place to decide which retailers to visit is to look back to the places you have visited in the past. Where do you tend to get most excited? What stores seem to get you through their doors to actually buy? Your patterns for past shopping trips are good maps for future ones.

My guess is that at some point (especially once you finish this book) you will want to expand your repertoire for shopping. Rather than trying to peg each retailer's "FP appeal," go with your gut. Some boutiques strike you as gold mines as soon as you walk in. Department stores are a little trickier, as they tend to section off the specific styles, giving each a snappy name that will appeal to a certain personality type, but might contain many other kinds of pieces. Off-price stores are the most difficult because styles are mixed together. In any case, forage through, get the gist, and go with your gut. That's really all there is to it.

is it multiple personality syndrome?

You're classic, but you love to appear fashion-forward. You're relaxed, but you tend to wear bold colors. Maybe you're expressive, but you wouldn't dream of piercing your ears.

Even if you tested ten out of ten for your fashion personality, you may find yourself wandering around in one or two features of another one. No, it's not multiple personality syndrome. It may not even be a problem at all. For example, I have a classic-expressive fashion personality (six b's and four d's). However, in the spring, I am inspired by the beautiful floral prints that seem to puff away the gray and cold of the winter. Knowing my fashion personality prevents me from going wild for a whole bunch of romantic, floral pieces. (Gosh, I never even chose a c!) But also knowing how to cleverly incorporate one printed scarf or summer skirt in a *classic* way and into my wardrobe of *classic* pieces enables me to enjoy this style. (Remember, it's how an ensemble comes together rather than the individual pieces.) Although floral items are mostly romantic in nature, the romantic fashion personality does not have exclusive rights to floral prints. Hey, this is fashion; you can't help what you like. Just moderate what you buy.

Also, staying fashion-forward is extremely important in my profession. Rather than becoming completely expressive, I opt for classic pieces that have been updated. Again, being fashion-forward is a major feature of the expressive, but the expressive fashion personality does not have a monopoly of the fashion-forward.

You'll know when you've wandered too far away from your fashion personality: Items will sit in your closet untouched because they just don't "do it" for you. This chapter is all about preventing that from happening.

the me I always knew I was

Your personal style is very much characterized by both your fashion personality and your tastes. What you do with this self-knowledge makes all the difference. Enjoy it!

FASHION MOMENT OF TRUTH

wardrobe analysis for fashion personality

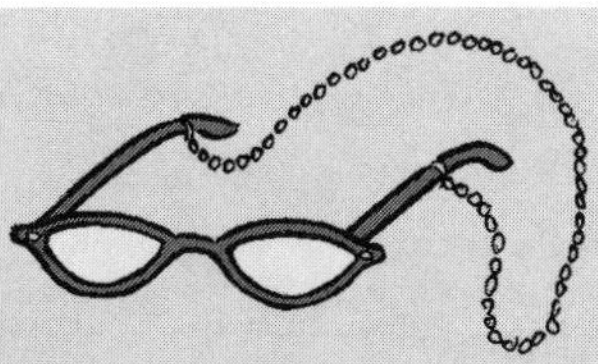

Return to those clothes in your bedroom. Now, add to it all of your shoes, purses, belts, jewelry, and other accessories. Stick to this season's wardrobe for now.

Ready?

Again, take another deep breath and detach yourself from what you see.

Check out each garment. Put it on if necessary. Decide if what you see is really you. Does it fit in with what you found out about your fashion personality? Does it fit well with the style you described for yourself?

Stay consistent. You want to have a theme to your wardrobe that goes along with your personality. Remove anything that doesn't. Also, check for wear and tear. Remove items which are permanently stained, pilled, completely out of style, or in general disrepair. (You've already done much of this!)

TRY THIS: Take notes based on the labels of both the items you keep and the items you discard. Which brands or designers tend to go with your style? Which ones didn't work for you? Also, look to see which names gave you the quality you expected and which names failed miserably.

Once finished, prepare for the third *Element of Style* in the next chapter. This is the last step for clothing analysis.

CHAPTER FOUR

the elements of style
color palette

do you have the flu, or is that just a really bad color for you?

During the course of any given seminar and to drive home my point on choosing optimal colors for a wardrobe, I often hold up my least optimal colors (olive, brown, and orange) below my face and ask the crowd for some opinions.

"Ewww," the pinched faces say.

No further explanation needed.

a colorful history

If you were just awake in the 1980s, you probably noticed all the fabric color swatches and skin color analysis systems that floated around like the high maintenance rayon of the period. In fact, you might even know a little about the color analysis methods. Unfortunately, however, you may have to leave some of that knowledge behind.

That's because the original good idea has been smothered by a countless number of new, sometimes more marketable color analysis systems that work for the fashion color consulting industry but *against* you. No matter what label you use for how to best remember the palette of colors, the colors either flatter, or they don't.

So, I'll boil it all down to the original theory without the famous seasons we all have heard so much about. Here's how it goes:

Examine your hair and describe its color. You might say that it is light brown with red highlights or jet black, or blonde with ash tones. You might also be able to describe highlights and lowlights and other such things, but generally these qualities are pretty easy to see.

Now look at the skin on your face. It's a little more difficult to describe its color because of its multidimensional character. You wouldn't say simply brown, black, or white. Rather, you would say something like "dark brown with ashen areas" or "olive with dark brown freckles and sallow tones." You would speak in terms of the dominant color, the varying shades of color, and the colors of all your little imperfections.

Beauty will save the world.

FYODOR DOSTOEVSKY

One way to simplify the description is to point out the *undertones* of skin color. The undertone is the tone of your skin that is not readily apparent until certain colors are held up to it. The concept was first put to good use in the Western world when portrait painting became popular during the Renaissance, and painters realized that rendering a more accurate representation of their subjects involved adding either blue or gold hues to the dominant color they were using to represent skin. They were noticing *undertones*.

Very generally, there are two undertones to human skin: cool and warm.

These undertones become apparent when colors are put close to the skin. Each color either works against (or *argues with*) the skin tone and causes a dull, flat, and an overall unhealthy look, or it complements the skin tone with a glow that appears healthy and vibrant. So, skin with warm undertones will appear healthy and vibrant next to warm colors, and skin with cool undertones will appear healthy and vibrant next to cool colors. The colors work with nature.

Color labels in and of themselves don't always signify their warmth or coolness, and most colors have warm and cool variations. For example, if you were to take out a tube of red paint and dab it onto a canvas, there's no mistaking the color you see: red (probably bright and true). But add just a tiny bit of blue to the red – just a dab (too much and it's purple!), and begin to mix. Suddenly, your red is cooler and deeper. This red is a *cool* red.[1]

Squirt out another bit of red and add a little yellow this time. The effect is dramatically different, but the color could still be called red. Now, however, the red is closer to the color of a tomato and nearing the color orange. It's a *warm* red.

Both of these reds, the warm and the cool, can be darkened (shades) and lightened (tints) by adding black or white paint. Still, they remain either warm or cool because of the original mixture.

Knowing your skin's undertone, and, in turn, knowing the difference between a *brick* red and a *tomato* red, is essential for effectively choosing color for your style.

The color palettes, or the colors grouped according to how they flatter undertones, are categorized in four ways: cool, light cool, warm, and light warm. (See the color palettes on the back flap of this book.)

the only problem is that I'm allergic to yellow

In my work with women, I have found color analysis to be the second most emotional issue for women. (The *most* emotional issue is weight changes.) This is because we each love certain colors and have developed connotations for them. Pink might have been the dreaded (or the welcomed) assigned color for childhood. Green might have been a uniform color. And, black may have become synonymous with freedom and expression or death and mourning. I can honestly admit that I have developed an aversion to the color dark green because I spent eight less-than-ideal years wearing a uniform in this color. (It had yellow, blue, and red pin stripes forming a plaid across a pleated skirt. It was actually kind of cute, but I think I reached saturation point.)

Just remember, though, color is more than what you wear. You can enjoy them on other people, in your home, or in nature. (See *Post Color Analysis Counseling* later.)

The point of knowing your color palette is to understand what looks *optimal* on you. Folks used to joke that my colleagues and I were just "color season police" whenever we recommended specific colors for them. There's no issue of control here. It's only an issue of sharing what we honestly observe.

How I wish that someone had shared what she had honestly observed on me while I was in college. I fancied myself a euro-earthy type and wore tons of olive, rust, and black. The black was good for me; the others made me look like I had chronic fatigue syndrome. No wonder I went for a nine-month spell without dates.

My mentor Patti owned a clothing boutique that would have served me well. She displayed all clothing by color season, so that any customer (after a color analysis, of course) could go straight to her best colors without confusion or heartache. *Seasonal Impressions* became one of the most unique and customer-friendly places in the Baltimore area, and people lament Patti's retiring still.

Unfortunately, what you will be completing within this chapter is not a color analysis in the fullest sense. You need an in-person color consultation for that. On the other hand, you will arrive at the same conclusion if you follow the directions very carefully. If ever you doubt how a color looks on you, ask an honest friend who won't simply tell you what you want to hear.

OBJECTIVE: determine your color palette so that you can select wardrobe items in your optimal colors.

STYLE PROFILE #7

painting with my palette

First, remove your makeup so that you get the most accurate reading of color against your skin. Then, gather some garments in the color orange, and others in the color pink. If you don't own garments in these colors, borrow them or use large pieces of construction paper. You will need other colors later on, but you will not know which ones until you reach the end of this profile.

Answer each question below by circling the appropriate number:

1. My *natural* hair color now (or before I turned gray) is or was:
   1. dark brown to black
   2. reddish blonde
   3. medium to light brown
   4. light red
   5. ash blonde
   6. medium red to auburn (dark red)
   7. golden or light blonde

2. My skin tone could be described as:
   1. dark brown to black
   2. light and very ruddy
   3. sallow or olive to light brown
   4. very pale and peachy "peaches and cream"
   5. very pale with pink tones

3. If I spend too much time in the sun I tend to:
    1. tan very easily (or become darker) or be unaffected
    2. burn or freckle and remain pale
    3. freckle or burn but later tan

4. If I were to wear the color orange without makeup I would look: (Hold up the color orange to your face before a mirror in full daylight if you can't recall and don't worry; it doesn't matter what you think of the color. No one will force you to wear it even if it looks good.)
    1. overwhelmed, sallow, or sick
    2. healthy and glowing

5. If I were to wear the color pink without makeup I would look: (Hold up the color pink to your face before a mirror in full daylight if you can't recall and don't worry; it doesn't matter what you think of the color. No one will force you to wear it even if it looks good. This is objective observation here!)
    1. healthy and better than orange
    2. overwhelmed, sick, or harsh

Now, examine your answers. **If you answered by choosing mostly odd numbers, your skin has cool undertones.** To be sure, stand in front of a mirror either outside or in a very well lighted room. (Ensure that there are no shadows on your face.) Hold up the colors bright pink, white, black, and royal (bright) blue to your face. They should be flattering on you and bring out a glow in your cheeks.

If you answered by choosing mostly even numbers, your skin has warm undertones. To be sure, stand in front of a mirror either outside or in a very well lighted room. (Ensure that there are no shadows on your face.) Hold up the colors orange, brown, olive, and cream (ivory) to your face. They should be flattering on you, better than the colors above, and bring out a glow in your cheeks.

To continue finding your best palette, you must determine if lighter colors are better on you after all.

For example, a woman with cool undertones may have dark brown hair and light brown skin. She may look stunning in royal blue, hot pink, and black because her dark coloring is not overwhelmed by these strong colors.

Another woman with cool undertones, perhaps someone with very pale skin and ash blonde hair, will look overpowered by these same colors. She requires lighter, more muted versions of the same colors. For example, periwinkle (light blue), pastel pink, and mauve would work better for her. Her face is more noticeable than the colors of her garments, and that's exactly what she needs: Her face should be the focal point!

STYLE PROFILE #8

adjust the color

A. If you determined that you have *warm* undertones to your skin, turn to page 142. If you determined that you have *cool* undertones to your skin, gather together garments or large scarves in the following colors: bright pink, pastel (light) pink, black, and light blue

Hold each color up to your face. If your face is overwhelmed by the bright pink and the black but flattered by the pastel (light) pink or light blue, you are a light cool. This means that your features are lighter and should not be upstaged by bold colors. Avoid colors such as black, bright red, royal blue, or deep purple up against your face.

If the bright pink and black are flattering, you have cool undertones.

Return to the color palettes on the back flap to find your best colors. They may not all be your favorites, but you can pull out your favorites for any wardrobe you decide to build. Use the palette for your next *Fashion Moment of Truth*.

Here are some tips for both the cool and light cool palettes:

COOL

Use these guidelines for choosing colors:

- Choose cool colors with blue undertones and *no* yellow undertones for staple items in your wardrobe.
- Choose neutrals such as white, black, navy, gray, or charcoal gray for your ensembles. The darker neutrals are ideal for shoes and boots.
- Choose gem colors such as red (bright red, not tomato red), blue (especially cobalt, royal, and navy), purple, aqua, turquoise, bright pink, and emerald green (not hunter green-too much yellow).
- Avoid yellow, orange, olive, rust, brown, hunter green, peach, and lime green.
- Lighter cool colors are best used as complementary colors in prints or accessories.
- Silver-tone accessories are optimal for you.
- Stay with colors which are close to your natural hair color rather than choosing an artificial blonde or red color.

- Pay attention to the shades of makeup you buy. Don't try to "balance your coloring" with warm colors. Rather, work with your natural skin tones using foundation in cool tones.
- Choose cool shades such as pinks, mauves, and reds rather than corals or mochas (brownish colors) for your lipstick shades.
- Choose cool shades such as plums (purples), icy blues, or neutrals for your eye shadow. Use charcoal, navy or black for eyeliner.
- Choose a background color from your palette when having a color photograph taken of you.

LIGHT COOL

Use these guidelines for choosing colors:

- Choose cool *muted* colors with blue undertones and *no* yellow undertones for staple items in your wardrobe.
- Choose neutrals such as bone (eggshell) white (bright white is too stark), navy, cool taupe, gray, or charcoal gray for your ensembles. These neutrals are ideal for accessories.
- Choose muted colors such as red (muted brick red, not tomato red), mauve, blue (especially periwinkle and navy), violet, aqua, turquoise, muted emerald green (not hunter green – too much yellow), and light blue-green ("seafoam").
- Cool pastels look marvelous on you. Try powder pink and light blue.
- Avoid yellow, orange, olive, rust, brown, hunter green, coral (peach), and lime green.

- Black overwhelms your face and washes you out. If you must have black in an ensemble, do not place any around your face.
- Silver-tone accessories are optimal for you.
- Stick close to your natural hair color or dye *ash* blonde.
- Pay attention to the shades of makeup you buy. Don't try to "balance your coloring" with warm colors. Rather, work with your natural skin tones by choosing a foundation in cool tones.
- Choose cool shades such as pinks, mauves, and reds rather than corals or mochas (brownish colors) for your lipstick shades.
- Choose cool shades such as plums (purples), icy blues, or neutrals for your eye shadow. Use charcoal, navy, or soft black eyeliner.
- Choose a background color from your palette when having a color photograph taken of you.

B. If you determined that you have warm undertones to your skin, gather together garments or large scarves in the following colors: coral (peach), orange, brown, and beige

Hold each color up to your face. If your face is overwhelmed by the orange and brown but flattered by the coral (peach) and beige, you are probably a light warm. This means that your features are lighter and should not be upstaged by bold or heavy colors. Avoid colors such as olive, rust, orange, brown, or hunter green.

If the colors orange and brown are flattering, you have warm undertones.

Return to the color palettes insert to find your best colors. They may not all be your favorites, but you can pull out your favorites for any wardrobe you decide to build. Use the palette for your next *Fashion Moment of Truth*.

Below are some tips for both the warm and the light warm palettes:

WARM

Use these guidelines for choosing colors:

- Choose warm colors with golden or yellow undertones for staple items in your wardrobe.
- Choose neutrals such as cream (ivory), beige, brown, or rust. These neutrals are ideal for accessories.
- Choose warm colors such as hunter green, true green, teal, bright yellow, yellow-green, olive, warm red, warm wine, or rust.
- Avoid black, especially around your face.
- Gold-tone accessories are optimal for you.
- Stick with your natural red hair color.
- Pay attention to the shades of makeup you buy. Don't try to "balance your coloring" with cool colors. Rather, work with your natural skin tones with foundation in warm tones.
- Choose warm shades such as corals (peach) and tomato-reds rather than pinks or mauves for your lipstick shades.
- Choose warm shades such as creams (ivory), beige (as dark as "tan" or as light as "vanilla") warm greens, and browns for eye shadow and brown for eye liner.
- Choose a background color from your palette when having a color photograph taken of you.

LIGHT WARM

Use these guidelines for choosing colors:

- Choose light warm colors with golden and yellow undertones for staple items in your wardrobe.
- Choose neutrals such as cream (ivory), camel, celery, or beige. These neutrals are ideal for accessories.
- Choose brighter warm colors such as tomato red, yellow, kelly green, soft green, chartreuse, and coral (peach).
- Completely avoid black because it can totally overwhelm your face.
- When choosing reds, go for tomato-red rather than brick or blue-red. Light oranges and light yellow-greens are good for you as well.
- Turquoise is a good color for you. It is a universally good color.
- Avoid stark white. This will wash you out.
- Gold-tone accessories are optimal for you.
- Stay with your naturally light-red hair color.
- Pay attention to the shades of makeup you buy. Don't try to "balance your coloring" with cool colors. Rather, work with your natural skin tones by choosing a foundation in warm tones.
- Choose warm shades such as coral (peach) and tomato-reds rather than pinks and mauves.
- Use brown colors for eye liner. Keep eye liner subtle.
- Use muted green, brown, cream (ivory), or beige (as dark as "tan" or as light as "vanilla") eye shadow.
- Choose a background color from your palette when having a color photograph taken of you.

SEMINAR FAQ
beautiful people and color palettes

QUESTION: I see fashion models and actresses wearing what should be colors that don't flatter them. But they *do* flatter! I see this with some teens and younger women too. Isn't it true that some people look great in all colors?

ANSWER: Yes. It's true. I admit it. There are some very beautiful people out there.

These very same women also have their *optimal* colors. When pressed, they often will admit this. In regard to fashion models and actresses, just remember that it's one thing for a woman with a tremendous amount of resources to choose colors that aren't her best. It's quite another issue for a woman who is living in the real world.

Alas, one disadvantage to being a movie star or even a news anchor is that other people are choosing the clothing (or costumes) they wear on the set or stage. You better believe that these wardrobe professionals ensure that their subjects look fabulous by using makeup and lighting techniques.

Also, since entertainers are fashion leaders to a certain extent, they tout the colors that are considered the fashion of the moment. There is a whole industry that dictates what colors are "in" and entertainers are a critical part of it.

Rather than color analyzing Hollywood, learn to recognize *your* best colors.

what color do you feel?

A favorite color is like a fun-loving friend. When you wear your favorite color you tend to feel a little bit happier, more confident, and more attractive. If that color is also one from your color palette, then you *look* a little happier and more confident, and – here's the bonus – you actually *are* more attractive. So, the favorite color is both a fun-loving and *reliable* friend.

Colors have the ability to stimulate physical reactions or inspire feelings. In fact, there is a whole science around what colors convey which moods and even influence behavior. Although there is no magic in color, it is fun to remember that color is more about perception than reality. Different colors have come to signify many different virtues, vices, seasons, aspirations, and events in every culture on the planet, and the business of color forecasting is greatly regarded in the fashion industry.

Look around the world to see how color is used in fashion. In the West, we generally attempt to coordinate or even match colors in our ensembles, and we rarely mix prints. In Africa, however, bright colors of completely different palettes are mixed in a single dress. The effect is striking, beautiful, and perfectly appropriate in that part of the world. Thankfully, the more international flavor of recent fashion has altered some of our own notions on color. (Sometimes, I envy their unrestricted creativity.)

In Asia, colors carry significantly more meaning, and business travelers are often advised by employers to avoid the ones that have the potential to cause trouble. I have several friends from Southeast Asia who speak their minds about the colors anyone chooses to wear.

Isaac Mizrahi, one recent designer success story, is noted for his use of color in design. "I love Technicolor," he's exclaimed. "It's wildly beautiful."[2] Below is the science on which this guy (and many others) cashes in.[3]

color fun facts (and theories)

- Our understanding of the human perception of color is rather recent (late nineteenth century) and was developed through the sciences of physics, physiology, and psychology.
- One hundred thirty million light-sensitive cells called rods and cones fill the eye's retina. Rod cells pick up shapes and lighting, and cone cells pick up colors.
- The colors we *perceive* are simply wavelengths of light that are not absorbed by an object but rather reflected back to the eye.

- The human eye can see millions of colors. An artist named Albert Munsell developed the first methodical labeling system of colors in 1905 and influenced all of us in the way we identify color.
- Primary colors are the most basic colors on the color wheel and cannot be created by mixing colors. There are only three: true yellow, true blue, and true red.
- Secondary colors are created by mixing the primary colors. Red mixed with blue is purple, red mixed with yellow is orange, and blue mixed with yellow is green.
- The term "shade" refers to a color or "hue" created by adding black.
- The term "tint" refers to a hue created by adding white.
- Monochromatic color schemes are variations of tints and shades of the same color.
- Complementary colors are colors which lie opposite of one another on the color wheel (you know, the one you learned about in art class) and are used by graphic designers to create eye-catching documents.
- Yellow is the first color the eye notices and at its brightest can be physically irritating.

- Researchers have found that blue rooms increase productivity for the people who work there. Blue can also curb the appetite. Put a blue light bulb in your refrigerator and see.
- Green has traditionally been considered to have healing benefits and has been found to be soothing. It is also considered to be the most relaxing color. (Have you ever noticed it at the dentist's office?)
- Red can make you hungry. Ever notice that red is used in food packaging and signage?
- While white implies purity and innocence in Western society, white is the color of mourning throughout much of Asia. Many widows wear it.

People often ask me if I think that any one *element of style* is more important than the other two. The answer is no, but color has an edge in that it can help to make an immediate impression. It's usually the first descriptor people use for explaining the outfits they see.

> *I can live for two months on a good compliment.*
>
> MARK TWAIN

Below is a little more information on each of the basic colors. These tidbits are especially important if you are holding fast to one set of colors for your wardrobe or deciding to opt for a monochromatic look. Keep in mind that there are variations across cultures and subcultures. Most importantly, these are only connotations and, obviously, are not qualities intrinsic to the colors themselves. I am convinced that some strong personalities can actually undo the effects of certain colors (e.g., the glorious person who makes black look spunky)!

NOTE: (This is an important one!) When I use a color label, I am envisioning a very specific color. You may think of a completely different hue. These differences are normal and are due to where we live, our experiences, and even our education. This is one reason why you have things like the *Munsell* system or the newer *Pantone* system that visual artists use. If you are in doubt as to how a color really appears, check the palettes in this book. They have the popular names listed beside them.

TRY THIS: Dig into a new box of Crayola crayons (sixty-four is best). Pull out a few and read the labels. You may actually find yourself arguing with the things! That's pretty typical. Color labeling is a subjective thing, so always use a reference to determine true colors.[4]

black

Color palette: Complements cool undertones.

Connotations: Sophistication, forward fashion, art, death and mourning.

Cautions: Can wash out even someone with cool undertones, especially as she gets older. If over-used, black can be depressing or morbid.

Good for: Evening, business, business casual, personal casual, and accessories.

Fits into an ensemble as a: Neutral or dominant color; avoid pairing with navy.

Shopping notes: Easy to find. Women with light cool undertones may have trouble finding their best dark neutrals and may come to rely on black. They should keep it away from their faces.

white

Color palette: Complements cool undertones.

Variations: Bone white (egg shell) is good for a woman with light cool undertones. Creamy-white (ivory) is better for a woman with warm undertones.

Connotations: Purity, freshness, youth, medicine, cleanliness

Cautions: If overdone or styled with too much structure, can appear clinical or in the very least a bit boring. Not empowering in the business environment.

Good for: Warm weather personal casual, daytime parties in the summer.

Fits into an ensemble as a: Warm-weather neutral or dominant color.

Shopping notes: Easy to find. Buy in durable, natural fabrics as white items must be cleaned often. Cotton fabrics can be bleached; synthetics cannot be bleached.

gray

Color palette: Complements cool and light cool undertones. This color can be warmed up if it is mixed with warm colors.

Variations: Light gray works well for the warm weather seasons; *charcoal* is an excellent neutral for cool weather seasons.

Connotations: Business, reliability, sobriety.

Cautions: Can appear boring or drab.

Good for: Business and business casual, personal casual, any season.

Fits into an ensemble as a: Neutral or dominant color. Pairs well with any shade of pink.

Shopping notes: Always check the coolness or warmth of a gray. A "muddy" (heather) gray is usually either warm or very drab.

red

Color palette: True red or red in the blue range is cool and complements cool undertones; red in the yellow range is warm and complements warm undertones.

Variations: A muted *brick red* or *mauve* is better on a woman with light cool undertones.

Connotations: Risk, boldness, passion, vibrancy, luck, sex appeal.

Cautions: Could be interpreted as forward or presumptuous in a solemn setting.

Good for: Personal and business casual, evening, small doses for some business wardrobes, speaking engagements, sports, any season.

Fits into an ensemble as a: Dominant or complementary color if paired with black, white, beige, cream, or navy as the neutral.

Shopping notes: Always check the warmth or coolness of a red. Do not remove the tags from an item until this can be checked in full daylight.

blue

Color palette: Complements cool undertones; *teal* blue is a warm blue and complements warm undertones.

Variations: Both *cornflower* or *powder blue* are better on a woman with light cool undertones.

Connotations: Serenity, comfort, the sea, boyhood.

Cautions: Blue coordinated with pink can look like a baby's layette.

Good for: Just about every occasion, photographs, speaking engagements, uniforms, any season.

Fits into an ensemble as a: Dominant or complementary color if paired with white, gray, beige, or cream.

Shopping notes: Match your blues in the daylight. If you are attempting to match your shoes to a bottom, be sure that both are of the same shade of blue.

navy

Color palette: Complements cool undertones.

Variations: A bluer navy, often called *French navy* works well for women with light cool undertones.

Connotations: Authority, safety, reliability, classic, stiffness.

Cautions: Can become boring or masculine.

Good for: Personal and business casual, business, uniforms, neutral for a wardrobe color story for any season, accessories.

Fits into an ensemble as a: Neutral or dominant color.

Shopping notes: Match your navies in the daylight. If you are attempting to match your shoes to a bottom, be sure that both are of the same shade of navy.

yellow

Color palette: Found mostly as a warm color and complements warm undertones, although a bluish-yellow (*lemon*) is technically a cool yellow. Generally, women with cool undertones should still avoid it.

Variations: Bright cool yellow will create a beautiful contrast against very dark brown or black skin. It is a beautiful contrast only and often not complementary to the skin.

Connotations: Spring, new beginnings, childhood, innocence.

Cautions: Little-girlish in a business environment.

Good for: Warm weather personal casual or, in its most mellowed versions, business casual.

Fits into an ensemble as a: Dominant or complementary color

Shopping notes: Yellow is easy to find only during the warm weather shopping seasons.

green

Color palette: Green in the blue range is cool and complements cool undertones; green in the yellow range is warm and complements warm undertones.

Variations: Sea foam or *pastel green* is better for women with light cool undertones; *olive* or *hunter green* (very dark warm green) is better for women with warm undertones.

Connotations: Nature, serenity, spring, summer (depends very much on hue).

Cautions: Can look clownish at its brightest in business settings.

Good for: Personal and business casual, casual speaking engagements, any weather season.

Fits into an ensemble as a: Dominant or complementary color.

Shopping notes: Always check the warmth or coolness of a green. Do not remove the tags from an item until this can be checked in full daylight.

purple

Color palette: Complements cool undertones.

Variations: Violet is better for women with light cool undertones. Cool *wine* or *plum* works well for women with cool undertones as well. A *burgundy* with a touch of brown works better for women with warm undertones.

Connotations: Royalty, creativity, enthusiasm, non conformity

Cautions: Can appear clownish at its brightest in business settings.

Good for: Personal or business casual, evening, photography, casual speaking engagements, any season.

Fits into an ensemble as a: Dominant or complementary color.

Shopping notes: Keep in mind the warm versus cool burgundy issue. Do not remove the tags of an item until you are sure of its warmth or coolness. Examine in full daylight.

pink

Color palette: Complements cool undertones.

Variations: Peach is better for women with light warm undertones. *Pastel pink* is better for women with light cool undertones.

Connotations: Femininity, romance, light-heartedness, girlhood.

Cautions: Little-girlish in some business environments.

Good for: Personal and business casual, evening, any season.

Fits into an ensemble as a: Dominant or complementary color.

Shopping notes: Muted and bright pinks are more easily found during cold-weather shopping seasons; light pinks are more easily found during warm-weather seasons.

orange

Color palette: Complements warm undertones.

Variations: A very light orange or *peach* is better for a woman with light warm undertones.

Connotations: Autumn, harvest, warmth, coziness (when muted), agitation (when bright).

Cautions: Can be very harsh or agitating.

Good for: Personal casual, evening, sports, very small doses in accessories.

Fits into an ensemble as a: Complementary color.

Shopping notes: Even if you have warm undertones, avoid investing a lot of money in the brightest variants of this color.

brown

Color palette: Complements warm undertones.

Variations: A dark *chocolate* brown is technically a cool brown, but is very rarely flattering on a woman with cool undertones.

Connotations: Uniformity, classic styling, reliability.

Cautions: Can appear masculine if an item is man-tailored.

Good for: Personal and business casual, business, any weather season, accessories.

Fits into an ensemble as a: Neutral or dominant color.

Shopping notes: Always available in accessories. More available in garments during cold-weather shopping seasons.

beige

Color palette: Complements warm undertones.
Variations: Also called *tan*. A darker variant is often called *camel*, and a lighter, more neutralized variant is called *cream*, or *khaki*. The cool variant of khaki is really a light gray, often called *stone*.
Connotations: Naturalness, friendliness, approachability.
Cautions: Can appear boring or unnoticeable. Avoid whole ensembles in hues which approximate flesh tones.
Good for: Personal and business casual, accessories, any weather season.
Fits into an ensemble as a: Neutral or complementary color.
Shopping notes: Easy to find all year around.

Since we can see millions of colors, this list is obviously not exhaustive! The trick to this art is to train your eye to recognize the warmth or coolness of any garment or accessory color. A nice way to train your eye is to play with tubes of paint until you see the variants. If you're not into making messes but still want to train your eye, always compare the colors you see in the brightest lighting possible.

GREAT COLOR TECHNIQUE: Try wearing three colors (from your own color palette) around your face (blouse, collar, scarf, earrings, necklace, etc.) This will add vibrancy and interest and keep the eye on your face. More colors than this can distract from the face.

Certain colors can also conjure up certain associative feelings. While I was living in Spain, a rusty brown color became the wardrobe choice for every sophisticated woman in Madrid. It looked fantastic to me (perhaps because I was enjoying myself so much), and the color came to imply all the most exotic things in my own little universe.

So, back in the States I chose the color for my clothing despite the fact that I need colors from a cool palette. I am sad to say that it didn't conjure any images of sophistication or beauty for anyone with whom I came in contact. Eventually, I came to understand that fashion color preference is a highly individual and subjective thing and that my future choice of color should be based on how much it flatters me. Now, color choice is one hallmark of my style. I wear my best every single day, and it makes me appear healthier and younger.

can I keep this?

Not all women grasp color analysis the first round. One may hold up an item in a warm color and tell me that it's cool. Others will hold up an outfit and ask me with pleading eyes, "Can I keep this?" They know that the color is wrong for them, but are hoping that there may be a way to reinvent it. I like to call this "post-color-analysis denial." Many who are in denial may actually see things that aren't there.

Then there is the seemingly gray area (so to speak). A pair of pants or a skirt in an unflattering color is held up as a *Can I keep this?* in the hopes that since it is away from the face, I'll agree that it's a keeper.

Technically, there's no clash with skin tone. It's placed too far from the face for this to be an issue. The issue is *color harmony*. It will usually not harmonize with the optimal colors you have placed around your face. Remember, a woman should wear the colors; colors shouldn't wear the woman.

If, by chance, a great neutral seems to bridge the offending color and your face, you may have a quick fix. There's little chance, however, of establishing *total color harmony* in your wardrobe. In fact, that one unflattering color from an opposite color palette will become a handicap to your wardrobe technique. (See the next chapter.)

post-color-analysis counseling

Many of my clients through the years have complained that their favorite colors are not the colors of their palette. It can be a terrible predicament for someone who is really into using their unflattering colors for self-expression. But it doesn't have to be!

eight ways to enjoy colors that aren't in your color palette

1. Smile when you see them on someone else. (But don't smirk if it's not her color!)
2. Wear the colors in your sleepwear.
3. Buy a big bouquet of flowers in those colors and place them prominently where you live.
4. Decorate your home in those colors.
5. Get a blanket in those colors and snuggle up in it.
6. Dress your small children (not your teenagers) in those colors. (Generally, children can wear any color.)
7. Buy a car or a bike in one of those colors.
8. Paint the shutters of your house in those colors. Paint the whole house in one of those colors!

Remember that your wardrobe doesn't exist to decorate an object. It's there to bring out the best in a beautiful person!

FASHION MOMENT OF TRUTH

wardrobe analysis for color palette

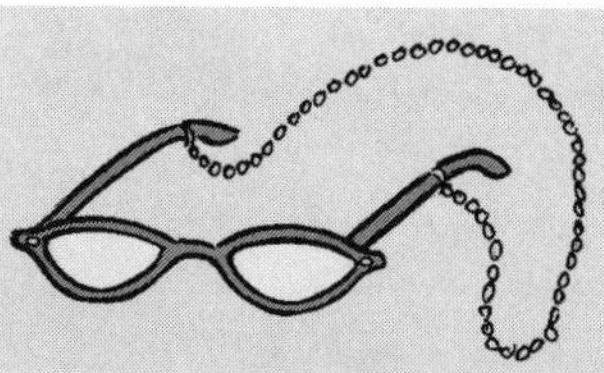

At last! The final stage. Now it is imperative to maintain your objectivity. Return to your wardrobe and examine it for color. (I know, it's pretty depleted by now, but you are starting to see what you own!)

Check each garment one at a time. Decide if its color is right for you. If you have difficulty determining its true color, try it on in full light and let it speak for itself. How does it look on you?

Remove any item which is not a flattering color for you. You are going only for the best.

NOTE: You may have an item in a print that contains some unflattering colors. If they are extremely subtle and the other colors clearly dominate, it may be a keeper. More often, however, discordant colors (although used brilliantly in graphic arts as "complementary") will muddy the waters and dull the overall color of the garment when placed up against your skin.

A good way to check this affect is to view the outfit from a slight distance to see which color dominates.

Continue on to accessories, including shoes, handbags, scarves and jewelry, and use the guidelines above to clean out.

In the end, you may be left with very little. But don't fret! You will design your new style in the next chapter!

CHAPTER FIVE

total style
wardrobe planning I

now I *really* have nothing to wear!

Once a wardrobe has been purged for body type, fashion personality, and color, women may start to become light-headed, a bit dizzy, maybe a little slap-happy. I often respond with assurances that after a thorough wardrobe analysis, the only direction left is up and out of this closet of darkness!

All glory comes from daring to begin.

ANONYMOUS

Others claim to feel exhilarated by the thought of living on the edge with nearly nothing to wear. Perhaps it's some primeval desire to get back to nature.

You might not have either extreme feeling. Very often, after an extensive wardrobe has been pruned, you might be pleasantly surprised to find a beautiful one waiting inside like a pearl in an oyster shell.

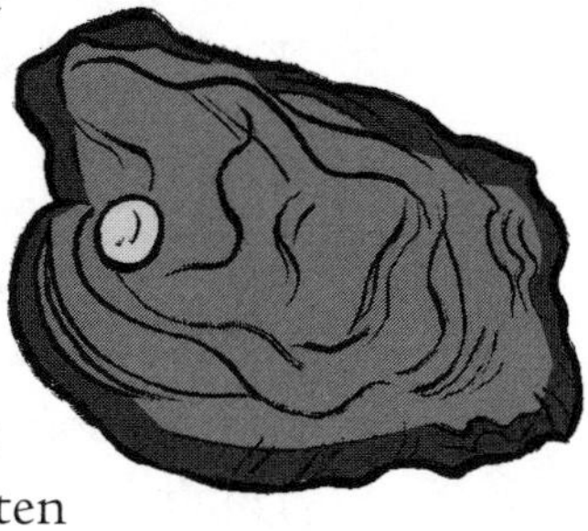

My colleague Jeannette once had a client who had enough clothing to open a small department store. They pulled out each item until they had stacks up to their shoulders and had to delay dinner for their families. The client laughed heartily at the items she had forgotten about or couldn't recognize. She just never wore most of them.

Not surprisingly (due of course to the laws of probability), many items were kept as optimal pieces for her revamped wardrobe amidst the ton which went to charity. By the time each optimal piece made it back into the closet, Jeannette and her client had discovered that not only was the closet completely full with just the optimals (how the heck did it all fit in there?) but that the client had a lovely wardrobe all along. She just couldn't see it.

How many things I can do without!

SOCRATES

No matter where your feelings hover, take advantage of this opportunity to design your most fabulous style.

In this chapter you will lay the groundwork for your new wardrobes by deciding exactly what *kinds* of wardrobes you need and how to meet your demands for each. In the next chapter you will actually plan out those wardrobes using your choice of three techniques.

okay, so maybe I don't need that much

Before we begin to envision your perfect wardrobe, we need to spend a little time dispelling some common assumptions and adopting some time-tested habits.

1. Less is more.
2. Keep or plan out only items about which you are *absolutely excited.*
3. Less is more.
4. Keep or plan out only items in which you look *absolutely fabulous.*
5. Less is more.
6. Don't think in terms of replacing an item you have removed from your wardrobe.
7. Less is more.
8. Don't keep or plan out items for your wardrobe that you simply "like."

9. Less is more.
10. You should be able to see your entire wardrobe in one glance.

Here's another little tidbit for your consideration: There are billions and billions of pieces of clothing out there. *Why should you own even just one mediocre thing?*

> *Darling, you don't need that. You have enough already.*
>
> **HALSTON**

Practically speaking, it's best to be able to account for everything in your closet and drawers. For maximum bang for the buck, you should use 100 percent of what you own and look fabulous in each and every ensemble.

I once read a statistic sometime in the mid 1990s that the average woman wears only 25 percent of what she owns. Imagine how that statistic has changed long after that decade of economic boom propelled us into an era of cheap labor and low-cost products. American women have been buying tons and tons of stuff!

I would argue that now the statistic may be 15 to 20 percent. That's an extremely small number of useful things and a huge waste of time and money.

OBJECTIVE: decide what kinds of wardrobes you need and how to get each to work with your lifestyle and priorities.

decisions, decisions

Let's begin the fun. We'll start with some vocabulary.

1. **BASE NUMBER** — The number of items (not including accessories) which make up a wardrobe. All the wardrobe techniques that I use work with the magic number *eight.*
   Recommendations: You need a lower base number than you think. Eight is simple and will work in any kind of wardrobe for any season. Remember, less is more.

2. **COLOR STORY** — The planned colors of a wardrobe.

Recommendations: One to three colors work best in most wardrobes. A color story should be chosen from your color palette.

Example: A woman with cool coloring *could* (not must) choose black and white as neutrals and pink as a dominant color. A woman with warm coloring could choose brown and cream as neutrals, and green as a dominant color.

By the way, a neutral color is any color that can be coordinated with a great number of other colors. Generally, it can be coordinated with all the colors of its palette.

Neutral cool colors are black, white, gray, and navy.

Neutral light cool colors are navy, gray, taupe, and bone (chalk white).

Neutral warm colors are brown, beige, cream (ivory), and olive.

Neutral light warm colors are beige, cream (ivory), and celery.

3. **COORDINATION** — Any two or all base items and accessories of an ensemble "relate" to one another in color, texture, or print, but not all three. (If they were identical in color, texture, *and* print, that would be "matching.")

Recommendations: Base items will coordinate if you choose a neutral and other colors from your color palette. Also, two or three textures can work in one ensemble, but rarely (though not never) can two different prints.

Example: Coordinate with flair by choosing a color story (see below) and then choosing an accessory such as a bracelet, watch, or handbag in a "surprise" color from another palette.

4. **TOTAL COLOR HARMONY** — Color coordination (i.e., all from one color story) across all items and all accessories in a

wardrobe. So every pair of shoes, every purse, every top, every bottom, and every whole piece can be worn with every other. If you really want to save time and money, choose all your shoes in the darkest neutral of your color story.

Recommendations: Any wardrobe designed on a tight budget should be done with total color harmony in mind. Also, total color harmony helps to make any woman polished and elegant. It's easy and quick.

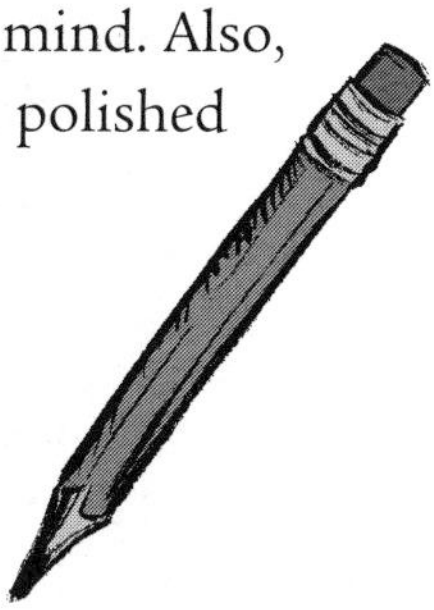

5. **ENSEMBLE** — A complete outfit, including top, bottom (or whole piece) and accessories.

types of wardrobes

Now you have to decide what kinds of wardrobes you need and if there are any special considerations.

Since you are an expert of your style and you are really beginning to know yourself, most of the information below will make sense. You will, however, see three terms that I haven't introduced yet. They are wardrobe design techniques that I introduce in the next chapter.

MIX AND MATCH — Items in a wardrobe mix and match, so every top goes with every bottom.

SPECTRUM — All bottoms are the same neutral color and tops are each any color that goes with the neutral

MONOCHROMATIC — Each ensemble contains only one color or two similar (monochromatic) colors from top to bottom.

While you may not know exactly how they work, you can take note of them while you read. One, two, or all three of them will work for the types of wardrobes you need.

WARDROBE TYPES
Personal casual
Business casual
Combination personal casual and business casual
Business
Evening
Athletic
Sleepwear
Travel

SPECIAL CONSIDERATIONS
Maternity
Nursing

SEASONAL
Cold weather
Warm weather
Transitional

Below are definitions for each term in the list above. I've also included very specific suggestions for incorporating your *elements of style* and reducing any related headaches you may have had in the past. Read through every list to decide which kinds of wardrobes, special considerations, and seasons you have to plan and how to plan them. Then, turn to page 182 for your next *Style Profile*.

PERSONAL CASUAL: A wardrobe used for personal time. This includes time at home and time at casual social events with either friends or family. This is fashion that is not worn at the workplace.

- Use everything you know about your *elements of style* for creating this wardrobe.

- Avoid tennis shoes as a uniform. They are a competing focal point for your face because they are clunky and usually lighter in color than the hem of your trousers. Think of function and form. (Newer athletic shoes in dark neutrals provide nice alternatives.)
- Do not forget details like accessories and makeup.
- Each woman has different and multiple environments for her personal casual time. Consider this when planning it out, rather than just copying other women.
- Consider age-appropriateness for any item or ensemble.
- Choose fabrics that breathe and make you feel comfortable so that you won't look for short-cuts in your style.
- Choose wrinkle-free items if you don't iron.
- Choose washable items.
- Stay polished because your personal casual time is your most important time. Most often it's the only time you spend with loved ones.

What one has to do can usually be done.

ELEANOR ROOSEVELT

BUSINESS CASUAL: A wardrobe used for days at work designated as "dress-down" or "casual." This wardrobe is also the default wardrobe for professional settings that don't require either suits or a uniform. It's the wardrobe you use when you need both to convey and command a bit more respect – in teacher conferences, community meetings, shopping (that's doing business, remember) or church services.

- Use everything you know about your *elements of style* for creating this wardrobe.
- Plan out this wardrobe with the dress code of your workplace in mind. If there isn't one, use the tips in this section.
- Leave jeans out of this wardrobe.

- Choose crisp dress pants, khakis, or skirts for your bottoms. Never choose shorts.
- Choose structured knit blouses, turtlenecks, sweaters, man-tailored shirts, appropriate blouses, and twin sets for tops. Do not choose T-shirts or sweatshirts.
- Choose short or long sleeves for your tops. Never go bare-armed to work. (No halters, sundresses, tank tops, or tube tops.) The guys can't. (I think it would be awful if they did.)
- Blazers and structured jackets are nice reliable pieces for this wardrobe.
- Wear hosiery with a short skirt or dress in the workplace.
- Choose loafers, fashion boots, or pumps. Never choose tennis shoes, flip flops, or sandals.
- Maintain a crisp and professional look. Choosing high quality fabrics for your wardrobe items will help with this.

COMBINATION PERSONAL CASUAL AND BUSINESS CASUAL: A convenient and economical wardrobe. It incorporates items for both personal casual and business casual. While there is no crossing over of one venue to the other for whole ensembles, individual items can be matched in ways that will work for both.

- Use everything you know about your *elements of style* for creating this wardrobe.
- This wardrobe is especially good for part-time workers, women who have to dress *business casual* only one or two days a week (wearing suits on the other days), or at-home mothers.
- Use the *mix and match* technique to get the greatest number of different looks.
- Carefully read through the guidelines above for business casual.

- Maintain total color harmony for this wardrobe so that it truly is a combination wardrobe.
- See page 199 for more details.

BUSINESS: A wardrobe used for the business environment. Most often involves suiting (sometimes called *corporate*) but can be completed with structured separates which work like suits. Often, the level of dress referred to as *executive* is suiting in the strictest sense and is not the level at which you should take any shortcuts.

- Use everything you know about your *elements of style* for creating this wardrobe.
- Know the dress code for your workplace.
- Invest in a great number of appropriate hose.
- Invest in at least one pair of versatile, closed-toe, low or medium-heeled pumps.
- Choose well-made suits in fine fabrics such as gabardine wool or silk. See page 278 for details on choosing a suit.
- Accessorize the suits you choose according to your fashion personality but always with a little restraint.
- If opting for separates rather than suits, choose only crisp, structured, woven pieces in neutrals or muted tones. Leave the strong colors for the accessories.
- If opting for separates, use the *mix and match* wardrobe technique.
- Launder professionally.
- Don't forget to choose carefully your professional and elegant briefcase and watch.
- See page 313 for more details.

EVENING: An item or wardrobe used for semi-formal or formal events in the evening.

- Pay very special attention to your *elements of style.* You want to look spectacular.
- Pay special attention to what is appropriate for when. Generally, long length skirts are acceptable for evening. (Hemlines move up and down with the times, but you can get a feel for an appropriate length by looking in the department stores and fashion magazines.) Weddings are still skirt and dress territory in most regions of the U.S., but holiday and special occasion parties are appropriate places for beautiful pant styles as well. The opera is still a dress-up affair in many cities.
- There are seasons of the year when you are suddenly attending several evening events with many of the same people. So, you can plan out a simple wardrobe technique for these seasons (usually Christmas and spring). For example, you could buy a cashmere blouse, a sequined blouse, a long taffeta skirt, and a velvet pair of palazzo pants for a mixed bag of Christmas events. Mix and match these for different events – a party, a ball, a show – and you'll be presenting a great array of different looks.
- See page 285 for how to buy a special occasion ensemble.

ATHLETIC: A wardrobe used strictly for sports or exercise.

- Yes, even when you sweat, you should be concerned with your *elements of style.* Exercising takes motivation, and there's nothing like the knowledge that you look your best to get you going.
- Choose pieces in fabrics that breathe and keep moisture away from the skin. (cotton, some cotton combinations, and newer synthetics designed for athletes.)

- Choose pieces according to the temperature. If you run outside all year long, this is especially important.
- Keep underwear as underwear. Ensure that you are getting the support you need from your underwear.
- Bring a robe to the locker room and avoid exposing yourself to fellow athletes.
- Use your athletic wardrobe *only* for exercising.

SLEEPWEAR: Maybe it's a bit of a stretch to include a list of points for sleepwear, but you're giving up a lot of fun if you neglect it completely. Sleepwear should be a lot more than an afterthought and a little less than an intentional, coordinated wardrobe.

- Choose items according to comfort while sleeping. Don't force yourself to wear long, old-fashion night gowns just because you think you should as a romantic. (Many women don't like long nightgowns because they bunch up while sleeping.) Instead, choose something that works for you *and* has romantic touches.
- If others see you before you actually sleep, choose items according to the message you want to convey to the person or people you see. You want to be sexy for your husband (especially the longer you are married) and presentable to a roommate. My fellow fashion consultant Patty once met a woman on an airplane who explained that her career was all about saving marriages. "So you are a marriage counselor," Patty concluded. "Oh no," the woman answered. "I sell lingerie."
- Decide what you want others to see when they look at you late at night or early in the morning. I know many a woman whose husband only sees her early in the morning before dressing and late at night after taking day clothes off, so sleepwear poses an especially interesting challenge. These

women could benefit from investing in a comfortable "twilight" personal casual wardrobe that works well for picking up around the house, snuggling with children, and getting into bed. They should adhere to their *elements of style* for this wardrobe to make it a success.

- Continue to choose items according to your fashion personality. (Yes, a relaxed can still wear something silky and sexy. She just might choose it in a muted color and simple cut. An expressive might go for animal prints.)
- Buy two beautiful robes, one for snuggling up in winter and one for staying cool in the summer.
- If people insist on buying you clothes that don't fit into your wardrobe designs, request sleepwear as an alternative.

TRAVEL (AND HOW TO PACK FOR IT): A wardrobe usually borrowed from other wardrobes and packed for travel. It may be personal casual, business casual, business, evening or a combination of any or all of them. It's important to stick with a base number of eight or ten for this wardrobe to reduce the weight of luggage (see below).

- Pay close attention to your *elements of style* when planning this wardrobe.
- Consider the full scope of activities for any given trip. Write out what you will be doing and when. Then, write a list of all needed items. Pack this list as a record for what you are bringing.
- A travel wardrobe can be created with any of the three techniques; however, the *mix and match* technique is the easiest and uses the smallest number of items for the greatest number of looks.
- Choose knit garments for your personal casual wear. (This is only if you have knits; perhaps your fashion personality

doesn't allow for it, or they don't flatter your figure.) Knits can be rolled and tucked tightly into your suitcase. Rolling or folding tissue paper into the garment will lessen wrinkles.

- Pack extra hose. Place in baggies and label what the color is. (Imagine a groggy morning in a dimly lit hotel room.)
- Pack one pair of versatile shoes in a bag (and also a pair of evening shoes if needed). The ones you wear on the plane are your second pair. (For a business trip you could wear loafers and pack pumps. For a personal trip you could wear comfortable shoes such as loafers or low-healed boots and pack tennis shoes, sandals, or another pair of loafers.)

He who would travel happily must travel light.

ANTOINE DE SAINT-EXUPERY

- Wear valuable accessories such as jewelry onto a plane. Never pack them.
- Plan out the handbag you will carry. It should be conducive to the type of travel you are planning. By the way, if you can, pack your makeup, tooth brush, and an extra pair of panties in your purse in case you are ever separated from your bags.
- Pack a stain removal stick or wipe.
- Plan in your travel wardrobe your summer bathrobe (it rolls up), sleepwear, and slippers.

- Ensure that liquid toiletry remains tightly sealed, bagged, and stowed into a compartment of your luggage away from your garments. I use small containers of shampoo and soaps gathered from previous hotel stays. If I am staying in a hotel, I don't pack them at all since almost all hotels have toiletries (and hair dryers and irons). I've been known not to risk packing liquids and opting to buy them upon my arrival.
- Choose your luggage with your most common type of travel in mind. Remember, luggage is an accessory for your travel

wardrobe. Suitcases (hard and soft) are good for plane travel. (Make sure that your carry-on fits in the overhead luggage compartment. You might have to call ahead to check the maximum permitted size for a particular airline.) Large and small duffel bags are appropriate for car travel. You can usually buy these in sets and get a lot value for your money. They are, of course, beautifully color coordinated nowadays.

- The old-fashion cosmetic boxes are wonderful for car travel as well. I love how the lid pops up with a mirror underneath. Such glam!
- A good guideline for most plane travelers going on vacation for one week or more: one carry-on case and one large suitcase. If your carry-on case is as large as permitted, you may be able to use just this.
- If you are handling children on a plane, just put everything through baggage. Carry a stylish back pack or large purse to stow what you need. Older children can carry their own backpacks (stashed with reading material and coloring supplies), which will slow them down while you stay a bit more mobile. That's important if you have a little darter (as in "darts" into crowds).
- A good guideline for most plane travelers going on a two to three day *business casual* business trip: one carry-on case (in addition to a laptop computer).
- A good guideline for most plane travelers going on two to three day business trip requiring a business wardrobe: one carry-on case (in addition to a laptop computer) and one hanging garment bag for suits.

what wardrobes do I need?

Everyone needs a personal casual wardrobe. If you work in an office setting you need a business casual wardrobe or a business wardrobe. A combination personal casual and business casual wardrobe is a great option if only one or two days of the week are business casual and you'd rather not invest a great amount of time or money into creating a separate business casual wardrobe.

If, after a thorough wardrobe analysis, you find that you have many wonderful items to work with (especially if they come in many colors) you may want to create two or even three personal casual wardrobes or two or even three business casual wardrobes. You can do this economically with the eight base wardrobe techniques I introduce in the next chapter. It will be especially cost-effective if you don't need to make more than just a few purchases to complete it.

Most women borrow from other wardrobes to create their travel wardrobes. I had a client who wanted something special for her two-week trip to Paris, so we designed something completely new which had to be purchased. Of course, she very cleverly incorporated these items into her personal wardrobe when she returned from her trip because she had designed the wardrobe with total color harmony.

In regard to an evening wardrobe, most women need only one or two ensembles. Women with high-profile jobs or who have husbands with high-profile jobs often need an entire evening wardrobe.

special considerations

MATERNITY: A wardrobe designed for a pregnant woman. It may contain maternity items, plus size tops adapted as maternity, or tops to be worn open over maternity items.

- For starters, never give up on your style. You'll not only need it to help boost your morale when things get tough, but also to maintain your perspective so that things don't get nearly as tough as they could. Maintaining perspective also means remembering that there is a little person growing inside you. All the more reason to look your best! I think that Ben Franklin was so popular with women because he once said that pregnant women are the most beautiful of all!

- Although a pregnancy is only a short period of time, thus making it seemingly hard to justify the expense of a new wardrobe, it still spans across either one complete fashion season or parts of two. That's a justifiable expense anyway. If finances are a worry, use a versatile *mix and match* technique. See the tips for an affordable wardrobe on page 188.
- Use layering to get the most for your money and work with your body's constantly changing size and temperature. Also, keep in mind that single pieces may work well for a time, but there is always the possibility that you will outgrow a dress or a jumper if you become exceptionally large. There is really no way of predicting.
- Plan out an updated maternity wardrobe even if a pregnancy is not the first. So what if you have cute things from the late 1990s? They are out of date.
- Stick to your *elements of style*! You need them during pregnancy at least as much. (You are a pear now, dear – even if you weren't before you were pregnant.)
- No matter what your fashion personality, add a bit more structure around your face. You need to pull attention up to your eyes. This can be done with collars, scarves, or necklaces. It all depends upon your style and comfort level.
- Revel in your accessories. Carry a really smart bag to perk up your look.
- Don't go for too many buttons in front and don't rely on the buttons to keep a garment together. My good friend Mary, while nine months pregnant, once turned to get her three year old only to freeze in horror as every single button on the front of her dress popped right off and onto the floor.
- If you know that your ankles have a tendency to swell, invest in trousers. It will help you feel a lot less self-conscious. I get swollen ankles only during the last few weeks of pregnancy,

but I choose trousers over skirts even for the early months because they give me a little more confidence.

- Don't bare your belly. A baby is a great focal point, but the little sweetie will get plenty of attention after she is born. Remember to keep your focal point on your face!
- Check that your belly button isn't noticeable through your outfit. Some women use large adhesive bandages or adhesive nipple covers to smooth out the belly.
- Invest in all new undergarments and maternity (or Queen-size) hosiery. Support hose is a must if you have any problems with varicose veins. (Remember to budget for these items in the early stages of wardrobe planning.)
- Shop at maternity stores or online with maternity retailers. Some department stores work well, but it always bugged me that the maternity section is behind the lingerie at these places. You might have to ask an associate to find it.
- Always ask about the return policy of a retailer when buying any item. Maternity stores often have the strictest of return and exchange policies.
- If you find that your shoes don't fit anymore, don't worry; it's normal. It's okay to have to buy a new pair of shoes a size larger. You may or may not be able to fit in them after the pregnancy, but that shouldn't be a concern. You are buying for the duration of the pregnancy.
- Have fun! Buy several inexpensive shoes one size up. Shoes can be the quickest way to add style to an ensemble.

POST PARTUM OR NURSING: A wardrobe designed for a woman in the post-partum period. It generally consists of comfortable separates matched for an infant's easy accessibility to breasts for nursing.

- I have rarely seen a good-looking nursing top. (True, things are improving.) I used to call the tops "immoral," but I have since calmed down because my friends would cringe when I said that. I nursed my babies in separates, and I managed to keep it a private affair even in public. Come to think of it, I used regular wardrobe design techniques to plan a wardrobe for this period. Don't feel pressured into buying nursing tops or anything specialized for this time. Continue your fabulous style in separates with a ready supply of nursing pads for your bras. (The ones with the adhesive strips will spare you any embarrassment.) Add a beautiful receiving blanket to use as a cover up while nursing in public if this makes you feel comfortable and be sure to always burp a baby with a cloth or towel between you and little darling.

- Do not – I repeat – do not carry a diaper bag that screams "diaper bag!" You know the type: pastel plastic with teddy bears or building blocks. You are the one carrying the bag, not the baby. I'd wager that the baby doesn't care about Dumbo or Pooh. True, hospitals still give them out. (I gave them to my preschool girls to use as "purses.") However, you should always think before you do free marketing for Walt Disney or Warner Brothers.
- Choose a structured bag in a larger size or opt for some of the new styles of bags now sold by some retailers who specialize in baby equipment. Their bags are often designed to look like purses. They tend to come in all the dark neutral colors and are often very nicely styled and current.
- Guard your bag. Never let it become lumpy or smelly. It's a tough habit to start, but try to clean out your bag every time you return home.
- Wear washable garments. I guess this goes without saying because I've never known a woman to stick with dry-clean-only when home with a baby.
- Treat color like your best friend. Wear your absolute best medium and dark colors. This not only livens up your ap-

pearance but helps to minimize the chance of going out in public with obvious baby stains. (You will go out in public with stains because that's what babies do best. Just try to keep them from becoming obvious.) Of course, if given the chance, change your stained outfit.

- Continue to wear accessories. Wear pretty earrings and an attractive watch. Why not?
- Continue to wear makeup. You may even need a little more now since going through something as physically intense as childbirth. Even just a little lipstick can do wonders.
- Revisit your undergarments. Purchase well-made nursing bras with plenty of support. Check that your nipples aren't poking through the bra and top. (See p. 79 for information on bras.)

SEMINAR FAQ

dress code of honor

QUESTION: I work in an office that has no dress code, and it really shows. Some wear suits, others wear khakis and shirts, and a few even wear jeans. We can't look to our boss because she is the worst dresser of the bunch. How do I begin to design a wardrobe that will work in an environment that's this casual?

ANSWER: There is really only one approach that addresses the dignity of both your profession in general and your career in particular: Be the "cream that rises to the top." Just wear the highest form of appropriate attire for your field in general. So, for example, if suits are the tradition in your field, design a wardrobe of suiting despite what the others are wearing. If, generally, your field has a tradition of dressing down, design a great business casual wardrobe. Who knows? You may actually influence the way others are dressing.

I have known women who were directed by their supervisors to never wear suits to the office. Indeed, one company was actually kind of neurotic about it all. The way these women stepped around the mandate was to choose structured separates for a business casual wardrobe that worked a lot like suiting. So they opted for pieces like dress trousers, twin sets, man tailored blouses, and jackets, and they stuck to all the standards like neutral hosiery, closed toe shoes, and brief cases no matter the day of the week or the time of the year. The market offers many beautiful options that work well for this kind of situation, so these women were very happy in the end.

weather seasons/climate

COLD WEATHER: A wardrobe designed for winter or a cold climate. Special considerations include a "dress" coat, personal casual coat, gloves, scarf, hat, etc.

- A cold weather wardrobe is more expensive than a warm weather wardrobe. Budget accordingly.
- Pay special attention to the warmth of the fabrics. Wools and cottons both breathe and warm up nicely. Avoid wool if you tend to itch a lot or if you are always holding a child (or man) who itches a lot.
- Avoid acrylic-cotton blend sweaters. Most tend to pill after the first wash.
- One hundred percent acrylic in an especially soft fabric will

pill a lot less than a combination. This makes a nice, inexpensive alternative.

- Invest in thermals if you tend to get cold but want the thermostat to stay low. There are many pretty styles that will fit as well as a second skin. Thicker thermals add the appearance of weight to your look. Opt for silk thermals. They are thin and wonderfully warm.
- Consider your workplace. I have always found the office to be overheated, so I avoid using heavy wool for business and business casual dress. Wool gabardine works well when the heat is too high or uncontrollable.
- Plan out your dress coat, day coat, and inside jacket (blazer or sweater for inside). See page 281 for tips.
- Check out the cold weather tips on page 325.

WARM WEATHER: A wardrobe designed for summer or a warm climate. Special considerations include a swimsuit, shorts, hat, etc.

- Summer is a time for loosening up a little bit. Just don't loosen up your style. Keep it elegant.
- Remind yourself that you don't have to show all the body parts that others are showing.
- Do not create a personal casual wardrobe that consists of nothing but shorts.
- Choose shorts carefully. The hems of the shorts should fall to the thinnest part of your thighs. Ensure that shorts never rob the focal point from your face.
- Cheap fabrics seem to sneak into our garments during this time of the year. Be vigilant. Read labels and feel items while shopping.
- Avoid using flip-flops as your primary shoe, even if you don't have to work.

- Do not shop for all summer apparel while it is extremely cold or while it is snowing. You can choose a few items at this time of year because you will benefit from getting the first dibs. However, if you go wild, you will make mistakes.
- Check out the warm weather tips on page 326.

TRANSITIONAL: A wardrobe designed for spring and fall that "transitions" from one extreme season to another. Special considerations include a raincoat, umbrella, light jacket, etc.

- You need a transitional wardrobe even if you think you don't. In some climates, like those in Canada or the Northeast, the wardrobe may need a very low base number. (This excludes you folks in the Arctic Circle and the tropics.)
- Don't give in to the quick-solution-sweatshirt for running out of the house. Invest in something snappy and uplifting.
- Use layering such as the kind facilitated by the *mix and match* technique.
- This is a very important time that says "upcoming season" with its color but "current season" with its weight.
- Without the appropriate pieces we lose confidence and many women stumble along during the transitional fashion periods. Pay attention to your wardrobe needs with all the care you would take for the other seasons.

STYLE PROFILE #9

a month in my life

Decide how you spend your time each month so that you can design your wardrobes accordingly.

Note the sample calendar for Sheila below. Sheila works part-time in a business casual setting. She determined that she needed a combination personal and business casual wardrobe because of her part-time schedule and because so much of her personal time is taken up with school meetings and social events.

The abbreviations B (business), P (personal casual), BC (business casual), and E (evening) each represent a wardrobe type that she wears for that day of the month.

SEPTEMBER

S	M	T	W	T	F	S
BC/P	P	BC	BC	BC	P	P
BC/P	P/BC	BC	BC	BC	P	P
BC/P	P/BC	BC	BC	BC	P	P
BC/P	P	BC	BC	BC	P	P/E

This method is what I call the *method of liberal arts majors.* In other words, there is no math (no percentages; no pie charts!). What you need is the following:

1. Your regular calendar. Open it to the three or four months that constitute the next fashion season. If you are at the beginning of one, use this season.
2. Blank calendar pages (you can use the ones below) for each of those months.
3. A pencil or pen. Color coding with color pencils or crayons work the best.

MONTH:

S	M	T	W	T	F	S

MONTH:

S	M	T	W	T	F	S

MONTH:

S	M	T	W	T	F	S

INSTRUCTIONS: Decide your wardrobes for all of the kinds of activities you do. For example, personal casual time requires a personal casual wardrobe. PTA meetings, parties, dinner dates, and serious shopping trips need the structure of a business casual wardrobe. Time at work requires a business casual or business wardrobe or both.

Designate a symbol or color to represent each of these types of wardrobes. Don't forget to create a key for what you chose!

Fill in the blank calendars on the facing page with your symbols or colors to show when you wear these wardrobes. See Sheila's calendar for an example.

Stand back and examine how the calendars appear. Check the following.

- How many types of wardrobes do you really need? Business, business casual, and personal casual? Can you combine the business casual and personal casual wardrobes? Do you have so many evening events that you need an evening wardrobe? Do you have some trips coming up?
- How many wardrobes do you need for each wardrobe type? For example, if you have a long winter ahead of you and you will be working long hours in a business casual wardrobe type, maybe you need two of them, each in different color stories.
- Is total color harmony called for? Should it be across one, two, or all three types of wardrobes?
- Any other special considerations? Any big-time events like an anniversary dinner or a television appearance? While it is not wise to purchase an ensemble only for

a specific event, it is a good idea to figure out how a wardrobe will accommodate the event.

- Are there any accessories that need to be purchased? Is this the year you will replace your coat? Your bathing suit? Your work pumps? Your handbag? Is it time to unveil your signature accessory? See p. 217 for more details.
- Learn the science of budgeting. See p. 267 for more details.

what's a busy woman like you doing in a chapter like this?

You are not off the hook yet! You *almost* have all the information you need to begin planning, but there is some vital information missing. Since you are not like everyone else in the world, you need to analyze your unique demands for fashion. They are extremely important for choosing which wardrobe planning technique you will use, whether or not you will go for total color harmony, or what particular items are must-haves. Below is a *Style Profile* which contains some issues about which you may never have given much thought. They constitute the *consciousness* you give your wardrobe.

STYLE PROFILE #10
my needs assessment

Read each statement below and choose the appropriate rating. You must decide how important each issue is for selecting clothing and accessories and plan according to your priorities.

1. I must purchase clothing and accessories as economically as possible (*an affordable wardrobe*).

   not important at all — not very important

   important — very important

2. I must wear the most fashionable clothing possible for my budget and my circumstances (a *fashion-forward wardrobe*).

   not important at all — not very important

   important — very important

3. I must wear the most comfortable clothing possible for my budget and my circumstances (*a comfortable wardrobe*).

   not important at all — not very important

   important — very important

4. I maintain a high profile within the community and must be ready for impromptu appearances before an audience (*a reliable wardrobe*).

   not important at all — not very important

   important — very important

5. I must have flexible wardrobes which work with my constantly changing size (*a flexible wardrobe*).

   not important at all — not very important

   important — very important

6. I must have a great number of different types of clothes for the great number of tasks I do in any given week (*a versatile wardrobe*).

   not important at all — not very important

   important — very important

7. I must have a wardrobe which is conducive to quick and thoughtless mixing and matching for effective time management (*a time-efficient wardrobe*).

   not important at all   not very important

   important   very important

Next, rank them in the order of importance.

1. ______________________
2. ______________________
3. ______________________
4. ______________________
5. ______________________
6. ______________________
7. ______________________

How you prioritize these issues and, in turn, apply them to your fashion choices will add to the overall flavor of your style.

Examine your answers and ***read only the sections below that rank as very important or important for you.*** Once you finish reading the tips for your priorities, return to page 193 of this chapter.

PRIORITY CHOICE #1: I must purchase clothing, accessories, and cosmetics as economically as possible *(an affordable wardrobe).*

If financial limitations are an important consideration for designing your wardrobe, you are certainly not alone. Most women want to save money even if they have a relatively generous amount of disposable income. After all, there are a great number of other things on which you can spend your money.

In planning the items you need for this wardrobe, try the following:

- Buy items in good quality but easy-to-maintain fabrics. Dry cleaning can be expensive. (Remember to check labels while shopping.)
- Plan out *total color harmony.*
- Use either the *mix and match* or *spectrum* technique.
- Buy items that work through several seasons of the year. Microfiber items, clothing in lightweight wool, or cotton knit separates work well.
- Learn shortcuts for updating a wardrobe. Replace buttons, use vests and jackets, and adjust hem length to give ensembles a new life.
- Avoid buying fast-track fad items with short expiration dates.
- Buy solid color outfits rather than outfits in prints.
- Plan out timeless wardrobe items and rely on accessories to update and vary the look of your ensembles. (Tops in solid colors, add-on jackets, a sheath dress, etc.)
- Create a budget for your wardrobe. (See chapter eight.)

PRIORITY CHOICE #2: I must wear the most fashionable clothing possible for my budget and my circumstances (*a fashion-forward wardrobe*).

If, objectively speaking, this a high priority for you, you are a lucky woman! What fun it can be! Try the tips below:

- Educate yourself. Check high-end catalogues and fashion magazines for ideas and browse before you buy.
- Leaving your credit card at home, tour quality retailers for ideas. Then, choose your price range and retailer according to your budget and keep those images and your *elements of style* in mind when you plan.

- Opt for your absolutely best colors rather than the faddish ones for your wardrobes.
- Pay very close attention to your handbag and shoes. If you are planning for winter, coordinate your winter coat with these accessories. Spend quality time searching for these things so that you get the most fashion for your money.
- Get a really fantastic, fashion-forward haircut to go with your new wardrobe.
- Become very skilled in makeup application.
- Groom your eyebrows and extinguish facial hair with the best resources available to you. In other words, if you can afford to visit a salon, do so.
- Plan out a signature accessory that updates your look instantly.

PRIORITY CHOICE #3: I must wear the most comfortable clothing possible for my budget and my circumstances (*a comfortable wardrobe*).

This is just about everyone's priority. Of course, you may be of that particular type (probably a relaxed!) who would die without it.

- Plan out ensembles that use separates by using either the *mix and match* technique or the *spectrum* technique. (See below.)
- The advantage of the *spectrum* wardrobe solution is that you will be able to buy multiples of your favorite (i.e., most comfortable) bottoms.
- Buy items made of fabrics that breathe (cotton, acrylic, lightweight wool, linen, etc.).
- Buy comfortable shoes that have style. Save the tennis shoes for athletics.
- Never err on the side of schlepping out. Rather, add structure or detail in ways that don't compromise your comfort.
- Accessories do not hurt. After a while, you won't even know they are there.

PRIORITY CHOICE #4: I maintain a high-profile within the community and must be ready for impromptu appearances on television or before an audience (*a reliable wardrobe*).

- Read the tips for Priority #2. You will have to be fashion-forward in your appearance for your own credibility.
- Read the tips regarding a business wardrobe on page 169.
- Go for total color harmony so that you always look put-together.
- Take time choosing your wardrobe colors. If you are appearing on television, avoid wearing black around your face (use navy as an alternative dark color if it's from your color palette). Extremely bright colors such as yellow, red, or pink can be a bit much for television or photography as well.
- Also, choose color so as to project the mood you want to convey.
- Check background color scheme for a television studio from the set coordinator before dressing for the day.
- Avoid printed (especially striped or checked) tops. The busier the top, the more it distracts viewers or moves on the screen.
- Wear earrings, but choose conservatively according to your fashion personality.
- Avoid overwhelming accessories. Pins are beautiful but choose them the same way you would choose earrings.
- Stick to only one noticeable (head and shoulders) accessory. Choose large earrings or a necklace but not both. Or, choose a pin or a scarf but not both. A fussy look is distracting and can make you appear frivolous.
- Meet with a makeup consultant to master makeup techniques. Wear makeup every day.
- Carry your makeup bag in your purse for touch ups.
- Keep an extra pair of hosiery in your purse or glove compartment of your car. See page 319 for details on an emergency kit.

- Keep a dressy pair of shoes and an exciting accessory such as a scarf or beads at work for any surprise evening functions.
- Study chapter nine.

PRIORITY CHOICE #5: I must have flexible wardrobes which work with my constantly changing size (a *flexible wardrobe*).

- Use a *mix and match* wardrobe technique.
- Go for total color harmony in any given wardrobe.
- Coordinate similar color stories across all your wardrobes for easier mixing and matching across weather seasons and types.
- Budget for undergarments in your size now.
- Tackle only a wardrobe for your size now.
- Buy items that work through two to three weather seasons.
- Buy ribbed-knit tops that ride over the top of your trousers if this is good for your body type.
- Invest in a blazer, sweater, or outer coat that can be left open or closed to create different looks.
- Keep this blazer and a pair of polished loafers or boots by the door.
- Become a master at accessorizing. Rely on accessories to change the look of an ensemble.
- Keep in mind that there are plenty of fashionable yet washable clothes. There's no reason to wear rags because you are cleaning or taking care of children.

PRIORITY CHOICE #6: I must have a great number of different types of clothes for the great number of tasks I do in any given week (a *versatile wardrobe*).

- Use the *mix and match* technique with plenty of layering.
- The *spectrum* technique will allow you to simply change your top for any change in activity.

- Use simple accessories that add beauty.
- Choose items that are machine washable.
- If some of your tasks include cleaning and mothering, buy a really great (fashionable), oversized apron. Hey, if it's now acceptable for men to wear them, why not for women to continue wearing them? Just don't forget to take it off when you head somewhere!
- Keep a fantastic blazer and pair of loafers or boots by the door for running out to personal or business casual events.

PRIORITY CHOICE #7: I must have a wardrobe which is conducive to quick and thoughtless morning decision time for effective time management (*a time-efficient wardrobe*).

- Create a list of your combinations. (Polaroid photos or illustrations work well.) Post it in your closet, perhaps on the back of the door.
- Pay very close attention to your color story. Stick to a one to three color story.
- Go for 100 percent mixing and matching if you choose this technique. *Spectrum* and *monochromatic* techniques are optimal. (A wardrobe of only dresses provides what we call "twenty second dressing.")
- Avoid prints in your wardrobe.
- Go for *total color harmony*. This is an absolute must!

parting thoughts

You're ready to design your new wardrobe now. You know what you need and how it should work for you. Some parting thoughts:

1. Consider your *elements of style.*
2. Be creative.
3. Less is more.

CHAPTER SIX

total style
wardrobe planning II

confessions of a former fashion victim

During my first year of teaching, I had a supervisor who was an amazing dresser. Every single day she wore what appeared to be an expensive outfit in beautiful colors and with all the right accessories. She was gorgeous, and hearing the clothing report for Cathy every morning was like checking in on the weather forecast. Only this forecast was always bright and sunny.

Clothes make the man. Naked people have little or no influence in society.

MARK TWAIN

I was only twenty-two and fresh out of school. I looked to her as a great fashion example, as I'm sure just about every woman who knew her did. But she was intimidating. If I wanted to have great style, how would I, a first-year teacher in a public school, ever be able to afford a different dress for every single day of the year? She seemed so high up there that I just sort of gave up.

Later on, while I was working for a technology company, I met another one of these fashion intimidators. Her name was Debé, and she was very exotic and French (French Canadian, anyway) and in a league of her own. Just like my first supervisor, she had a different outfit for just about every day of any fashion season. However, Debé was a peer rather than a supervisor, and people began to compare her to me and other women (never the men) in the same position for qualities that went beyond fashion. You can imagine all the confusion I had as a young, impressionable fashion victim.

You know exactly where I'm going with this. Yes, these women had fashion. They even had style. But their *style* did not come so much from clothing. What I eventually learned is that beautiful style comes from *quality* rather than *quantity,* and that, at its best, style incorporates creativity, professionalism, and elegance. If either Cathy or Debé had only a *fraction* of all those outfits, they would still have looked fantastic.

But they would have to learn a few things. This chapter explains those things.

OBJECTIVE: plan a fantastic wardrobe!

three wardrobe design techniques

There are three wardrobe design techniques that I have used for myself, my friends, and my clients. They are easy and adaptable and will work for women of every body type, fashion personality, and color palette. (Some of these techniques are better than others for particular *elements of style.*) You may find yourself using three different techniques for three different wardrobes, or you may adopt one as your favorite for every wardrobe you need.

1. THE MIX AND MATCH TECHNIQUE — A wardrobe technique that facilitates complete mixing and matching of separates. A low base number of eight items is disguised by a great number of looks created by layering and accessorizing. ***Good for:***

- all body types, especially the pear and the heart because of their dependence on separates.
- all personality types, especially the classic.
- an affordable wardrobe. The limited number of items used will be disguised in a great number of combinations.
- a fashion-forward wardrobe. Its heavy reliance on accessories is a sure-fire way to stay current.
- a reliable wardrobe. This is especially the case if accessories are used in clever ways.
- a flexible wardrobe. Items such as blazers and man-tailored blouses that can mix and match well also transition nicely across two or three sizes.
- a versatile wardrobe. A wardrobe with the possibility of layering can be modified to meet daily demands.
- cold weather and transitional weather wardrobes. Layering techniques also keep you warm.
- personal casual, business casual, combination business casual and personal casual, business, and travel wardrobes.

2. THE SPECTRUM TECHNIQUE — A wardrobe technique that has an abundance of colors for tops and a single neutral color for the bottoms. *Good for:*

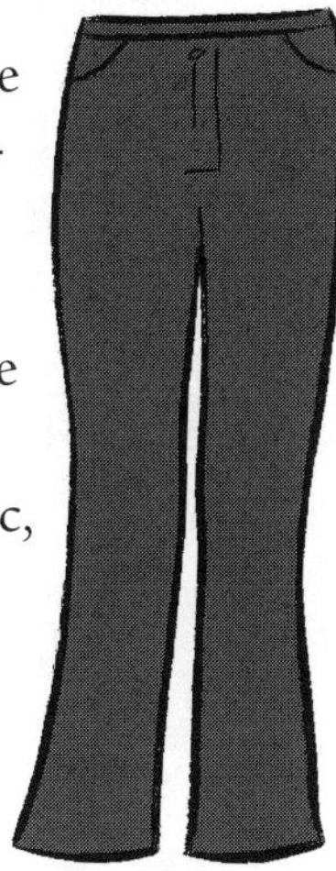

- all body types, especially the pear because a single dark color can be used for all bottoms.
- all personality types, especially the relaxed, classic, and expressive.
- an affordable wardrobe.
- a fashion-forward wardrobe. Bottoms can be chosen to work through many fashion seasons, and tops can be updated frequently.
- a reliable wardrobe. The broad spectrum of color in this wardrobe is excellent for varying the look for television or public appearances.

- a comfortable wardrobe. You can buy multiples of your most comfortable bottoms.
- a wardrobe that is being constructed from a mixed assortment of colors in a purged closet. (This can happen even after the most thorough of wardrobe analysis; tons of items in tons of colors that still look fabulous.)
- a time-efficient wardrobe. This wardrobe requires no thought in the morning.
- personal casual, business casual, combination business casual and personal casual, business, and travel.
- overcoming any boredom related to the designated colors of a color story; especially good for women in climates where one weather season is particularly long.
- women who have professions greeting the public from behind a desk.
- warm weather and transitional weather wardrobes. If you love sweaters, this solution is excellent for a winter wardrobe as well.
- a wardrobe with printed tops (excellent for women with the pear shape body type). There's always a neutral bottom with which to match them.

3. THE MONOCHROMATIC TECHNIQUE — A wardrobe technique that uses only one color for any single ensemble. This wardrobe could consist of only one color throughout the entire wardrobe. ***Good for:***

- all body types, especially the box body type.
- plus size women if darker colors are used.
- all personality types, especially relaxed, expressive, and romantic.
- a fashion-forward wardrobe. (Some suit styles always stay in style.)

- a reliable wardrobe. Suits are always appropriate for public appearances.
- a time-efficient wardrobe. This wardrobe requires little thought in the morning. (Often called *twenty-second dressing*.)
- all seasons.
- personal casual, business casual, and business wardrobes.

from eight to infinity

Eight is the magic number for these techniques. That's a total of eight items, not including accessories, for any wardrobe. And it's not just me – it's mathematics! Turn the number eight on its side and you have the symbol for infinity. That's just how eight works in your wardrobe.

instructions for the mix and match wardrobe technique

Below are the steps to follow for designing any kind of wardrobe using this technique. A wardrobe solution worksheet is provided on page 211.

1. Conduct a thorough wardrobe analysis on the wardrobe you currently own (just like you did in your *fashion moments of truth* for chapters two, three, and four). Consider the items you saved as optimal pieces for designing this wardrobe.
2. Decide your color story either by using the colors from your optimal pieces left in your wardrobe or by choosing from your palette. Decide on at least one neutral for this color story. A total of three colors will work to keep it interesting without diminishing its simplicity.
3. Using eight as your base number, decide the ratio of tops to bottoms. Usually four tops and four bottoms is best, but three and five (or five and three) is a safe bet as well.

4. Keep in mind your fashion personality for the cut and styling of each piece, and later for your accessories.
5. Keep in mind your body type for where you will place colors, prints, and the direction of lines. Limit prints *either* to tops or bottoms.
6. Imagine how items will mix and match and layer.
7. Keep in mind your priorities to stay honest and realistic.

MIX AND MATCH TECHNIQUE (This sample wardrobe is intended as an instructional tool for *any* wardrobe. This one happens to be a combination personal-business casual type for a transitional weather season.)

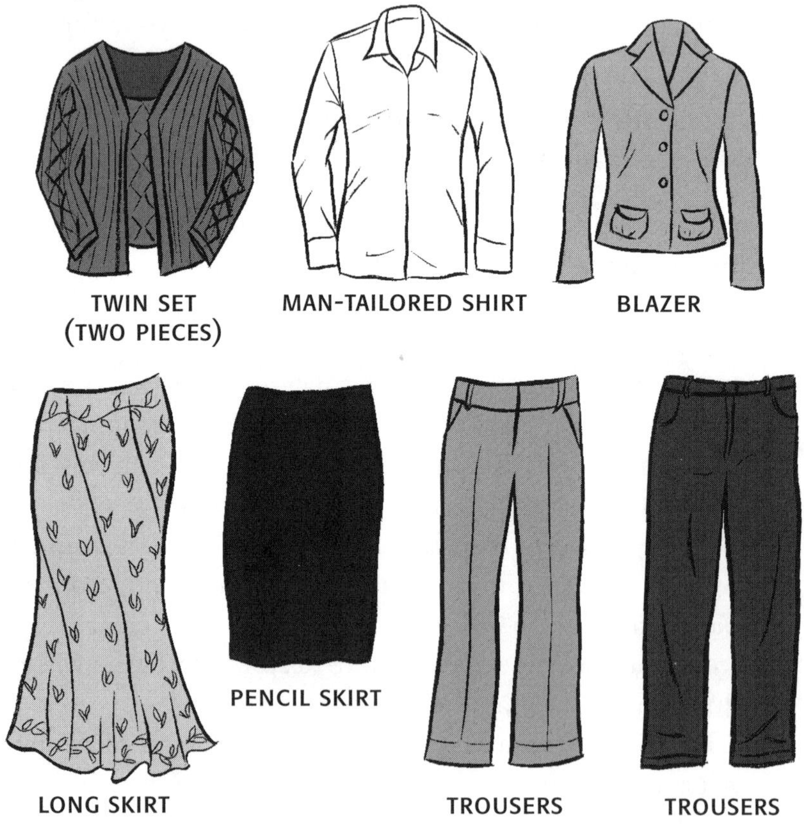

The trick to making this wardrobe technique work is layering and accessorizing. Here are some of the possibilities. Remember, eight is infinity!

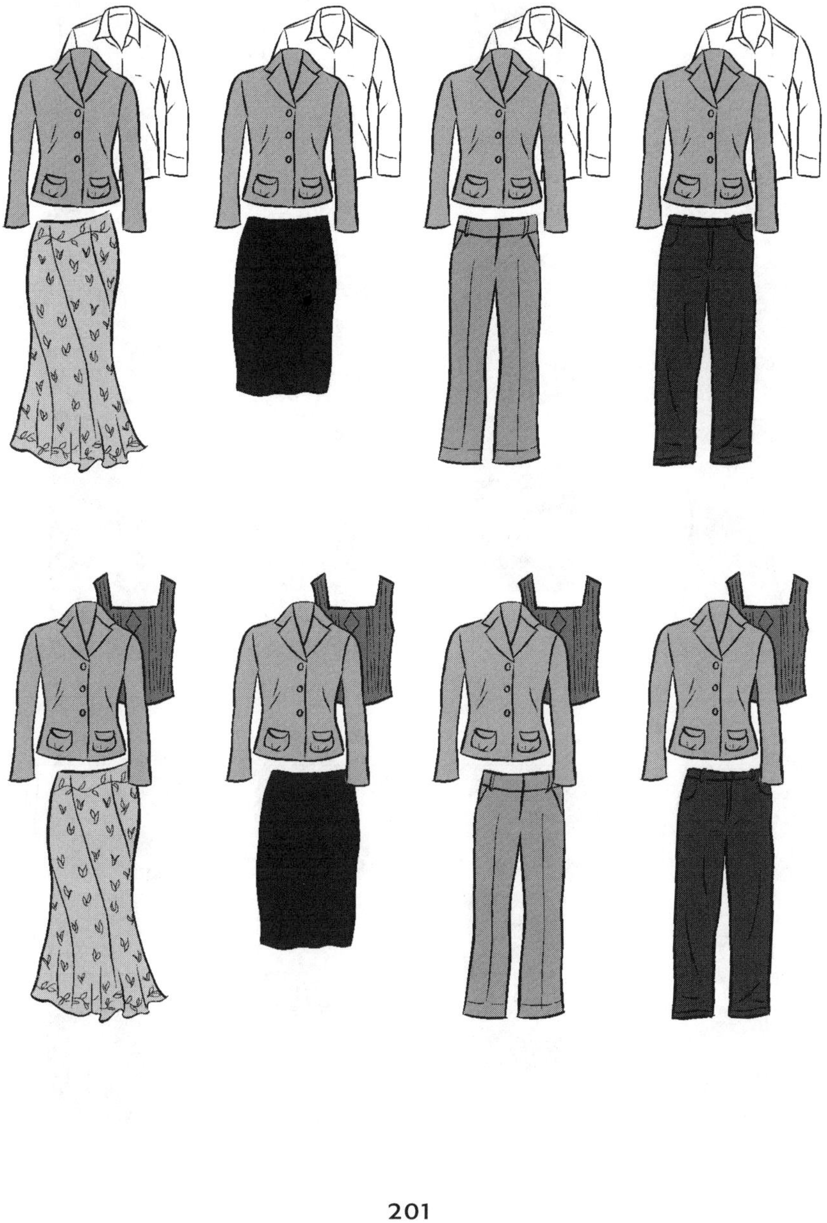

instructions for the spectrum wardrobe technique

Below are the steps to follow for designing any kind of wardrobe using this technique. A wardrobe technique worksheet is provided on page 211.

1. Conduct a thorough wardrobe analysis on the wardrobe you currently own (just like you did in your *fashion moments of truth* for chapters two, three, and four). Consider the items you saved as optimal pieces for designing this wardrobe.
2. Decide your color story. Decide on at least one neutral for all the bottoms. Each top can be in a different color. Be sure to choose from your color palette.
3. Using eight as your base number, decide the ratio of tops to bottoms. Since all your bottoms will be solids of the same color, you might want to try five tops and three bottoms or even six tops and two bottoms.
4. Keep in mind your fashion personality for the cut and styling of each piece, and later for your accessories.
5. Keep in mind your body type for where you will place colors, prints, and the direction of lines.
6. Keep in mind your priorities and lifestyle to stay honest and realistic.

SPECTRUM TECHNIQUE (This sample wardrobe is intended as an instructional tool for *any* wardrobe. This one happens to be a personal casual type for the cold weather season.)

TURTLE NECK | V-NECK TOP | BOAT NECK | SHAWL NECK | MAN-TAILORED SHIRT

A-LINE SKIRT
(in chosen dark neutral)

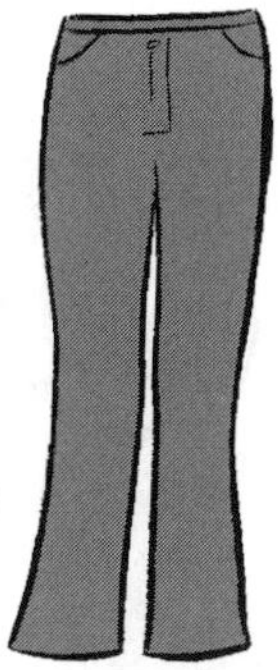

TROUSERS
(in chosen dark neutral)

JEANS
(in chosen dark neutral)

Using accessories and the great variety of colors for tops multiplies the number of looks. Here are some of the possibilities for a spectrum wardrobe:

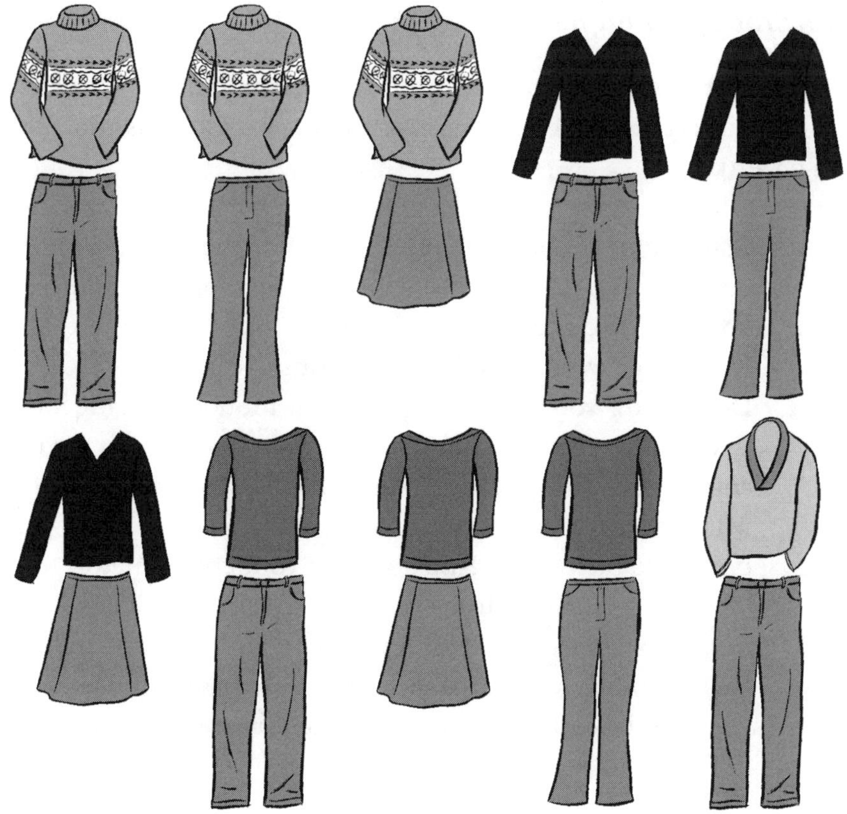

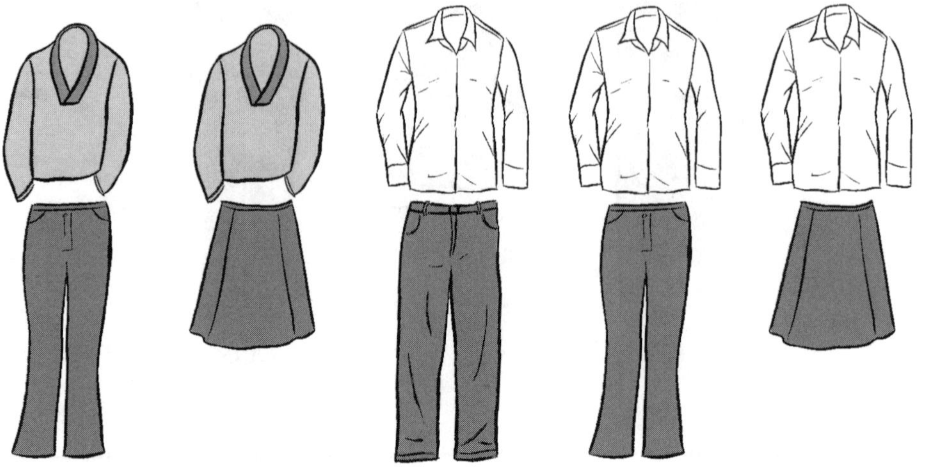

instructions for the monochromatic wardrobe technique

Below are the steps to follow for designing any kind of wardrobe using this technique. A wardrobe technique worksheet is provided on page 211.

1. Using eight as your base number, decide the ratio of tops to bottoms. If you are using mostly suits, four tops and four bottoms is your ratio. Three and five (or five and three) is a safe bet for wardrobes that don't consist of suits.
2. Decide how you will accomplish your monochromatic look. Use either a specific color for each outfit or one color for the entire wardrobe. (Multiple wardrobes each of only one color will keep several colors available to you across the year.) Just be sure to pick your best color from your color palette.

   NOTE: If this wardrobe does not consist of suits and you decide to choose one color for the entire wardrobe, you have the flexibility to mix same colors and shades of the same color in different textures within different ensembles. This will allow you to mix pieces, yet still maintain a monochromatic look.

3. Keep in mind both your fashion personality for the cut and styling of each piece, and later for your accessories.
4. Keep in mind your priorities and lifestyle, so stay honest and realistic.

MONOCHROMATIC TECHNIQUE using one color for the entire wardrobe. (This sample wardrobe is intended as an instructional tool for *any* wardrobe. This one happens to be a combination personal-business casual type for the cold weather season.)

Here are some of the possible looks for a monochromatic wardrobe:

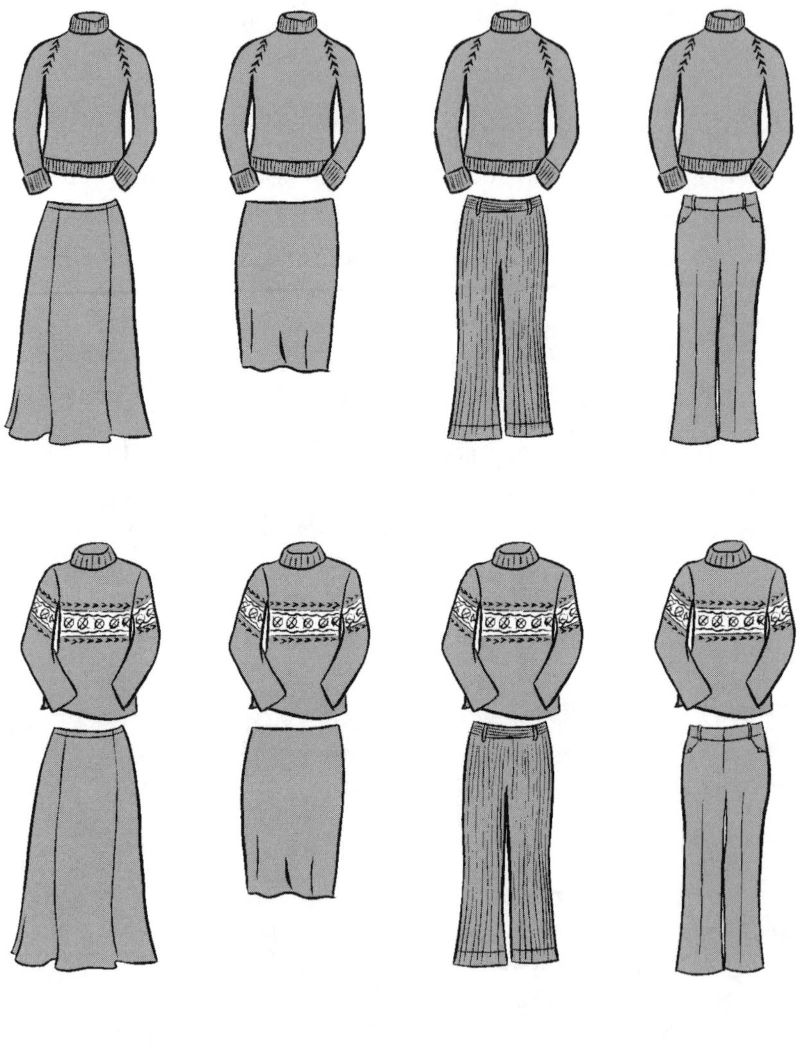

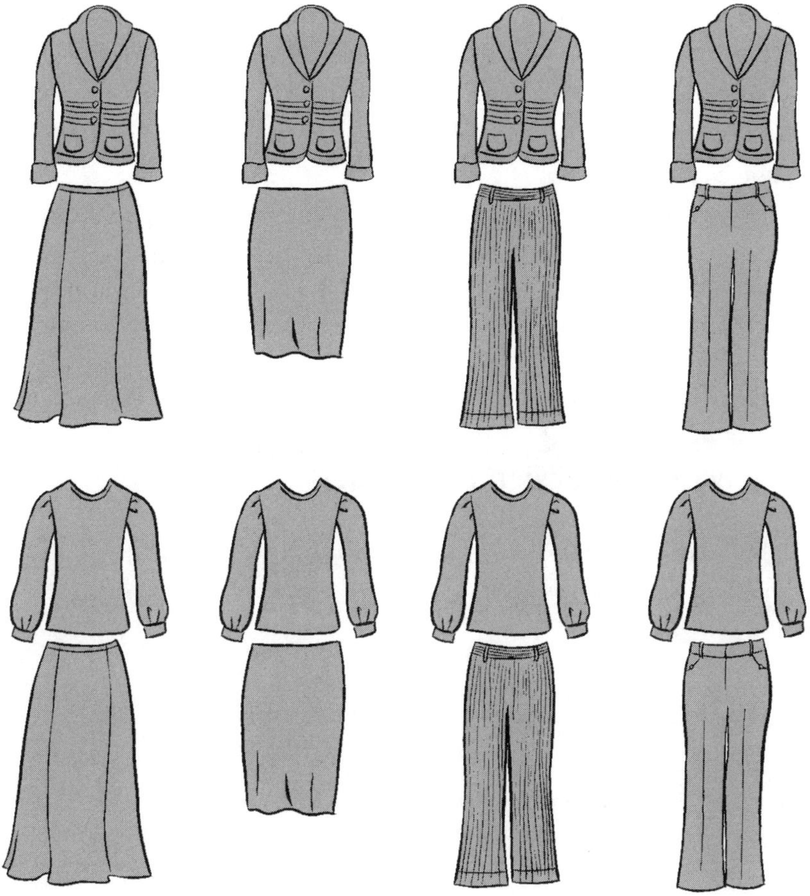

I'm changing my life!

It's now time to get down to business. In the next *Style Profile* you will plan your own wardrobe. Walk through the preliminary steps even if you think you know exactly what you are jumping into. I've found that in planning ideal wardrobes you have to lay the groundwork *first*. Using the worksheet is like getting all the instruments of an orchestra to work together for beautiful music. You will be singing a sweet tune in no time!

The chances are pretty good that you may have to purchase one or two (or more!) items for the wardrobes. Save your shopping stress for chapter eight. You'll learn to get what you need with no blood, sweat, or tears, and you'll be able to use the *Shopping Strategy Worksheet* on page 293.

Also, while planning your wardrobe, you will realize what kinds of accessories you need. Save the real planning for the next chapter. *Style Profile #13* will revisit this wardrobe planner with an eye toward accessories.

STYLE PROFILE #11

my wardrobe design techniques

The worksheet on the following page will walk you through planning a wardrobe. You will need:

1. a pencil
2. the back flap of this book, which illustrates the colors of your color palette.
3. the instructions for your wardrobe solution of choice if you can't remember how it is done.
4. optimal items from your closet *after* your wardrobe analysis. (You need to go through all three *fashion moments of truth*!)

IMPORTANT: Revisit the tips for the wardrobes and your priorities in the last chapter. Many of the suggestions imply specific techniques for choosing items.

To create additional worksheets, photocopy the following two pages. You won't always have to use a worksheet, though. In fact, after just one try with a particular technique, it should become second nature.

wardrobe technique worksheet Date: ______

MY ELEMENTS OF STYLE (circle one for each)

My body type is: *Pear Heart Box Hourglass*

My Fashion Personality is: *Relaxed Classic Romantic Expressive*

My Color Palette is: *Cool Light Cool Warm Light Warm*

MY WARDROBE SPECS (circle one for each)

This wardrobe is: *Personal Casual Business Casual Combo (Personal Casual/Business Casual) Travel Specialized*

The season is: *Cold Weather Warm Weather Transitional*

Special Considerations: *Maternity Post Partum*

MY WARDROBE TECHNIQUE

My technique of choice: *Mix and Match (see page 199) Spectrum (see page 204) Monochromatic (see page 206)*

MY COLOR STORY (from your color palette)

Mix and match color story: ______________________________
____

Spectrum color for bottoms: ______________________________

Monochromatic color: ______________________________

8 ITEMS

Tops:

Bottoms:

Accessories:

Combinations:

stories from the other side

Teaching about fashion continually reminds me how very different people are from one another. Every woman I've known has added her personal touch to her wardrobe techniques, and I'll bet that you will too.

Yvonne is a classic who uses the *mix and match* technique for her business casual wardrobe. I saw her closet after she finished designing one such wardrobe, and she proudly showed me how she had discovered layering in her own way: "I take this vest and turn it around to get a different look. Then, I layer away." Her simple red, black, and white wardrobe looked stunning with coordinated pieces that fit beautifully and keep impeccably.

The same Yvonne loves the twin set. She has a white cotton one with a short sleeve shell and long sleeve cardigan. Not only can she use it for her winter wardrobe, but she wears it almost as much in the summer with her pink, plum, and white color story.

I have a client named Heidi who took to the *spectrum* technique for her personal casual time like a kid to candy. "Why would I do it any differently?" she said to me once. "I love my turtlenecks and jeans while I'm working at home, and that technique makes it easy and interesting." So Heidi chooses well-fitting black jeans for her pear shaped body and adds interest by choosing her best cool colors in cotton turtle necks: purple, red, white, etc. If she needs to run out of the house, she simply throws on a pair of neat loafers and her perfect jacket.

Believe it or not, I even have a friend who uses the monochromatic technique for her warm weather, personal casual wardrobe. And she's a relaxed! Her warm coloring allows her to wear a rich creamy-color linen. So, she has a cream-colored wardrobe of cotton blouses, linen pants and skirts, and a versatile matching jacket. She added a straw bag and a pair of brown sandals, so she always looks put-together.

so, that's what's on the back wall of my closet!

Maintaining a beautiful wardrobe is a lot like working out (but not as difficult, as far as I'm concerned). You have to stick with it! You'll have to:

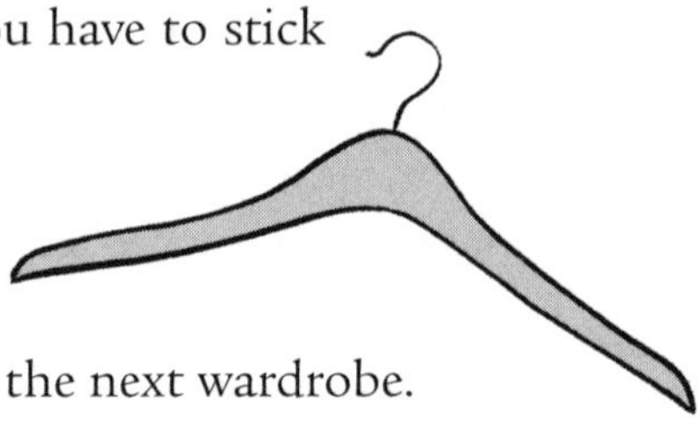

1. maintain what you own.
2. resist unnecessary additions.
3. assess what to do differently for the next wardrobe.

Below are some tips to meet those objectives.

- Keep all your wardrobe items easily accessible in one area.
- Keep nothing but your in-season items in this area. In other words, if you use a closet, get rid of the children's clothes, the picture frames, and the ping-pong table.
- You can begin the process of living with less by investing in a sturdy garment rack, placing it in a well-lighted area of your bedroom, and hanging your in-season wardrobe(s) on it. This is how I live even today because I find that I can more easily see everything in one glance. Also, since I am actually using every item, I don't have to worry about dust collecting on anything.
- Designate an area for tops, another for bottoms, and still another for dresses. Keep color families together within each section so that it's conducive to your wardrobe technique.
- Store shoes carefully. Use transparent, shoe-size boxes if you can; otherwise, shelves and racks are better than just tossing shoes on the floor.
- Keep the area well-lit. Make it a beautiful place to visit each morning and evening.
- Remove all wire hangers from your closet. Invest in some wooden or hard plastic ones.

- Fold sweaters.
- Always hang or fold clothes when finished with them. Okay, maybe that's a bit unreasonable for all you free-spirits. At least designate a launching pad like a men's valet for the next morning when you can call it an exchange. You can justify this by saying that you are airing out your clothes before placing them away. (Using a garment rack helps to fight this bad habit.)
- Paint the interior of your closet white so that you can see item colors clearly.
- Keep a lint brush close by. Many are constructed to hang.
- Create a ready-reference box for the maintenance of some wardrobe items. Remove tags from scarves and keep them along with the extra buttons included with new garments in this box. Keep needle, thread, and scissors close by for quick repair. Keep a stain removal product here or near your laundry hamper.

It's now or never.

ELVIS

- Always follow instructions for garment maintenance. This includes instructions on ironing.
- Replace your iron if it is leaving stains or burning clothing.
- Stay on top of laundry. (I know, easier said than done: it's my personal struggle as well.) I know of women who buy more clothing because they are overwhelmed by the laundry situation in their homes. Look to page 287 for tips on an effective laundry system.
- Keep your laundry separate from the rest of your household's. Invest in one of those divided stand-up net hampers to divide by color and carry around with ease. Some items are hand washable and need to stay separate. Select a separate system for these.
- Invest in a handy reference book on stain removal and keep it where you do laundry or in the reference box. The best place for information is the Fabric Institute.[1]

STYLE PROFILE #12

reflective wardrobe design

Remember how in chapter one I mentioned the qualities of creativity, professionalism, and elegance? Let's revisit those ideas for a moment. Reflect upon how your newly designed wardrobe incorporates (or could incorporate) these qualities:

Creativity:

____

____

____

Professionalism:

____

____

____

Elegance:

____

____

____

CHAPTER SEVEN

functional style accessories

looking for mr. good bag

We must be living in a crazy culture. It's the only way to explain why a woman would claim not to *find* a simple handbag after viewing literally hundreds. In some ways it's like looking for a soulmate: The bag must be strong, patient, loyal, kind, good looking, and, well, *perfect*!

An acquaintance of mine caught me in a parking lot once and dangled two handbags in front of me. "Okay, which one?" She asked, clearly suffering from that kind of anxiety that only fashion shopping can bring (without my help). One bag was a twenty-nine dollar brown and black saddle bag style with lots of structure, if not strength. The other was nearly $150, still inexpensive to some bag ladies, but clearly over the top for my friend. It was a black buttery-leather hobo with contrast stitching and very current styling. I knew which bag I would have chosen for myself, but that was completely beside the point. I had to walk her through her own process.

"Which one do you really, really like?" I asked.

"I don't know." She answered. That, to me, was a perfectly appropriate response.

Mind you, this friend did not at the time know her *elements of style*. She was at a disadvantage in even the fundamental decisions.

So I could only lay out the bag facts for her. "The black one will last longer, but it will go out of style pretty quickly. The brown one will always stay in style, but may not last for more than a few seasons. Frankly, those bags aren't the only options in the world. Do you have a little more time to shop?"

Great necessities call out great virtues.

ABIGAIL ADAMS

Some serious groundwork needed to be laid. It was just too big an issue to tackle in a parking lot!

Admittedly, other women may be baffled by this seasonal ritual and wonder why we spend the time doing it. In an online survey I conducted on handbags a few years back, one gal said that her favorite bag "must be deep and sewn into the sides of skirts or pants." She's probably just laughing at all the rest of us.

accessorize your life

When thinking of a *complete* wardrobe, picture your accessories as one-third of it if you have a classic, romantic, or expressive fashion personality. If you are a relaxed, accessories constitute less than that. Accessories are a major part of your personal style, and, for some seasons and fashion personalities, they can make up 75 percent of your style budget. Accessories are:

- shoes and boots
- socks and hosiery
- handbags
- jewelry
- sunglasses
- eyeglasses
- briefcase
- wallet

- portfolio
- cosmetics bag
- belts
- gloves
- hats
- scarves

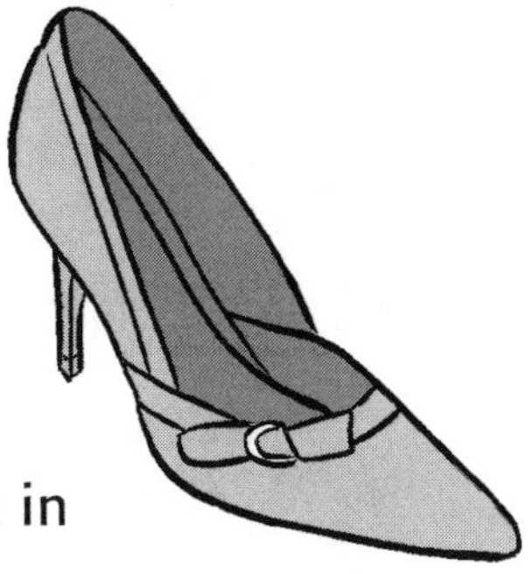

OBJECTIVE: plan how accessories work in your wardrobes.

It's easy to see how they can form a significant part of the budget as many of these items are relatively higher in price. Each requires heavier materials and more specialized construction. Use accessories effectively by:

- choosing according to your *elements of style*: body type, fashion personality, and color palette.
- choosing high quality, especially shoes and handbags.
- being creative.

I discussed accessories extensively for each fashion personality, but I would like to add that shopping for them should be approached with resourcefulness. Jewelry can be found at wonderful alternative places such as antique or second-hand shops, while handbags and shoes are best found at specialty shops or department stores. Of course, you never really know when you'll trip over your "it" bag for the season.

Make your accessory choice an art form and see how many clever things will come your way!

sole searching

I'm sure you've heard someone say, "I'm a shoe person." Usually it's confirmed by looking down at her feet. Her wonderfully attired tootsies inspire you to imagine all the other treats at the bottom of her closet. It's an art form, a kind of self expression.

I rarely attempt to temper the shoe choices of these folks. They usually have that part right. Their – shall we say – *issue* is that a good percentage of their shoe purchases end up stored away in the original boxes for years and years, sitting there lonely and dejected.

What a waste of money. Smart shoe choice prevents that and helps the rest of us polish our wardrobes. In fact, good shoe coordination (color and style) is so important for overall personal style that a badly chosen pair of shoes can ruin the look of the best ensemble.

In the interest of preventing mistakes with your shoes, I'll let you in on a few definitions.

anatomy of a shoe

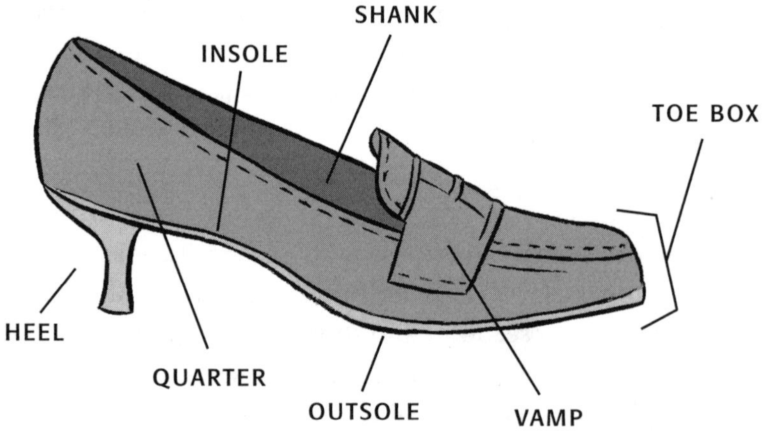

True, every woman needs a good pair of pumps. It's difficult (but not impossible) to buy a pair of pumps that will stay in style for the next twenty years. Pumps and other shoe styles have variables which change with the fashion seasons. Two of the most basic variables are *heel* styles and the shape of the *toe box.*

variations in heel

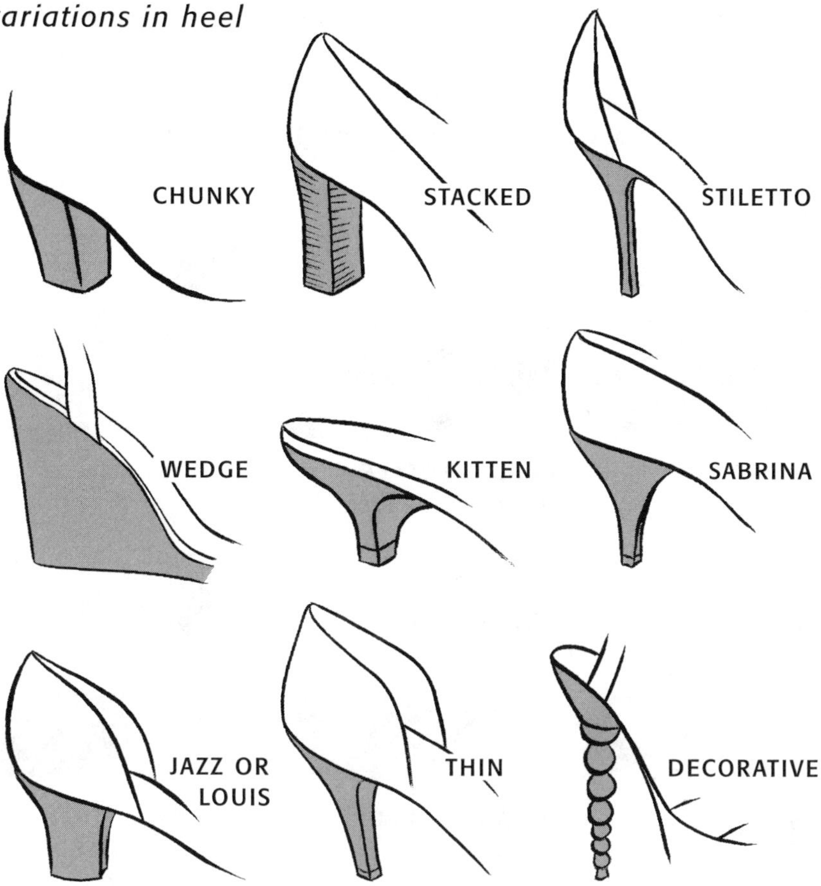

variations in toe box

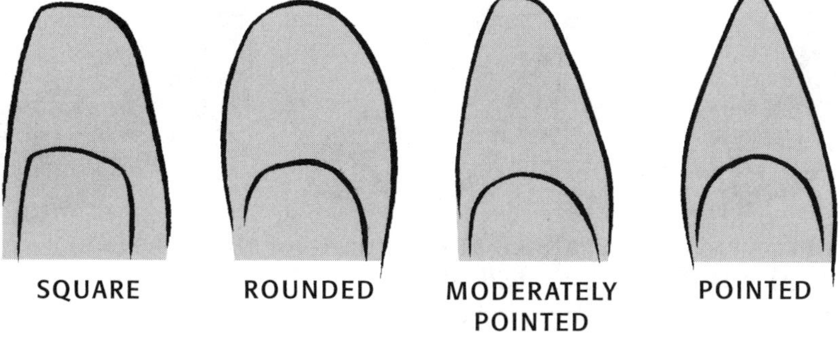

Before shopping for a pair of shoes, you need to not only determine what the current trends in shoe styles are, but also which is the most flattering for your feet and legs. (Remember p 92?) Then, plan the shoes into your wardrobe using the following guidelines:

Shoe Types

FLAT PUMP
best with trousers or shorter skirts

CASUAL LOAFER
best with trousers

DRESSY LOAFER
best with dress trousers

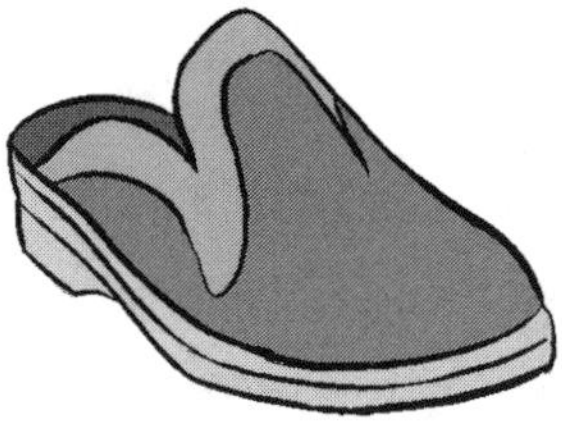

CLOGS
best with trousers

MEDIUM PUMP
best with trousers and skirts

D'ORSEY PUMP
best with skirts and dresses

HIGH HEEL (STILETTO) PUMP
best with skirts and dresses

ANKLE STRAP PUMP
best with skirts and dresses

BALLET FLAT
best with trousers or shorter skirts or softer, fluid dresses

FLAT MULES
best with trousers

MEDIUM MULES
best with trousers

HIGH MULES
best with trousers and skirts

ESPADRILLES
best with trousers and skirts

HIGH WEDGE
best with trousers and skirts

FLAT SANDALS
best with shorts and trousers

FLAT THONGS
best with shorts, trousers, and casual skirts or dresses

MEDIUM SLIDES
best with trousers, skirts, dresses

HIGH SLIDES
best with skirts and dresses

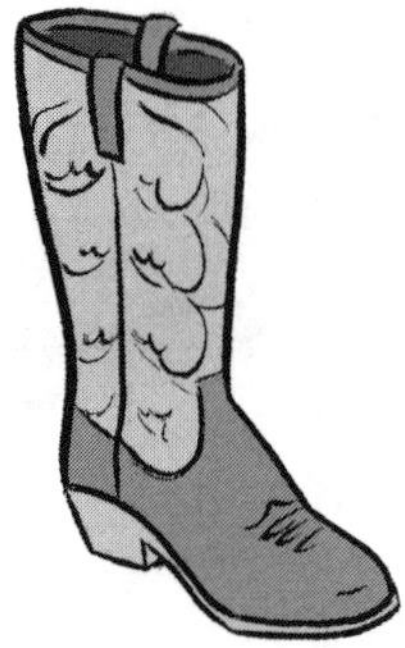

WESTERN BOOTS
best with trousers and long skirts

MEDIUM ANKLE BOOTS OR "BOOTIES"
best with trousers

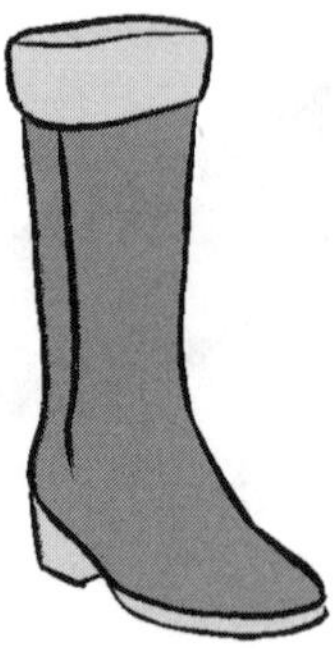

MID-CALF BOOTS
best with trousers and long skirts

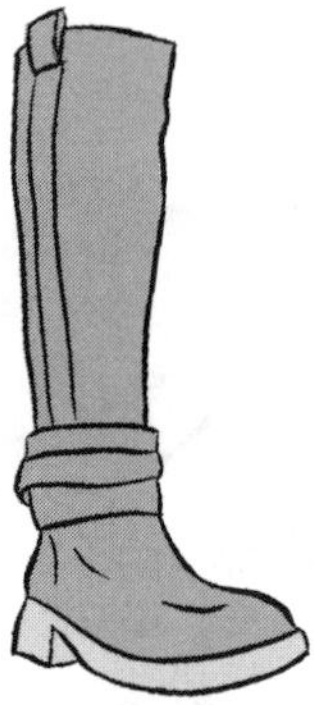

EQUESTRIAN BOOTS
best with trousers and long skirts

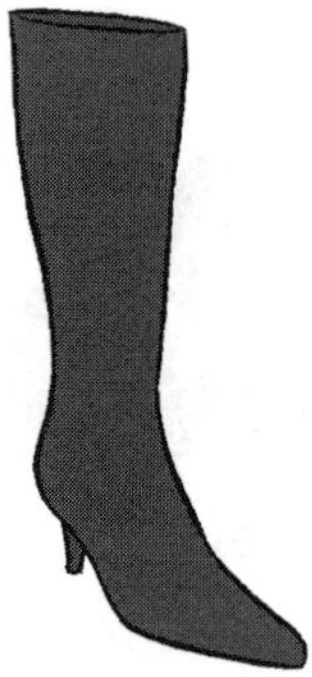

FORM-FITTING FASHION BOOTS
best with trousers and skirts

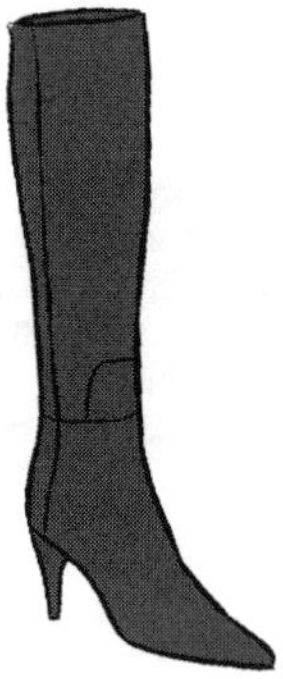

STILLETTO OR "FASHION" BOOTS
best with trousers and skirts

FLAT ANKLE BOOTS OR "BOOTIES"
best with trousers

ATHLETIC SHOES OR "TENNIS" OR "RUNNING" SHOES
best with athletic outfits

CANVAS ATHLETIC SHOES
best with athletic outfits, cropped trousers, and shorts

think on your feet

- You must be happy in your shoes. So choose shoes that are both comfortable and stylish. If you have never been able to marry these two qualities, change retailers. There is a whole new breed of manufacturers who specialize in just this.
- If you are trying to stick to a rather strict budget, go for total color harmony with your shoes (all black shoes or all brown shoes, etc.) Choose according to your color season.
- It's fun to have a shoe color that breaks the mold. A hot pink pair of sandals will work well if your wardrobe has hot pink somewhere in its color story. A red pair of pumps is great if you can match it to the red in several skirts and dresses.
- Always be sure to match up the navy of your shoes with the navy of your outfit. The other option is to go for a darker navy in your shoes.
- As a general rule, keep shoe color choice for a particular ensemble as dark or darker than the hem of your trouser, dress, or skirt. In the summer, a pair of sandals that matches your natural skin tone looks good as a neutral under any bottom. Very white legs are not flattered by black sandals or shoes even if the skirt or shorts are black.
- Keep shoes in good repair. Occasionally complete a heel-and-sole check while putting shoes on. I find that my shoes become worn without my noticing it.
- Choose heel height according to three things: the garment with which you are wearing the shoes, the condition of your legs, and your fashion personality. Wear at least an inch of heel with any skirt or dress or if you have thick calves.
- Avoid chunky heels if you have thick calves or ankles.
- If you wear boots with a skirt, go for at least an inch high heel.

- Choose a form-fitting ("clingy") boot with a higher heel if you are wearing it with a shorter skirt.
- Keep a separate pair of stylish boots for severe weather. (Never give up on style even in a blizzard!) Fashion boots are meant for the dry indoors.

how to buy a pair of shoes

- Decide which wardrobes will incorporate the shoes. For total color harmony, choose a neutral or dominant color from your wardrobe color story (cool – black, navy; warm – brown, cream, tan) and choose shoe style and heel height according to what you have learned above.
- Begin shopping by trying your most trusted brands of shoes.
- If at all possible, shop toward the end of the day, when your feet are at their largest.
- Try on the shoes you are considering in the kind of hosiery you would normally wear with them.
- Walk around the store in the shoes you are considering.
- If possible, walk up a few stairs or simulate this with a stool to check for comfort and fit. Ensure that the vamp does not cut into your foot as you step up.
- Never buy a pair of shoes that need to be "broken into" or a pair that wrinkles when you flex your feet.
- Leave about a one-half-inch space between your longest toe and the inside tip of the toe box. (Being measured by a professional ensures the best fit.) Check for heel comfort as well. You shouldn't feel a strong pinch within the quarter part of the shoe.
- Examine each shoe by holding up the heels side by side to make sure they are the same height and that the backs are of the same size.

- Feel around the insole for bumps (nail heads) that give away the fact that the wrong size nails have been used in construction. It's a sign of a cheap and potentially uncomfortable shoe.
- Evaluate the "slip factor" and decide what could be done to prevent slipping while wearing the shoes. (Usually scuffing the soles or adding skid pads work well.)
- Check that stitching is straight and tight.
- Consider the maintenance factor for the shoe. If you know that you'll be wearing the shoe in the winter or during the rainy season outdoors, choose something that is durable and easy to wipe off.
- Know what you are buying: leather? plastic? microfiber? Learn how it is best cleaned.
- When you finally walk out of the store, make sure that you have the right and left shoes of the size upon which you decided.

Numquam poetor nisi podager. (I only spout poetry when my feet hurt.)

ENNIUS

hosiery

- Choose nude or taupe hosiery for summer. Never wear white hosiery unless you are a nurse.
- Choose sheer black hosiery for a cold weather business or evening ensemble. Choose opaque black, blue, or brown hosiery for winter ensembles that are either black, blue, or brown.
- Completely avoid prints in your hosiery.
- Fishnet hosiery is only appropriate for evening wear. Don't wear it with a very embellished or lacy dress. It's overkill.
- Be sure your nails are trimmed, your hands are moisturized, and your rings are turned in when putting on hosiery. I know, that's a lot of work. But it's worth the extra effort.
- Keep hosiery in separate, plastic baggies. Knot hosiery with runs so you know only to use them under trousers.

- Wash hosiery using the hand-wash cycle of your washer and hang dry.
- Stock up on the good stuff when it goes on sale.

the joy of bagging it

Have you ever seen a woman reach into her back pocket and take out a man's wallet to pay for her groceries? It's a rarity, isn't it? We just all know that women have the better deal than men. Every now and then the fashion world tries to bring out a "carry all" or a "work bag" for the fellows, but it never quite takes. Poor things: they are really missing out. The irony is that in the history of mankind, the guys had the bag first.

Although some women may view the handbag like a burdensome anchor, it's the one accessory that embodies our freedom to move about in ways we had never been able before. Up until the latter part of the nineteenth century, women simply stuffed things into the deep pockets of their skirts, or, very early on, they carried "almoners" for alms giving or sported reticules or "work bags" for knitting. There wasn't much more than this for hundreds of years. After all, where were they going? Train travel revolutionized the way women carried things (in addition to expanding their mobility), and guys like Louis Vuitton promoted the corresponding bags amongst the highest levels of couture.

The handbag expanded and contracted throughout the last century, serving a bit like a decorative object held away from the body for a long while, then as a functional body part later on. The absolutely wonderful thing about all of this is that even now we can choose from just about anything in the history of the handbag and still look put together. Here are a few of the prototypical styles (there are literally thousands of variations of each).

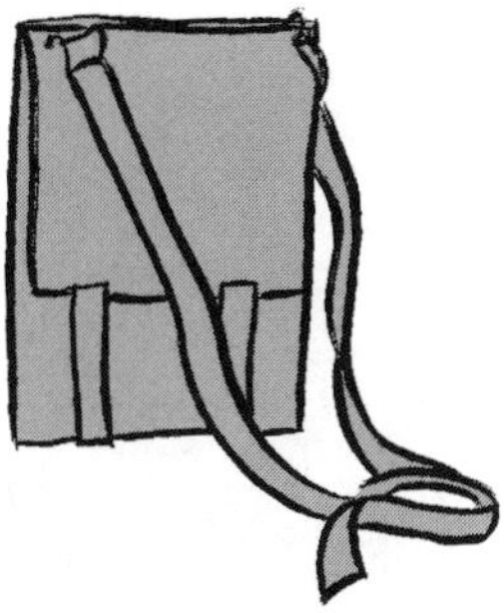

MESSENGER

"BASKET" OR SHOPPER

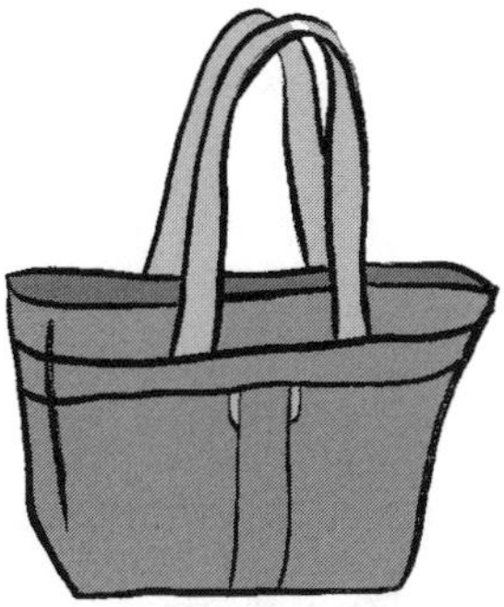

TOTE

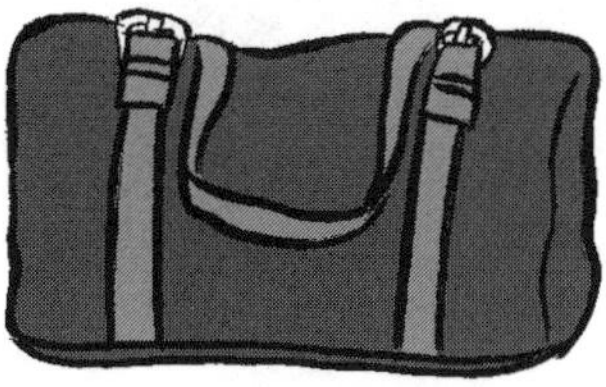

SATCHEL

HOBO

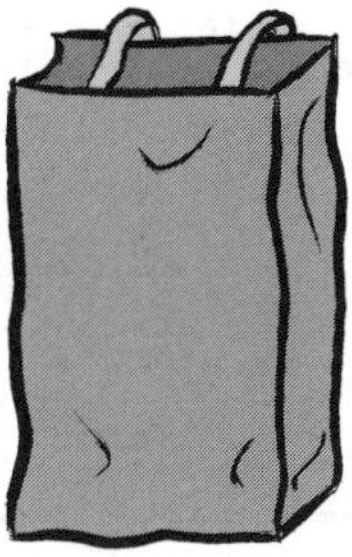

LUNCH SACK

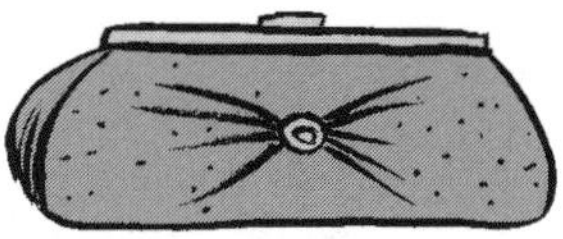

CLUTCH

WRISTLET

Often, designer names or the bag names they dubbed have become styles in and of themselves. Some of these were actually remakes of old favorites and all of them are legendary:

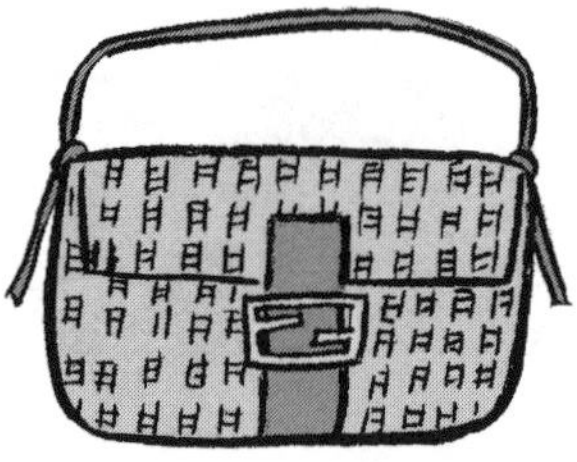

FENDI "BAGUETTE"

HERMES "KELLY"

HERMES "BOLIDE"

CHRISTIAN DIOR "LADY DIOR"

CHANEL "2/1955"

VUITTON "NOE"

bag angst (say *that* three times quickly)

Handbag choice should be related to three things:

1. your *elements of style* (Of course! What were you expecting me to say?)
2. occasions and seasons
3. functionality and lifestyle

your elements of style

- Here's a quick test to see if a handbag is good for your silhouette: Stand in front of a full- length mirror with the handbag directly in front of your torso. If the bag is wider and taller than your abdomen, it's too overwhelming for your figure. Of course, the "Kelly" bag (as in Grace Kelly) is an elegant, rectangular bag (see above) that the princess wore in the early part of a pregnancy she wasn't ready to announce. She was on to something. Use a larger bag if you are pregnant so that your belly looks balanced with your purse. If you wear a plus size for garments, avoid choosing an exceptionally small one.
- Buy your purse with the color story of your wardrobe in mind (including the metal used for the hardware). Your handbag can be the "wildcard" in your wardrobe, but ensure that it doesn't actually clash with your clothes.
- Consider styles that go with your fashion personality. Consider color, shape, theme, hardware, and the materials used for construction.
- Avoid overdoing a theme in your accessories. If your shoes are faux alligator in a cherry red color, it's best to choose a bag with a different kind of look.

occasions and seasons

- Most women need a bag for every day use and a separate bag for evening occasions.
- Evening bags are always small and may or may not be embellished. They must, however, be constructed from a more elegant material. Clutches, wristlets, drawstring almoners, and smaller lunch box styles work best.
- Darker neutrals are excellent for any time of year, but a bulky black or dark brown one will probably drab a cute summer outfit. An alternative summer bag is a good solution.

- Use fabric or straw for summer time only. Some of the synthetic straws are best because they are waterproof. I only recently discovered the beauty of these babies, and it has saved me from a lot of anxiety at the beach.

functionality and lifestyle

- Begin by studying your "purse behavior." Do you tend to overstuff? Do you tend to place a whole makeup bag in there or only a tube of lipstick? Do you carry around a novel? What's the general flow of hand from bag to wallet while paying with a credit card or writing a check? Do you scramble for change? Do you drop pennies all the time? Do you use a bulky calendar book or an electronic device? Watch yourself and hypothesize how some features may make your life easier.
- Consider which items you can live without. Where exactly are you going? Do you have a lot of wait time (great time for a novel or a stash of papers to grade)? Good rule: go for the smallest bag possible. Carry only what you need.
- Dream up a bag around your needs and behavior.
- If you need to pay for things in one movement because you are always holding a baby or watching a toddler linger in the aisle, try the built-in side wallet.
- Decide if a long strap or two shorter straps are best. (Straps should be reasonable for the size of the purse.) Avoid a strap that swings your purse right at the level of your buttocks.
- Avoid white or beige cloth at all costs unless you are a neat freak. (This is definitely a lifestyle issue!) Avoid suede if you can't clean it regularly.
- Get rid of your diaper bag. If you have an infant who needs a lot of baby stuff, keep a stylish bag for baby or hide the diaper bag in the car. Many friends of mine place a changing

station in their car because, let's face it, few moms change diapers in the grocery store.

- Decide how much of your fashion budget should go for your new handbag. If this is the year to find a new everyday bag that will last for years, you might have to lay out a good chunk of change. On the other hand, if you tend to grow tired of a bag pretty quickly, keep it under $100. This is especially the case if you keep several purses for a single wardrobe.
- Make finding a bag a science. Search around before you buy, but don't give into thinking that your dream bag is always "just around the corner." You could be looking forever with standards like that.

in-store checklist

Okay, so you are in a store and pondering a bag. After you have considered all of the above, check the following.

- Imagine how any purse goes with your coat. Try it out to see if it fits over the sleeve. Test it out to see if it stays on your shoulder.
- Check for the strength of the strap, especially if you tend to overstuff or continually hang it from hooks or chairs.
- Check the inside of the purse. Is the lining durable and attached to the outer material? Or, will holes poke through with one wrong move of a pen or finger?
- Check that the base of the purse suits the way you generally treat it. Can it sit up on a sink counter? Will it stand next to your chair?
- Avoid too many compartments if your purse behavior proves to ignore them and forget what's where.

- Ensure that the handbag closes securely so that you don't lose your mints or tampons on the escalator (or have them stolen!). Open-shut and open-shut and open-shut it just to check.

I am not exaggerating when I say that the purse alone can do an infinite amount of good for your overall personal style (not to mention ease of day to day living).

Recently, I met a mom at my daughter's preschool who seemed to have such great style. I couldn't put my finger on why exactly this was the case because her hair was so conservative and her coat was so plain. (I can't even remember her shoes.)

One day we got to talking about the spring styles that year, and she just shook her head and said, "Hey, I'm a girl who is all about accessories!" That's when it hit me: she carried different bags for her "different moods" and managed to add interest to dreary winter days. Her bag was like a ribbon on a gift with otherwise plain wrapping paper. What a treat!

briefcase, wallet, phone case, belts, etc

- Never carry both a handbag and a briefcase. Use one or the other. (Place your purse in your briefcase if possible)
- Opt for a feminine-styled briefcase rather than one designed for men. Also, invest in leather rather than canvas or plastic.
- Go for total color harmony for all these items.
- Check that your wallet is in good shape and speaks well of your personal style. This item often wears out the quickest because it tends to get stuffed. Designate times to clean out all those receipts and coupons and buy a firm leather style instead of a soft lumpy one.
- Remember that a belt creates a focal point around a waist. Never include it in an ensemble if you have a protruding

tummy. If you must use it to hold up your trousers, wear it under something.

- Replace a belt if its holes are misshapen from use. The exception to this is if you keep the belt hidden under garments.
- Belts that are sold with trousers are often cheap. Resist using them if they figure prominently in your look.
- Dark, neutral colors are best for a belt, unless, of course, it is a novelty piece.

give the lady what she wants

Each one of us wants to use scarves, jewelry, and all the little extras in the most flattering ways possible. Often, we will refuse things because we can't figure out how they work. Below are some guidelines.

all that sparkle: jewelry, sunglasses, eyeglasses

While many women either choose not to wear these items, or have the good fortune of perfect sight, jewelry, sunglasses and eyeglasses are often the most prominent of your accessories. When the choice is perfect, it adds a sparkle.

- Remember your color palette when purchasing jewelry, wrist watches, sunglasses, and eyeglasses. This will make coordination very easy as well. (Gold tone – warm and light warm, silver tone – cool and light cool).
- Stones in your jewelry that will be worn around your face should also be chosen with your color palette in mind. A good universal color for stones is aqua or bright blue. (Good tip for gift-giving.)
- If you have to worry about the cost of jewelry (and who doesn't?) purchase costume jewelry instead of precious stones and metals. You'll get a bigger piece that does more for your

ensembles, and you'll be able to buy other coordinated pieces. Also, the technology involved with producing colored stones renders truly genuine appearances. No one will know any better, and very few would care anyway.

- Choose jewelry for any ensemble by coordinating with embellishments on the garments. The more embellishment on a top or dress, the less jewelry you should wear.
- For evening wear, create a secondary focal point with your jewelry. Try just earrings, or earrings and a bracelet. If the earrings are subtle, add a necklace. Never clutter up with jewelry (earrings, bracelet, necklace, rings, *and* pin).
- Jewelry should be purchased with fashion personality in mind. Go with your gut. Spell out exactly what you want if you know you are getting a gift, especially from hubby. (No, you are not being selfish and demanding. You are being frugal and prudent. You can tell him that.)
- Check flea markets and antique shops for interesting pieces of jewelry. Both my sisters found their wedding rings in antique shops, and the praises still haven't stopped.
- Store jewelry so that pieces are easily seen and stay separated. Use one of those clear plastic hardware sorters (the kind with the little drawers) and place it so that light comes through the back. Or try a clear plastic children's shoe bag that hangs over a door. Novelty catalogues offer some very practical solutions.
- Clean your jewelry on a regular basis. (A soft toothbrush and a little toothpaste can work.) Dirty jewelry may just look lackluster to you, but dirty to others. That's a waste of your investment.
- Schedule regular cleanings for important pieces like wedding or engagement rings.

how to choose jewelry for your face shape

Aside from the guidelines that spell out how jewelry goes with your *elements of style,* particularly fashion personality and color palette, there are also guidelines that have to do with establishing symmetry and proportion. They work in a similar way to creating an optical illusion of proportion in your figure. Remember, the goal is to always have the focal point on your eyes.

EARRINGS should work with your face shape. They should simply frame the face without distraction.

1. If your face is long, or if you have any sagging from the advance of wisdom, you should avoid dangly or long earrings. The shape of the earrings should pull the eye up.

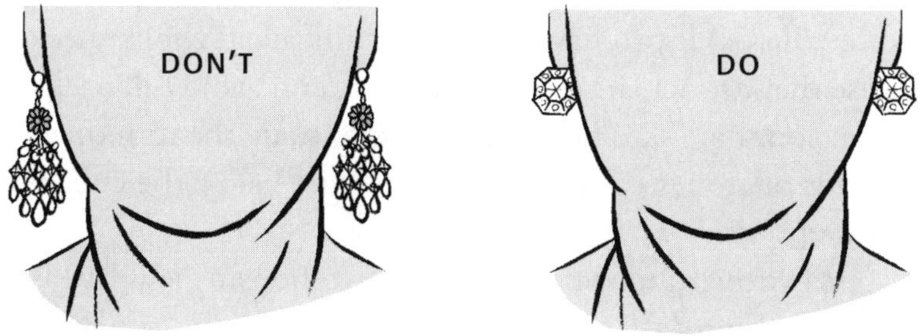

2. If your face is especially round, avoid repeating the roundness with circular earrings or overly large hoops. Longer earrings (but not excessively long), earrings in square shapes, and studs are excellent options.

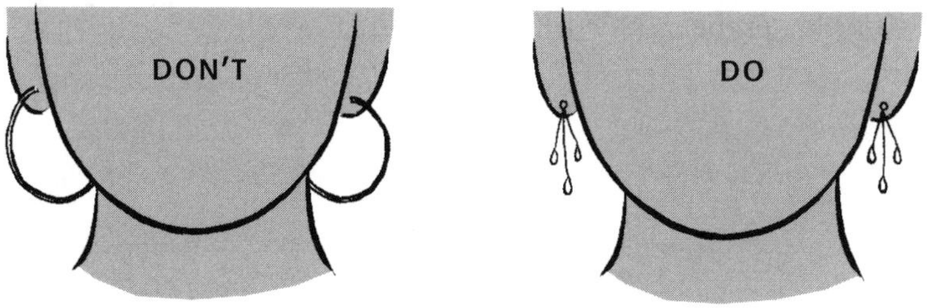

3. Finally, if your face is very short and boxy, do not repeat the shape with a pair of square-shaped earrings. Go for balance with something longer or rounder.

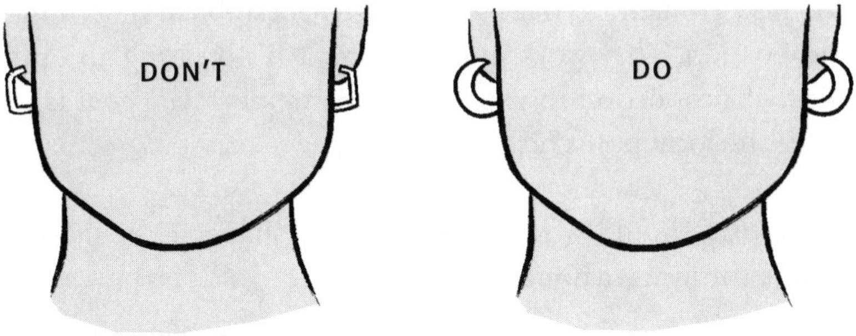

NECKLACES work in a similar fashion. Deciding on the right one involves looking at the length and condition of the neck and chin. (It also involves the styling of the outfit, your fashion personality, and color palette.) If you have a sagging chin, avoid choker necklaces because they attract the eye to your chin, and avoid bib necklaces that lie on your bare skin because they accentuate the roundness. Simple strands of stones or chains which lie just below the collar bone are good options.

As I've mentioned before, the key to choosing jewelry tastefully is an old-fashion dash of temperance. Never clutter up, never overdo it, and always keep in mind age appropriateness. If the neckline of an outfit works beautifully as a piece of art, choose more noticeable earrings and forgo the necklace. When a neckline needs a little something and the garment is not too busy, choose either a necklace or use a fashion scarf as a necklace to add a little zest. The earrings should then be a little bit restrained.

NO NECKLACE NEEDED

NECKLACE AND EARRINGS BALANCE OUT

SCARF AND EARRINGS BALANCE OUT

NECKLACE AND EARRINGS BALANCE OUT AND HARMONIZE WITH THE PIN STRIPES

Jewelry choice is a very personal art form, so after that, it's a matter of finding items you can wear with pride and joy.

SEMINAR FAQ

piercing

QUESTION: What are the rules for piercing, particularly around your face?

ANSWER: The rule is to keep your focal point on your eyes. Once when I was presenting to a group of teens, I caught a glimpse of a student's tongue that had a little hoop on the end. I was so distracted! I thought, "Hey, if I'm so used to this, why can't I concentrate?" That got me thinking about what would happen to this gal if she wanted someone to focus on what she was *saying*. She's blurred her proper focal point.

So, any piercing that distracts the viewer's attention from the eyes is a bad investment. Eyebrows, nostrils, lips, and chins are counterproductive places. True, the hardware can be removed, but some holes never close up properly, sometimes creating a scar.

Earlobes are good enough. One to two pierces per lobe is probably a good maximum limit. After that, you're pretty much mutilating the ear.

Body pierces (and tattoos for that matter) provide hours of adult moaning, but that's really why they're done. They too create a distracting focal point and send all sorts of messages about the victim – I mean *person*. The messages change according to the fashion trends, but they never connote the qualities of responsibility, intelligence, industriousness, taste, or elegance. Even Hollywood understands moderation in this area.

how to choose a pair of glasses

- First, examine how a pair works with your facial shape.
  1. If your face is round, avoid round glasses. Go for something that provides a horizontal line to balance the roundness.
  2. If your face is long, avoid large glasses. Go for something that provides a horizontal line to balance the length or choose "cat's eye" glasses to give a little lift to your face.
  3. Of course, you want to accentuate your eyes because of their importance in communication, so choose rimless glasses or glasses with very subtle rims if possible.
- Second, choose the metal of your glasses according to your color palette.
- Finally, choose glasses according to your fashion personality rather than mimicking a certain look. Continue to work with your facial shape.
- For sunglasses, go for the greatest amount of UV protection and opt for polarized lenses to cut down on glare.

cuddly duds: gloves, hats, scarves

One characteristic of the woman who has a natural ability with style is her knack for choosing those things that many of us take for granted. Accessories such as winter gloves, hats, and scarves are not only essential pieces for coordination, they are a lot of fun to plan out for a long and hard season. Let yourself be included amongst the ranks of those who have a knack. You'll just have to learn a few things:

- Check weather season checklists on page 325 for more information.
- Color *coordinate* (you don't have to match) your gloves, hats and scarves.

- Choose leather gloves for driving.
- Choose a micro fiber glove that is waterproof for snow play (like shoveling, scraping ice, and other fun stuff).
- Try on a hat before you buy it to see if it suits your face shape and fashion personality.
- Try a slightly loose fitting hat in a fabric that has less problems with static to avoid hat-hair.
- Avoid men's hats.
- Choose an absolutely beautiful scarf that will cheer you up in the depths of winter. Choose from your color palette, of course.

how to choose a fashion scarf

- Choose silk over polyester if feasible. It tends not to wrinkle as much when knotting and bunching and always looks sharp.
- Choose scarf size and shape according to how you most often style a scarf. Longer, oblongs are good for long styles, bows, and ascots. Small squares are best for choker styles. Large squares are excellent for over the shoulder looks.

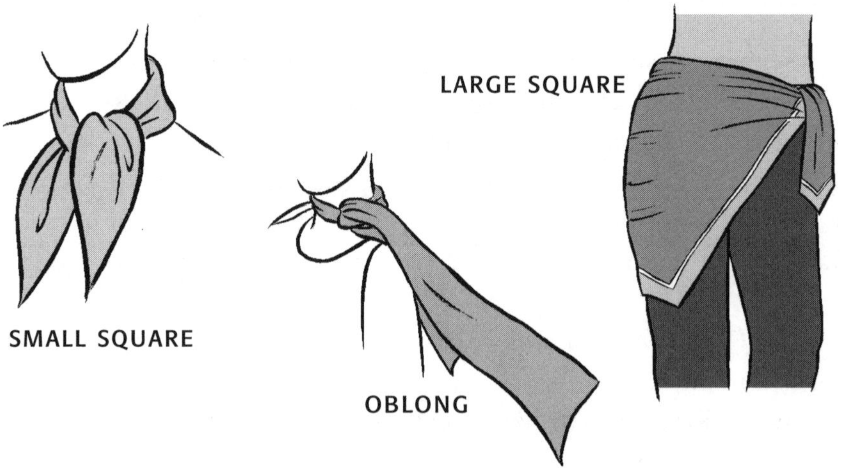

- Double the use of an oblong scarf by tying it around a summer hat or onto the handle of a handbag.

- Choose scarf color and pattern according to three things:
    1. How complementary a pattern it is for your wardrobe(s); if you have a *mix and match* wardrobe, you should be able to wear it with everything
    2. How much of a complementary color in your color story it has in its pattern
    3. How well it works with your fashion personality
- Once you buy your scarf, cut off the tag and store it away for reference. Be sure to store your scarves in a cool and dry place on hangers or folded in a drawer.

we should have kept that one in the family

Many women idealize a legendary accessory from family folklore. Usually it's a diamond ring, a string of pearls, or something else expensive and precious. It may just be the way we subconsciously root ourselves in royalty. (Hey, there's a little princess in all of us!) Why not? There's really no way to prove otherwise. And, if we all assume we are of royal blood, maybe we would more readily behave with nobility!

Sometimes, the accessory is a bit more esoteric: Aunt Sadie had a hot pink alligator bag from France, or Grandma smoked with a diamond studded cigarette holder. I specifically remember my Grandma's charm bracelet. It would jingle and chime as she raucously hit the back of Grandpa's bald head. (It was an expression of love.) But a kvetch begs the question: What would we *really* do with it if we had it now?

Well, it might stay in the closet. As with all items in fashion, trends never repeat themselves in exactly the same way. Accessories at least have a fighting chance. I really believe that this is a wonderful area for self-expression, and we should each set our own trends. Here are some tips.

- If you own a valuable heirloom (necklace, bracelet, set of earrings, or watch) which you think is really beautiful, wear it only if it flatters and when it is appropriate. You can enjoy the fact that you are putting to good use an item from your family history. (That item should never put *you* to good use.)
- If you own a lot of heirloom pieces, don't wear them all at once. Stick with *one* or *two* favorites, one ensemble at a time, and follow all the guidelines for combining jewelry as you would for newer pieces.
- The chances are pretty strong that the heirloom piece you have inherited doesn't fit with one of your *elements of style*. That's okay. If it's a small to medium-sized piece of jewelry or a tasteful handbag, it won't undo your look. Just keep in mind that if the piece is unharmonious to the rest of your ensemble, it can work counterproductively. I've come across some heirloom accessories that didn't look valuable and weren't very flattering. That is definitely counterproductive.
- Maybe you own absolutely nothing valuable from your family history. Create a tradition! Invest in an interesting piece that you plan to pass down to someone in the next generation. As always, choose with your *elements of style* in mind, but also go for what you think is nothing less than *breathtaking*.

Buying a vintage piece is a nice way to differentiate your look from the look of the every day boutique, but you must begin by deciding how much of an investment you can make. Fortunately, costume jewelry has always been around, and it shows up in abundance at everything from flea markets to high-end consignment shops.

and she lived happily ever after

You may have been waiting for this chapter to end so that you can get back to your wardrobe planner. (You may be either a shoe person or a bag lady!) You're excited! You're ready to add your personal touches to the basics you've already established. It's time to visit the *Style Profile* below.

STYLE PROFILE #13

icing on the cake

Return to your *wardrobe planner* on page 212. Then, plan the necessary accessories. It's okay to stay a little vague about the exact styling of the accessory, but you do want to think in terms of how it will coordinate with items upon which you have decided.

Also, a little check on your current inventory and a little fashion forecasting will do wonders for this step.

CHAPTER EIGHT

smart style
how to get what you need

born to love, not to shop

Watch a woman walk into the produce section of a grocery store, ignore the masses of fruits and vegetables bursting from the bins, bee-line straight to only what she wants, and leave with a confident, self-satisfied expression.

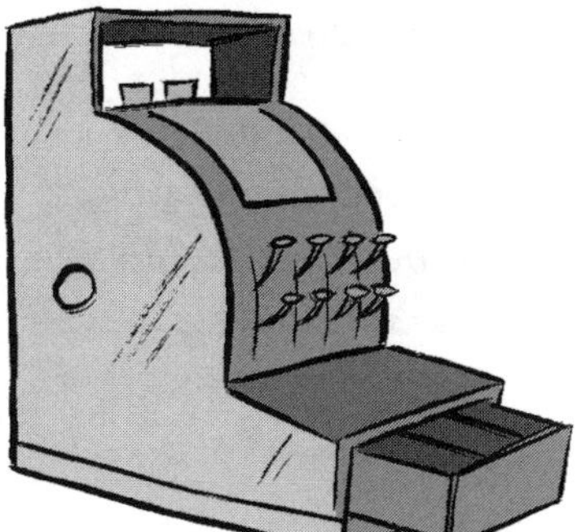

Watch the same woman head into a clothing store. Note the searching eyes, exasperated sighs, and shrug of shoulders.

Why the difference?

The difference is that you don't have to know much about yourself to buy a banana. You want it. You need it. You buy it. You eat it. You don't have to worry about the banana making you look fat, coming in your best color, communicating what you want, or being washable. Even guacamole is easier to buy than a plain white t-shirt.

Fashion is a $180 billion retail market nationwide, and women account for 80 percent of all purchases in this market.[1] You don't see the searching eyes, exasperated sighs, and shrug of shoulders because clothing stores are less inviting than grocery stores. It's just that despite so much apparent enthusiasm for clothes, women report dissatisfaction with their personal fashion, often admitting that much of what they choose for clothing is based only upon emotional or subjective reasons and impulsive responses to marketing.

A great number of us are absolutely confused and discouraged by the mere prospect of putting together a wardrobe. (But not if you're reading this book.) I've seen a stockbroker fall to pieces over a decision to buy a few suits, and I've watched a highly confident woman doubt her ability to make an intelligent decision while in the dressing room. What has happened to women as consumers of fashion? Why the agony?

The answer lies partly in the industry of fashion.

As seemingly fun-loving as fashion is and as much as we are all supposed to pretend that style is second nature to our sex, there are few unambiguous rules in fashion (or at least rules people can recall), and there's a nearly unmanageable assortment of ideas, services, and products barking for attention. It's chaotic.

Take care to get what you like or you will be forced to like what you get.

GEORGE BERNARD SHAW

Call it the beauty of the Information Age or capitalism run amok, this extreme number of variables confuses most women. Where do we even begin? Catalogues or department stores? Boutiques or the Internet? Is it wise to spend $450 on a suit at Nordstrom or only $125 at J.C. Penny? Or should I take out a loan for that $3,000 Armani suit? Is a wardrobe of knit separates the answer to dry-clean management? Is this cotton turtleneck in black more versatile than the one in navy? What's this new fabric and how is it different from *that* new fabric? And when are pants not appropriate?

This doesn't mean that having a greater choice in fashion is the corporate equivalent to crimes against humanity. (Although, just to confuse the issue, there are people out there who say that it is!) It's just that the average human being can take only so much. We simply don't have the stamina to sort through the choices.

The whole decision-making process is compounded by another good thing: women's greater economic power. Women today not only have a greater amount of money, but a greater amount of disposable income. We are the shoppers that retailers have in mind when they arrange their stores and stock their supplies. The times have definitely changed.[2]

looking for love in all the wrong places

And then there's the psychology of shopping. Not only does the mere act of shopping seem to work like therapy or chocolate, some brand names are emotionally charged with qualities that many women attempt to find in their soulmate. This "emotional branding" is not an accident. Manufacturers want to ensure more than a sale. They want a relationship with you.[3] They want you to believe that their brand of cotton swab is softer (even if it isn't), or that their cola is hipper (even if cola is never inherently hip), or that their T-shirt will turn heads (even if it doesn't). You will remain loyal to their label if you believe these things.

> ***But what, as marketing genius Sigmund Freud was moved to ask, do women want from shopping?***
>
> PACO UNDERHILL

Very clever advertising woos you into this relationship, and I can only shake my head at how frequently I'm bombarded. I often can't distinguish between advertising and entertainment. Sometimes I can't distinguish between advertising and news. One day, Heaven help us, we may not be able to distinguish between advertising and reality! To help you comprehend the vast universe of marketing, think of yourself as having two types of encounters with advertising: the inopportune and the opportune.

The inopportune encounter happens when you are not shopping. Perhaps you are just driving along and suddenly find yourself staring at a Gap ad on the side of a bus. It's inopportune because you aren't shopping at the moment. On the other hand – and this is how advertising can be so powerful – you are hooked. The image is so appealing that you subconsciously (or not so subconsciously) resolve to get a piece of the action. You want your jeans to hang just so, and your blouse to curve just so, and the guys to hover just so. Buying the product is the only way those things will ever happen.

For me, the most provocative advertisements had to do with getting "a great deal." I might not have been aiming for the spunky coed look, but becoming convinced that I will be on the road to economic prudence (i.e. take advantage of the 50 percent off everything sale) was one way any store would get me through its doors.

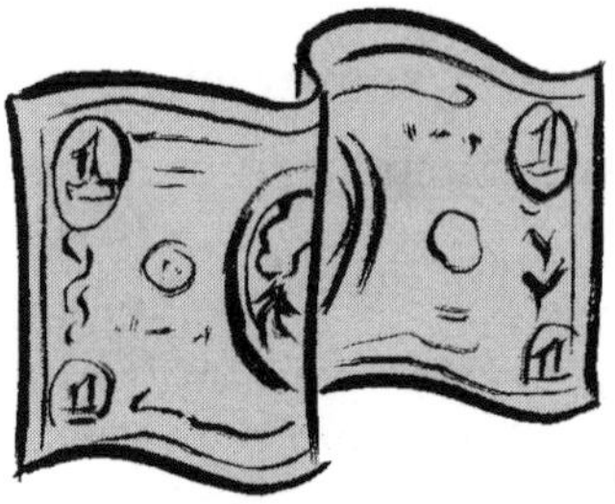

The opportune encounter happens when you are actually shopping and has the immediate potential of opening your wallet. You walk into a store and you are greeted by oversized posters of super-models sporting the wares like cats in heat. Then, there's that moaning, throbbing music charging the air. You are supposed to look cool and detached. And even if the music does sound like sex, you are not supposed to admit it or give away your suspicions with a startled facial expression. Instead, inside you, there's a storm: *Wow! THIS is what I buy when I buy here! Let me at it!* All thought as to what you need to communicate with your style goes right out the window display. (Remember what I discussed in chapter one?)

There's a reason why cosmetic counters greet you right in the front of a department store. All those giant-sized, airbrushed photos of unbelievably beautiful women are there to remind you that you need to improve yourself – a lot. Try to go past them without looking. If the sights don't get you, those wafts of olfactory nirvana may do it.

All of this happens on the gut level. Within seconds, minutes, hours, or days (for some) the old intellect kicks in to remind you that the promotion promises more than any garment or cosmetic can deliver. Unfortunately, for many, the intellect doesn't kick in until the garment (eventually a little bit aged and boring by then) *proves* that it can't deliver these things. Well, that's *why* advertising works this way.

But, even amidst the heavy breathing and heart pounding and impossible temptation, you do have the freedom to choose. You can:

1. Buy it.
2. Not buy it.

That's what it all comes down to. You can have all the feelings in the world, but it's how you act upon these feelings that really matters.

So how impulsive are you in a shopping moment? Return to *Style Profile #2* in chapter one (the one where you pulled three garments out of your closet) and determine if impulsive responses to advertising is a problem for you.

Knee-jerk buying can ultimately leave you miserable. Not only do you place yourself and your family at financial risk or even ruin by spending what you don't have, you can spoil relationships with the people you love. Unfortunately, it's common to find marriages in danger because shopping becomes the equivalent to an addiction for a spouse. If excessive shopping is a problem for you, you might already know that this is no help in finding your style and successfully applying it. You know that it is an absolute impediment. You must face the problem head-on and take action to change your behavior.

So how are you in the wild world of retail?

STYLE PROFILE #14

find your shopping style

What kind of shopper are you?

Answer 1 (never), 2 (seldom), 3 (occasionally), 4 (often), or 5 (always). Then, take this test again, after the next fashion season, to see if your score goes up.

1. Before I take a shopping trip I decide what items I need and where I am most likely to get them.
   1 (never) 2 (seldom) 3 (occasionally)
   4 (often) 5 (always)

2. I plan specific, optimal times to shop.
   1 (never) 2 (seldom) 3 (occasionally)
   4 (often) 5 (always)

3. My fashion purchases are made within a budget.
   1 (never) 2 (seldom) 3 (occasionally)
   4 (often) 5 (always)

4. When I shop I tend to stick with a plan for the items I am going to buy, and I don't purchase more than I actually need.
   1 (never) 2 (seldom) 3 (occasionally)
   4 (often) 5 (always)

5. When I unexpectedly find myself in a clothing store I totally refrain from making any impulsive purchases.
   1 (never) 2 (seldom) 3 (occasionally)
   4 (often) 5 (always)

6. While shopping, I try on every single garment I am considering for purchase.
   1 (never) 2 (seldom) 3 (occasionally)
   4 (often) 5 (always)

7. While trying on any garment, I check all angles in the mirror and attempt to walk, bend over, and sit.
   1 (never) 2 (seldom) 3 (occasionally)
   4 (often) 5 (always)

8. While shopping, I always check labels for fabric and care on every single garment I decide to purchase.
   1 (never) 2 (seldom) 3 (occasionally)
   4 (often) 5 (always)

9. While shopping, I examine for quality any garment I am considering.
   1 (never) 2 (seldom) 3 (occasionally)
   4 (often) 5 (always)

10. While shopping, I check the garment for any defects.
    1 (never) 2 (seldom) 3 (occasionally)
    4 (often) 5 (always)

11. After every purchase I place the receipt in a designated place in case I need to make returns or exchanges.
    1 (never) 2 (seldom) 3 (occasionally)
    4 (often) 5 (always)

12. If I am unsatisfied with any garment I have purchased, I return or exchange it as soon as I have decided.
    1 (never) 2 (seldom) 3 (occasionally)
    4 (often) 5 (always)

Now, tally up your points. Each answer is worth its number (1 – never = 1 point, etc.). Check below for your shopping style.

If you scored 12 – 24, you are clearly a fashion victim. Take heart, dear friend. There is hope. You just need to focus on your purpose for shopping and tailor your shopping habits to be more effective. Begin by reviewing each statement above and adjust your behavior so that you can score higher numbers on your next round.

If you scored 25 – 50, you may have some good shopping habits but you could tweak your shopping style a little. Reflect more on the way you shop and how effectively your wardrobe works for you. Check over those statements for which you chose the lowest ratings and try to bring those numbers up.

If you scored 51 – 60, Congratulations! You are an intelligent consumer of fashion! Check out any weak spots. Where were your lower scores (if any)? Focus on improving those scores.

I had my fashion spending under control – until I saw some clothes!

Need any help?

shopping therapy: tips for resisting impulse buying

- Continue reading this book.
- Limit the number of catalogues you receive to one or none.
- Never just "hang out" at a mall. If you must be in a mall, stay out of clothing stores unless you have a specific item to purchase.
- Allow places other than the mall or a department store to be the center of your social gatherings or quality time. Choose parks, galleries, museums, libraries, cafes, or gyms to meet with friends or get some down time.
- Don't allow a fashion item to stalk you. Get your mind on other things if you find yourself distracted by that "something."
- Avoid even needed shopping trips when you are moody or depressed.
- Look stunning when you go out for necessary wardrobe shopping so that you don't feel the need to self-improve every time you pass a mirror.
- Place yourself on a clothing budget.
- If you have credit card issues, leave the credit card at home and pay only with cash.

Your money must create peace of mind for you, not extra anxiety.

SUZE ORMAN

But you do have to purchase clothing sometimes! For some, impulse buying is far from the issue. There are some out there who have enough of an anti-shopping neurosis to cancel out the effects of all the full color billboards, clever video clips, and that throbbing, moaning music.

I once worked with a woman who was the antithesis of an impulse buyer. Her problem was that she became absolutely paralyzed when faced with shopping decisions. She chose never to respond to advertising, and she had problems setting aside the time to find even the clothing she desperately needed. It was crippling, and she knew she'd be naked if it wasn't cold or socially unacceptable.

You must do three things to become an intelligent consumer of fashion:

1. Know yourself.
2. Know the market.
3. Know yourself in the market.

Reading this book takes care of the first objective. We covered the third objective (*know yourself in the market*) in the last *Style Profile* (*Know Your Shopping Style*). The second objective, *know the market,* we will cover now. Don't worry, though; knowing the market doesn't mean spending hours in research on manufacturers, distributors, regulations, pricing, marketing, and all the stuff that FIT students study in heady textbooks. It's knowing what's available at any given time, what you can ignore, and what will work for *you.* This chapter concludes with a shopping plan, so it will all come together in the end.

A fashion victim is dressed in designer clothes from top to bottom.

DONNA KARAN

Keep in mind that one of your strengths is that you have shopped all your life. You already know a lot about the market and you can learn from the mistakes you have made in the past.

OBJECTIVE: develop strategies to modify personal fashion selection in the market to become a more effective consumer of fashion.

it's a jungle out there (know the market)

Fashion retail is like one big jungle filled with wild beasts, poisonous plants, quicksand, and pesky little insects. It is also, incidentally, filled with those rare orchids and exotic birds that add interest to your collection – I mean, wardrobe. The trick is to know which little critters can be brought home as pets. Let's step back and be logical for a moment. For starters, there are two basic choices to make once you have your wardrobe plan ready: where to shop, or *venues*, and when to shop, your *times*.

venues

Currently, you can shop for clothing and accessories using regular retail (department stores and boutiques) and alternative or "nontraditional" retail (discount or outlet stores, off-price stores, consignment or vintage shops, thrift stores, catalogues, television, or online).

Below is a handy reference to the types of retailers there are, their advantages and their disadvantages.

REGULAR RETAIL

Specific venues: Department stores, boutiques; usually found in malls or in downtown shopping districts.

Advantages: Well stocked with the latest fashions, generally higher quality, most or all sizes found, pleasant surroundings, on-site assistance.

Disadvantages: Marked-up pricing; upscale stores may be difficult to visit because they are found only in larger metropolitan areas.

Recommendations: Visit well into a fashion season for sales, if you do not need a hard-to-find size. Take your time trying on all items and accept help, but ignore the advice. For really great deals, look for items that are the department store's "private label."

OFF-PRICE

Specific venues: Large stores which advertise "designer names for lower prices."

Advantages: Well stocked with current fashions, lower prices, found in both suburbs and cities.

Disadvantages: Limited range of sizes available, confusing or even disorganized surroundings, no on-site assistance

Recommendations: Visit on a regular basis as these retailers stock constantly. Take your time trying on all items, bringing in as many sizes as possible. Or, bring a friend to be a "runner" to exchange sizes while you are trying on items.

DISCOUNT

Specific venues: Large stores that sell everything from housewares and hardware to cosmetics and stationary all at very low prices, found everywhere. (Many of these also sell light bulbs.)

Advantages: Low prices, large selection, most sizes available.

Disadvantages: Variable quality, variable surroundings, little or no onsite assistance, sometimes bland fashions.

Recommendations: Use for hosiery, undergarments, sleepwear, t-shirts, and jeans.

OUTLET

Specific venues: Clusters of boutique-like stores associated with a brand or designer name often found along interstate highways or tourist destinations.

Advantages: Sometimes lower prices.

Disadvantages: Items are usually leftovers from last season, unreasonable travel involved, limited range of sizes available, unpredictable inventory.

Recommendations: Buy out of season items and combine a visit to a women's fashion outlet with visits to other kinds of outlets to make the drive truly worthwhile.

SECOND-HAND

Specific venues: Consignment, thrift, and vintage
Advantages: Lower prices, access to otherwise out-of-reach high-end items.
Disadvantages: Dependence on the shop owner's ability to select only current and quality garments that are in excellent shape; thrift stores can be disorganized and unpleasant.
Recommendations: Be choosey as to which shops you visit and have a plan (see below).

CATALOGUE/INTERNET/TELEVISION

Advantages: Very convenient (too convenient sometimes), great variety of styles, all sizes available.
Disadvantages: Inability to feel for quality or try on items for fit. It can also be difficult to judge the true color of an item.
Recommendations: Choose only retailers that offer higher-quality items and take pride in their customer satisfaction. The best will pay postage for returns.

Here are some tips:

- Decide on your universe of retailers according to your *elements of style*. If a clothing store continually sells styles and colors that don't work for you, ignore it altogether. What great relief it is to save time in shopping!
- If you haven't visited several different *kinds* of venues, try some new ones. After a while, you will be able to decide your

tolerance level for shopping trips. Regular retail builds in the cost of nice dressing rooms, more staff, and pleasant surroundings, while other venues do away with many of these things. It's okay to decide that you just can't think and choose anywhere else but those places which pamper the customer. On the other hand, many women love the thrill of the hunt, and are willing to put up with chaotic clothing racks, messy dressing rooms, and absolutely no help. True, some alternative venues manage to provide low prices, high quality, and pleasant surroundings, but those same places are probably lacking on some other level (variety of styles and sizes, current looks, convenience, etc.). Know the options and be honest with yourself about what you can tolerate.

- If you choose *not* to buy from regular retail venues, still do not ignore them completely. They are the best places to do some fashion forecasting or to investigate what high quality involves. In fact, you should make it a point to visit designer boutiques from time to time to see how items are (or are not) set apart from the rest of the fashion world.
- To avoid a pre-packaged look, vary where you buy wardrobe items. You might find that one retailer is better for accessories, another for your business wardrobe, and another for your personal casual wardrobe.
- Relax. There are few true bargain stores anymore. Outlets offer discount prices some of the time, but there's usually a drive involved (which means extra expense), and the inventory is often limited or from previous seasons. Even consignment shops and thrift stores can produce sticker shock. Don't feel guilty if you make a decision to buy a planned item at a reasonable price but suspect that there might be a better price *out there somewhere*. The *out-there-somewhere* factor costs time. And we all know about time and money!

- The Light Bulb Rule: Avoid buying business wardrobe items at stores that sell light bulbs as well. These places may offer lower prices, but they often sell lower quality as well.

"hey, at twenty bucks, I'll make it fit!" (how not to use a second-hand shop)

Second-hand shops are great options and include consignment, vintage, and thrift stores. However, they are often the most abused places because bargain shoppers can undo their bargains. Apply all the same rules to second-hand shops that you would to any other venue.[4]

- Be choosy about the shop (consignment, vintage, or thrift) you visit. The store should be particular about what it chooses to sell and have reasonable prices.
- Different women consign different items for different reasons. True, downtown and higher-income districts tend to have the good stuff, but for a price – often a high price. Other, less affluent places will probably never see real couture come through their doors. The trick is not to assume anything about a shop until you actually inspect it for yourself. Snobs R Us may have the sweaters you love at reasonable prices because their consignees bring in so many. On the other hand, Rick's Pick and Save may overprice an item on the mistaken notion that it's worth something.

- Go into a consignment shop with a plan. Never binge on unplanned items.
- Don't get caught up in the seemingly low-priced designer label thing. Ask yourself the following questions when assessing a designer item:
    1. Is it part of my plan?

2. What is the price of the item *new*?
3. What is the price of its spin-off?
4. Is it in excellent condition?

Only buy the item if it is part of your plan, significantly lower in price than new, reasonable for your budget, and in excellent condition.

- Second-hand shops tend to be better for cold weather item purchases. Most fabrics used for these items are durable.
- Read care labels. If a garment is in great shape, it is because the previous owner followed care directions vigilantly (or she never actually wore it!). You may not be so disposed.
- Try on any garment under consideration. Don't visit a second-hand shop that provides temptation but not a dressing room!
- Examine the garment very carefully for the following:
  1. Stains, especially under the arms and on collars
  2. Pilling, especially on the elbows and under the forearms
  3. Dullness in color, especially whites and blacks
  4. Missing or damaged buttons and hardware, especially those that are difficult to replace
  5. Odors, especially on vintage pieces
  6. Worn fabric, especially delicate ones and vintage pieces

  Do not buy anything that has any of the above.
- If you repeatedly find a favorite style or brand in your size at the same store, it could be that the same person is consigning the items. Speak to the proprietor about being notified when this consigner comes into the store with new items. Consignment shops track inventory with codes that identify sellers so that they may be paid at the end of the month or season.
- Ensure that you are added to the shop's mailing list for announcements of sales and new inventory. Find out the best times to visit and make a date with yourself.

- Don't compromise on fit. This is the most common mistake in second-hand purchasing. Tailor if you must, but take into account the extra expense, add it on to the cost of the so-called bargain, and compare it to the equivalent purchase at another shop.

My sister Rose is the kind of woman you would call right before a major purchase. The chances are good that either she or her husband has researched the market. In regard to fashion, Rose knows how to get the most beautiful items from a variety of places. For any season, she may visit a high-end store for a good sweater and a pair of shoes; a discount store for her t-shirts and undergarments; and a consignment shop for a vintage pin or coat. No one can peg her shopping habits because they are varied and provide interest and appeal to all her wardrobes.

times

You can shop twenty-four hours a day, seven days a week, 365 days a year. But don't! Decide when you will shop with common sense.

- Regular retail offers prices that tend to wax and wane with the seasons. You will almost always pay full price at the start of a season. That doesn't mean you shouldn't. In fact, there may be reasons why you must.
    1. If you wear a hard-to-find size, you should consider pre-season or early-season purchasing. Your size is more likely to be available in an acceptable variety of styles.
    2. If looking fashion-forward is a high priority for you, get a jump on things. As seasons move on, variety decreases because items are picked over.
    3. If you want the most flattering and absolutely fabulous swimsuit, visit your regular retailers as soon as

the swimsuits appear. They are picked over early in the winter because of the cruise season and, of course, the regular, run-of-the-mill bathing suit panic. Do not feel guilty about spending a lot of money on a flattering suit. (That is unless you never swim!)

- Starting at around six to eight weeks into the season, items will begin to go on sale at regular retail venues. This is a good time to do the bulk of your shopping if you choose regular retail. Variety is still alive and prices are just a tad more reasonable (but not bargains).
- End-of-season and post-season shopping will have the deals, but it can be a very depressing experience and counterproductive for your *elements of style*. (Only the ugliest of colors are left!) You'll probably find something, but you may also spend way too much time bouncing from one retailer to the next.
- End-of-season and off-season purchasing is a good time for your neutral-color workhorse items if you wear easy-to-find sizes. For example, blue jeans, very basic trousers, classic solid-color skirts and jackets are good candidates. It's also a perfect time to buy undergarments, t-shirts, and workout apparel.
- Obviously, where you buy your wardrobe items will determine *when* you buy them. Avoid late-night binges on the Internet or with a shopping channel. Keep the time limited and your objectives clear.
- Never shop at the very last minute for an event or special occasion. The last minute may be impossible to avoid, but the *very last* minute tends to be the fertile period for big fashion mistakes.
- Keep a shopping trip for your needs a separate event from shopping for your husband or your children. Being the loving mother and wife that you are, you will shortchange your time for personal style.

- Reduce distractions while shopping. Hire a babysitter if necessary.
- Post-Christmas and some holiday sales are ideal for strict budgets, but often the inventory is picked over. Use this time as a secondary shopping excursion and not as your primary wardrobe-filler.
- Never buy something just because it is on sale. Buy only the items which you have planned to buy with your wardrobe plan, and, if they happen to be on sale, that's very nice.
- Don't take a sales associate's word for it. Most are only trying to make a sale. Bring a friend if you have a hard time deciding on items.
- Never confuse shopping and entertainment. Shopping is business. If it's entertaining business for you, then enjoy.
- You can, of course, make shopping more pleasant by scheduling lunch with a friend or by bringing him or her along for some help. This companionship is often very helpful.

to shop or not to shop (when to spend and when to wait)

If you are planning your wardrobe and trying to be proactive about what to buy, then planning a timetable for your needed purchases is a great money saver. You can feel secure about buying some things at full price and others on sale.

The best way to jump on the sales is to scan the newspaper on a regular basis or to get yourself on to the mailing list of your favorite retailers and watch for their circulars. The largest stores have their own inserts, and many stores print right on to the pages of the newspaper itself. Television is a good way to find out about sales as well, but unless you jot down the details, it doesn't provide a neat record for you to save.

Email notices are very convenient, but as with anything on the Internet, they may open the door to tons of unwanted email notices as well. Only fill out that "notify by email" card at your most favorite retailers. Don't bother with those that aren't your best bets.

Buy at full price, guilt-free

- anything that is difficult to find. It may include many of the things below.
- any hardworking wardrobe item for you business and business casual wardrobes, especially if being fashion-forward is a high priority for you.
- versatile, high usage items like business casual trousers, jackets, skirts, and blouses.
- winter coat.
- high usage shoes, especially for business or business casual
- swimsuits.
- high usage evening apparel.
- signature accessories.

Buy on sale

- anything that is always available.
- T-shirts.
- jeans.
- one-time outfits like gowns or glitzy blouses.
- work out clothing (unless, of course, you are a professional athlete).
- undergarments.
- non-signature accessories.

budget busters anonymous

Most of us don't bust the budget on fashion purchases. That's because most of us don't have budgets for our clothing anyway. We do spend money though. Often, however, we don't even know how much we are spending.

Over the last few years I have conducted a survey to get a feel for exactly how we behave in the fashion market. Although this isn't a scientific instrument, I probably have about one thousand anonymous questionnaires. The last question is the most revealing: "How much money on average do you spend on one wardrobe for one fashion season? (This includes tops, bottoms, whole pieces, undergarments, and all accessories.)" Instead of cuing them with multiple choice answers, I leave a long, silent, blank line.

The range of answers is quite eye-opening. In every crowd there are a few question marks. That's a bad sign. Right then I know I have a lot of work to do.

Then there are the $10 to $25 answers. These are the ones who don't understand the question, or hate fashion and may have been forced to come to the seminar, or don't know the truth. I can usually tell who these women are.

Most women write anything from $100 to $600.

There are also the daring ones. They write answers in the $1,000 to $5,000 range. It may be that they are buying good pieces, but even after all that investment, the pieces are still the *wrong* pieces (for them).

While I can't recommend specific amounts of money to set aside for any given wardrobe or wardrobe item, I can tell you what factors determine an appropriate amount.

- Income
- Lifestyle
- Season-specific needs
- General market conditions (prices and availability)

- Wardrobe techniques used that season
- Special needs

INCOME: The amount of money you take in for any given period of time. Now why would I even bring this up? Here's why:

- Obviously, the higher your income, the greater amount of money you will be *able* to budget for clothing. But – and this is a big one – you shouldn't feel pressured to spend more money. (Boy does the fashion industry disagree with that!) Your lifestyle should be a more influential factor.
- If, on the other hand, your income is relatively low, do not excuse yourself from creating a budget for clothing. Low income is all the more reason for budgeting.
- Income is tempered by the number of members in your family. So if you have a high income and many people in your family, the amount you will spend on your personal wardrobe will have to be less than if you were single. This phenomenon is fresh in your mind if you are newly married: single – large piece of the pie; married – smaller piece of pie because you have a *sweetie* pie.
- You will hear fashion consultants recommend that you spend up to around 25 percent of your total take-home pay on wardrobe needs. This is ridiculous unless you live with your parents and never intend to change that. Even then, that's not leaving much for living. If you are looking for a mathematical formula for fashion spending, don't hold your breath.

LIFESTYLE: What you do; how often you do it; where you do it.

- Lifestyle is often related to income. It can be the product of income, drives income, or (more realistically) both.

- Examine what you do and how often you do it. Are you mostly at home? Do you socialize a lot? Do you have responsibilities that make specific clothing demands? Do you work outside of the home? What are the dress requirements where you work?
- Generally, clothing for office work is more expensive than clothing for home life. So an at-home mother who rarely gets out will need less money for clothing than a woman with a high profile job. She still needs quality, but garments for personal casual time tend to be less expensive than suiting.
- If you work outside the home, then you need a business casual wardrobe, business wardrobe, or both (in *addition* to your personal casual wardrobe). That will involve more money unless you are very clever with a wardrobe technique.
- Lifestyle also determines priorities. If you need a fashion-forward wardrobe (priority #2) or a high-profile wardrobe (priority #4), then you need to appropriate a little more money to that wardrobe.

SEASON-SPECIFIC NEEDS: Things you need for any given season will affect the size of your budget.

- Season-specific needs may only be occasional, but they are cyclic. Coats tend to last from three to five years (a function of quality and frequency of use), so that amount of time will determine the cycle. You often can't predict a lifespan of an item, but you can prepare for the expense within a reasonable time frame (and then be pleasantly surprised if you don't have to spend that money.)
- Winter season-specific items tend to be more expensive than summer specific needs.
- Wardrobe shopping trips tend to coincide with the changes in weather seasons, so, ideally, clothing does not need to be a monthly category of the household budget.

GENERAL MARKET CONDITIONS: The average prices of items and their availability.

- You can't create a clothing budget in a vacuum. You have to have an idea of how much things are and if they are available. You also have to know how much availability is going to cost you in the form of driving expenses, time, shipping and postage.
- Survey what's out there, how much the items are, and where they are. You'll be doing this anyway if you methodically plan your wardrobe.

WARDROBE TECHNIQUES USED: Techniques vary on cost-effectiveness.

- The *mix and match* technique is cost-effective for a wardrobe created from scratch and worn everyday at the same place and among the same people. The mixing and matching and the accessorizing changes the look of all ensembles.
- The *spectrum* technique is also cost effective. Sometimes, this solution uses nothing but items you already own. (You may already have lots of great tops in many of your best colors!) In a season when this may be the case, budget some money for a season-specific need.
- The *monochromatic* technique will require relatively more money if you are starting completely from scratch. This is especially the case if you are buying suits.

SPECIAL NEEDS: You may have some needs which may affect the cost of individual items and therefore the size of your fashion budget.

- Often, plus-size fashion will cost more. Some of my clients complain that they can never find anything over a certain size on the bargain racks. This should be taken into consideration.

- Some women will require very hard-working bras. The better the bra, the higher the price.
- Items such as special shoes or support hosiery will bring up the cost of a wardrobe. Maternity items are also more expensive.
- Tailoring for any item adds to the cost of the item.

Your wardrobe budget should not be derived from the disposable income category. It should be up there with the grocery budget. (Remember, food, *clothing*, and shelter.) This doesn't mean that you should be spending what you spend on groceries (I would have a lot of fun on that level!). Clothing just needs its own category on a quarterly or semiannual cycle. (Choosing the cycle depends upon the climate in which you live.) Also, because you are a grown woman and your clothes are more costly than your children's, your piece of the pie should be larger than your young children's. It will probably be less than your husband's because men's clothing is relatively more expensive, especially if he wears suits.

> *Society drives people crazy with lust and calls it advertising.*
>
> JOHN LAHR

SEMINAR FAQ

fashion forecasting

QUESTION: How do I use fashion magazines? Whenever I spend the four bucks to get a copy, I may only find one useful photo or tip out of the whole thing. What do you recommend for someone who can't fashion forecast in person at high-end retailers?

ANSWER: There are two levels to fashion forecasting with fashion media. The level you choose will determine the source you use. First there is general fashion forecasting. This is when you try to glean the current colors, themes, silhouettes, styles, and accessories from the work of the designers. (Remember when we spoke about trends?) At this level you're not necessarily trying to build a wardrobe, but catch the mood of the season. It's a fruitful ritual for me as a fashion professional as it is for a fashion writer, designer, retailer, enthusiast, etc. I do get some ideas for my wardrobe, but I have to translate just about every image I see into my own language for fashion. Unfortunately, this often involves sorting through a lot of counterproductive, and, frankly, offensive images. That's the frustrating part.

The more practical method helps with personal fashion planning. High end catalogues and Internet sites afford some useful images for my planning, sometimes sparking actual buying decisions. Most high end stores offer catalogues by mail (often for a price) and while I may not actually buy a single thing, I can decide this season's colors, themes, silhouettes, styles, and accessories *for myself.*

So, to answer your question, hold that fashion magazine out at arm's length and with a critical eye, while you clutch the best catalogue to your bosom.[5]

the right stuff: finding the perfect item

Think of any garment or item you decide to buy in a multidimensional way. It has roles to play in your wardrobe, it has qualities of its own, and it speaks its own language. Consider the following after you have decided that an item fits your wardrobe plan and budget.

1. Materials and Construction
2. Care
3. Fit

materials and construction

The quality of garments and accessories is determined by the materials used and by the workmanship of the construction. Most items are machine made. Handmade items tend to be more expensive because they are usually better made and have taken more time to produce.

The best place to begin is with the material used to make an item. This includes fabric for garments and harder materials such as metal, plastic, and animal hides for accessories.

There are two types of fabric: natural and synthetic. Technically, there is a third type, man-made, but that might be a little too much information for our purposes.

There are also natural and synthetic *combinations*. I can firmly say that for some garments certain fabrics are a must, but then I'm amazed by technology and have to add to my list of greats. Perhaps a better way of capturing the basics on fabrics is to know which fabrics are best for which kinds of garments.

common natural fibers

COTTON

Features: Breathes well, strong, pills less, wrinkles easily (must be ironed constantly)
Origin: Harvested from plants
Care: Usually machine-washable
Good for: Tops such as man tailored shirts (especially when combined with Spandex) and tailored trousers and sweaters

WOOL

Features: Maintains structure well, breathes, wrinkle resistant, provides warmth, can pill easily, dyes easily, must be stored properly to resist insect damage

Origin: Harvested from fleece of sheep

Care: Usually hand-washable or dry clean; will shrink

Good for: Structured items, especially suits, trousers, sweaters, and coats

SILK

Features: Drapes beautifully, luxurious feel, breathes, wrinkles less, dyes easily (but will fade), doesn't pill

Origin: Harvested from silk worms

Care: Dry clean or hand washable

Good for: Blouses, dresses, fashion scarves, summer suits and sweaters

LINEN

Features: Drapes beautifully, breathes well, very strong, wrinkles easily (must be ironed constantly)

Origin: Harvested from flax

Care: Generally hand wash or dry clean

Good for: Summer dresses, jackets, and trousers

CASHMERE

Features: Drapes beautifully, soft and luxurious, expensive, can pill (short fibers)

Origin: Harvested from fleece of Kashmir goats

Care: Best to dry clean

Good for: Sweaters, coats, suits, and socks.

synthetic fabrics (among many, many others)

POLYESTER

Features: Can have luxurious feel, extremely versatile, strong, wrinkle resistant, can pill, washes well

Care: Usually machine-washable

Good for: Suits, tops, bottoms, dresses, scarves, and lingerie

NYLON

Features: Very strong, extremely versatile, wrinkle resistant, can pill

Care: Usually hand-washable

Good for: Swimwear, blouses, undergarments, and hosiery

SPANDEX

Features: Very stretchy, versatile, requires special drying care, no static, no pilling, resistant to perspiration

Care: Hand-washable

Good for: Swimsuits and work out wear; used with cotton in many tops (provides good structure and fit)

ACRYLIC

Features: Can have luxurious feel (wool-like appearance without the itch), pills extremely easily (including cotton-acrylic combinations), static problems, very versatile, dyes well

Care: Machine-washable

Good for: Sweaters, sportswear, and socks (great for athletic socks)

ACETATE
Features: Drapes beautifully, can have luxurious feel, tears easily, dyes well
Care: Dry clean
Good for: Dresses, evening wear and lining in coats and trousers

RAYON
Features: Drapes beautifully, highly versatile, no pilling or static, high maintenance (although less so nowadays), harvested partly from wood pulp
Care: Always read care label; usually dry clean *only*
Good for: Dresses, suits, and trousers

MICROFIBER
Features: Durable, versatile, insulates well, very fine
Not so much a fiber as much as a process; ultra fine knit or weave available in nylon, polyester, or rayon.
Care: Spot clean, machine washable or dry clean
Good for: Accessories such as handbags, shoes, and jackets

The quality of a garment is mostly determined by the fabric from which it was made. You can actually feel the difference. Good silks and rayons shouldn't wrinkle after being bunched in your hand, and anything knit should have a little substance to it. Loosey-goosey loops in what should be a tightly knit garment is a sign that the maker was trying to save on yarn. You can often pick up on poor quality in a knit garment by checking where the pieces of the garment have been attached, such as where the neck of a turtle neck connects, or along the top of the shoulders. Stitching at these sites should be tight and consistent.[6]

Accessories and even some garments may be constructed from the hides of all sorts of animals. Generally, the more exotic the animal, the more expensive the item. Cowhide, buckskin, kid (baby goatskin), snake, alligator, lizard, cordovan (horse rumps), kangaroo, and even shark are all a part of the fashion menagerie. Most of what you will find in the women's accessory department is made from cowhide (sometimes embossed with a pattern that mimics an exotic animal skin) so it's good to understand what to expect. Cowhide leather should always be soft and supple and stitching should be tight and consistent. Also, be sure that you are purchasing leather when you think you are. Labels will tell.

Faux materials no longer exist *just* to trick the eye. Nowadays they often stand alone as fashion statements. In fact, some designer lines, including even *haute couture*, tout the vinyl of their totes. Plastic is often not even disguised to look like anything other than plastic. The 1950s fashion icon Wilardy (Will Hardy) created curiosity handbags from a hard plastic called Lucite. These pieces are now very pricey collector's items and can easily compete with the beauty of anything made from precious materials.

Metal accessories such as buckles or jewelry should be checked for paint. If you assume that something is silver or platinum but you see paint-like chipping, something is amiss. Also, anything that is meant to be buckled, snapped, or twisted should be tested to ensure that it does exactly what it is supposed to do.

Always let your fingers do the work if a garment is up for consideration. Check stitching for snugness and consistency (the more stitches the better) and be sure that fabric lines up properly along the seams, especially for more noticeable prints like plaid and stripes. Lining should not sag inside a garment, and buttons should be secure with no loose threads.

ANATOMY OF A GREAT SUIT

- High quality and durable fabric
- Pattern is aligned over darts, seams, and pockets
- Good buttons in which hues are at least as dark as the fabric
- Uniform stitches
- No puckering on collars which lie flat,
- Attached lining
- Shoulders should fit perfectly
- Sleeves should fall to wrist bone
- Jacket should fall to flattering and current length

STYLE PROFILE #15
thanks, but I'm browsing

Need to learn a little about fabric? What about the difference between a quality button and a cheapie? Try visiting your local fabric store. Begin by exploring the differences in "notions" such as buttons and thread quality. (Note the prices.) Then, head out to the fabrics. Feel samples of silk, silk shantung, wool gabardine, wool flannel, and linen. Check prices too. Don't worry; no one will raise an eyebrow. This is just how good seamstresses shop.

care

Right after you examine a label for fabric, look for care instructions. (Labels are supposed to be there by law.) If it's dry clean only, you have to incorporate that cost into the long run cost of the garment. If it has any sequins, beading, or patchwork needing special care, those things must be included in the cost as well. Dyed leather products, suede, and shearling are also high maintenance items.

Take into account the cost of *time* for a garment. If you are not into ironing, then something with a million pleats just isn't going to cut it. If you can't seem to get a system started for hand washing (most clothes washers have a cycle for this, fortunately), then reconsider buying another hand-washable.

fit

Size numbers should never control the way you choose your fashion. They work well when deciding which garments to take off of the rack and into the dressing room, but you can't let them tax you psychologically. Besides, sizes manifest into different numbers amongst different brands. You may be a size 8 in one, but a 10 or even a 12 in others.

You must always try the garment on. Use the Checklist below the next time you head into a dressing room.

1. Does it fit in with my original plan?
2. Does its price fit in to my budget?
3. Is it worth the price? Make sure that

- the fabric does what it should. Feel it to make sure. (For example, a good rayon or or silk shouldn't stay wrinkled after scrunching in your hand.)
- the stitching around the pockets and seams is straight and finished.
- the printed pattern is matched up at the seams (especially plaids).
- the buttons are secure.

next, try on the outfit!

- Walk, bend forward toward the mirror (the best is a three-way mirror), and sit in the outfit. Check skirts for how high they ride when crossing your legs.
- Button up the first and second buttons to see how secure they are and how smoothly the garment lies against you.
- Check front, side, and back views. Reject anything which cups around the buttocks or generally doesn't flatter – even if it theoretically suits your body type.
- Tuck in any item that's meant to be worn tucked in to your trousers or skirt.
- Ask your shopping partner for his or her honest opinion. (Most sales attendants just want to sell the garment and are apt to be a bit less honest about how something looks on you.)

When you get home, double check your purchase and hang it up. Don't remove the tag immediately. You may find with a little reflection that the item may not work for you after all. That's when keeping a tag on comes in handy. You will be able to return it with no problem, under normal circumstances.

STYLE PROFILE #16
what to do in a dressing room besides panic

No, you should never panic. Nor should you perspire.

Think back to that last time you were in a dressing room. What were your feelings? Did you keep your head? Were you the least bit anxious or discouraged? Or, did your pulse race off to the heights of fashion ecstasy? (Okay, maybe that's a bit of exaggeration.)

Note your reactions in the dressing room during your next visit. What can you do to improve the experience?

cover me, I'm going in: suits, coats and special occasion dresses

Those women who never stress out about buying tops, bottoms, suits, or even shoes are often stopped frozen in their tracks at the mere prospect of buying those big ticket items that you only get once every few years. That's logical. After all, we are usually spending a relatively greater amount of money when we buy either a winter coat or an evening gown.

So I've decided to discuss the art of buying both. Below is a primer.

how to buy a winter coat

I spent most of my life happily braving the winter in a silly little coat. Then, I moved to the Upper Midwest. A person who lives in a climate where it actually dips below zero degrees cannot wear a silly little coat. She will not only be cold, but will be taken for a silly fool. I realize now why Middle America raises such tough people.

On the other hand, warmth and style are not mutually exclusive. Good heavens, they couldn't be because the coat is sometimes the only thing in which the others see you! It just takes a little extra effort to meld style with duckling feathers.

PLANNING

- Don't go near a store until you have decided which winter wardrobe to target (personal casual, business casual, business, etc.) Envision something that works with your *elements of style.*
- Decide length according to the wardrobe for which you are buying it. There are no hard and fast rules, but longer lengths tend to be more formal. Tailored wool coats are better for business and business casual wardrobes.
- A coat that will be worn over skirts or dresses should go past the length of the hemline of the skirt or dress.
- If you live in a mild or mildly cold climate, you will probably be able to plan out just one reliable coat to go with each wardrobe. If you live in a very cold climate, you should plan out a coat for cold days (kind of that silly coat thing) and another coat for seriously cold days. This also helps break up the monotony of wearing coats seven months a year; at least there's variety!

ANATOMY OF A GREAT COAT

- Fabric suitable for cold weather
- Flattering and coordinated color
- Durable lining
- Secure buttons in flattering style
- Streamlined silhouette

- Perfect fit in shoulders with ability to move arms
- Handbag fits over the shoulder (if that's your desire)
- Appropriate length for wardrobe
- Collar or hood allows ease to turn head while driving

SHOPPING

- Begin your shopping ventures by surveying several stores. Take notes on what you see and how much each coat costs.
- Return to the best selections. Don't wait for a sale because you will probably catch a cold by the time you buy, or the selection will be very much reduced.
- A coat which falls to your waist cuts your look in half, thus making you appear shorter or even heavier. Also, your fanny will get cold.
- Try on a coat over layers that you would normally wear in the winter. This may mean carrying a sweater with you to the dressing room.
- Try on the coat in front of a mirror and check all angles as you would for an outfit. See how well your purse slides over your sleeve. (This might mean *coordinating* your coat and handbag purchase.)
- Rotate your arms to check comfort around shoulders and arm pits.
- Check for snugness of stitching and security of buttons. Consider how easily a missing button could be replaced.
- Know the filling. Down is one of the warmest fillings around, but check for small holes where little feathers could escape.
- Check for care. Structured wool coats are dry-clean-only most often. Many sport coats and parkas are washable. Many coats have fur or faux fur trim or other types of detailing that need special care so include this into the overall cost of the coat. Fortunately, some of these details are detachable.

- While making the actual purchase, find out about the return or exchange policy for the coat. Save the receipt.

SPECIFIC GUIDELINES

If you need a coat for personal casual time:

- Remember that shorter lengths are better for driving and getting in and out of the car.
- Decide ahead of time if you want a hood, pockets, or zip-in lining for seasonal changes.
- Avoid coats with sports team logos or cartoon characters on them.
- Find a color from your color palette that won't bore you in a month. Or find a scarf or pin to brighten up the ubiquitous black or brown coat.

If you need a coat for business or business casual time:

- Go for more structure. Choose a flattering style that falls to below the hemline of your skirt or dress.
- Ensure that it is a coat in which you can commute comfortably.
- Avoid high maintenance coats. Fur, faux fur, or any kind of light trim needs to be cleaned in a special way. If you wear the coat every day, it may be hard to find the time.

If you need a really warm coat:

- Try a hooded down-filled coat that falls to your calves or longer and has cuffs that fit snugly around your wrist. Bulkiness is now obsolete, as newer technology in materials has allowed for very streamlined cuts. A cinch in at the waist or a generally fitted style is most flattering.

- If you go from your garage to a parking garage at work, a parka may be unnecessary. If you have any kind of walk outdoors in a cold climate, a warm coat is a must. It is possible to find stylish parkas but you may have to search several retailers to find the best and most streamlined.

how to buy a special occasion dress

Yes, at some point in her life, every woman finds her world standing still as she searches for the perfect dress for a high-profile occasion. It could be anything from a wedding or graduation to charity ball or simple cocktail hour. These are true fashion moments, memorialized in movies and novels, and are of epic proportions in the minds of those who live through the corresponding shopping excursions.

There are and will always be some clear dos and don'ts to this art. One major consideration comes to mind immediately: appropriateness. Consider the occasion: Will it be festive? Is it a church service? Will it be somber? Will you be among professional colleagues? Or, will you be surrounded by friends and family? Here are some guidelines:

- Plan according to your *elements of style.*
- Consider length according to current trends. Generally, full length dresses are for evening and are very formal.
- Always consider that your face should be the focal point of your ensemble. You will have a secondary focal point on your ensemble and it should not compete with your face. (Nor should it compete with the face of the bride, the graduate, the retiree, or the person of honor.)
- Survey department stores, boutiques and second-hand shops for inventory and prices. Don't forget to check vintage venues, but be sure that whatever you buy can handle the stress of dancing. Also, be sure that any vintage item you wear has

absolutely no odor. There's nothing like a bad smell to ruin the wonder of a special occasion.

- Attempt to time your shopping with the sales.
- Shop for this item with a sincere friend.
- Bring along shoes in the heel height you will wear for the occasion. (Shop in comfortable shoes and stash the high heels in a bag or your purse.)
- Try on the dress in front of a three-way mirror and check all angles. Avoid showing too much skin, especially cleavage and mid to lower back.
- Avoid sheer fabric across private areas.
- Check that you can raise your arms up (for dancing) or bend forward without the dress betraying you.
- Plan for the necessary bra. You will probably need a strapless. (This is often the case even if the dress isn't strapless.) Bra straps should never show, especially through sheer fabric.
- If the dress has a slit, check to see how high it is on you. It shouldn't reveal your upper thigh.
- Try walking in the dress with the shoes you plan to wear with it. The shoes should be the same color as (or darker than) the hem of the dress. Metallic strappy dress shoes are the exception.
- Check that the straps are secure on the dress.
- Don't forget your coordinated wrap or shawl.
- Read care instructions. If the dress has sequins or beading, cleaning may be complicated. This doesn't mean that it's a reason not to purchase the dress, just know what you are getting into.
- Ask about the return policy on the dress. This is not so that you can return it after the event. That's unethical. Rather, you may change your mind once you get home from the store. That's okay.

THREE TIMELESS SPECIAL OCCASION DRESSES

TEA-LENGTH WITH BATEAU NECK
Secondary focal point = bodice, may add earrings, formal

THE VERSATILE "LITTLE BLACK DRESS"
Secondary focal point = jewelry

WRAP DRESS
Secondary focal point = rosette

I lost my dog somewhere in my laundry system

A great wardrobe, like a great relationship, takes hard work to continue being *great*. Clothing requires maintenance, and no matter how high tech the fabric, a garment must eventually be cleaned, repaired, and stored.

I hate doing laundry – with a passion. When I go down into my basement to begin work, I feel as if I've been doomed to hard labor in a dungeon. Hanging pretty pictures around the room and throwing down a carpet has helped, but the radio was the most effective improvement because it eased that awful boredom that comes with folding towels

My friend Priscilla asked me what the big deal was. She's great with laundry because she's as serious about running an efficient home as she is about her personal style. She has also raised five children.

"I guess I have no self-discipline," I admitted. I'm just like many other people who have been raised with television: if it's boring, I'm not going to tune in.

"Well, it's easy and it really takes no time," she advised. "If you let it pile up, then it's hard and will take forever. Get a system going. Come on. Just do it."

just do it

So I have a system. It's the tried and true one that many of my friends use. Sure, it's a keeper, but as with anything worthwhile, I have to actually stick with it. This is how it works:

1. Provide each family member with an expandable net laundry bin that has three parts (or just one part can be enough). My friend Jeannette gave each of her children large ball bags – the kind from gym class – as an alternative to laundry bags. Also, give each person one rectangular laundry basket with sturdy handles. (Smaller children do better with square-shaped baskets.)
2. Explain to family members that as soon as they undress, they should decide if the outfit is clean or dirty. If it's clean, put it away. Okay, of course it's dirty. So, toss it into the *white*,

color, or *dark* section of the laundry bin or bag. This is called *presorting*. (This is also a good time to treat stains with a stain-removal product.)

3. Avoid letting dirty clothes sit around too long as mold and mildew can grow, causing a big stinky mess.
4. Wash clothes on a designated time or times of the day. Aim for what I like to call "meaningful" loads first (i.e. underwear, towels), but rest assured that even seemingly meaningless loads have great value too. This step could be completed by you if your family is very young (or a little too young at heart) or by each person. Be sure to write out directions for sorting and water temperature in very large print on a placard that hangs right at eye level above the washer (like the directions in the laundry area of a college dorm). True, they may not study it, but it's a reference to which everyone can refer in a pinch.
5. Train family members to read care labels on garments so that the dry-clean-only pieces don't end up in the general laundry.
6. Dry clothes immediately after washing. This means sticking around for the end of the washing cycle. Hang clothing that needs to dry on hangers. Lay flat the clothing that needs to lay flat.
7. Fold clothes right out of the dryer and place them into their respective baskets. I've labeled each basket with the names of each family member in permanent marker. I've even added happy faces and flowers for my more enthusiastic girls.
8. Have each family member put away his or her laundry each night. If each person has less (because less is better) than this shouldn't take very long.

I once heard the expression that a mother is only as happy as her unhappiest child. This especially applies to laundry: You are only as happy as the weakest link in the chain of your laundry cycle. In other words, someone will inevitably fall short and mess up the whole system. For these types you might have to modify the process and even help them along.

As for your clothing, sort it! Don't let your pretty little silk blouse get mixed in with the soccer uniforms. Designate a time for your laundry only. This little habit will help your wardrobe improve by leaps and bounds.

Finally, two little bits of wisdom will help you overcome your anxiety regarding laundry:

1. Laundry is a cycle. It's perpetual. It never ends.
2. Laundry is clothing. Clothing is what you wear so you aren't naked. (Well, there's actually a lot more to clothing, but bear with me here.)

Okay, maybe this doesn't ease your anxiety, but it may make you work a little harder!

STYLE PROFILE #17

the butcher, the baker, and the guy who repairs shoes

There are three things you must usually outsource when it comes to wardrobe maintenance: dry cleaning, shoe repair, and tailoring. Granted, you might be a great seamstress yourself, but I doubt that you have dry cleaning or shoe repair equipment down in your basement. Of course you might be married to a dry cleaner or shoe repair guy, but I'd love to find the woman who is married to both!

Locate the following services and write their phone numbers and/or addresses below:

Dry cleaning service ______________________________
____
____

Shoe repair service _______________________________
____
____

Tailoring service _________________________________
____
____

I'm a liberated woman

What a wonderful thing it is to be liberated. I know because I am. I now have the ability to walk past stores, racks, and individual garments knowing that they are just not me. I don't even look back. This shopping style has reduced my stress, saved me time, and protected my precious earnings. Then, when I do see the right item, I don't feel guilty about spending money on it. Liberation!

You may not be able to do this with ease at first, but you do have the freedom to do it. It just takes practice and determination.

smart style: a summary

Below is a description of the three things you should know before you begin shopping for wardrobe items: know yourself, know the market, and know yourself in the market. Go through this list and then complete the shopping plan in the next *Style Profile.*

KNOW YOURSELF

- Know your *elements of style*: body type, fashion personality, color season, and needs.
- Know what you want to communicate with your style.
- Know how to articulate your personal style.
- Know your particular wardrobe plans for this season.

KNOW THE MARKET

- Know what's available, when, and for how much.
- Know which retailers work best for you.
- Know that retailers will do anything to get you through their doors.
- Know the trends of the season but be able to choose the ones that will work for you.

ACT ON KNOWLEDGE OF YOURSELF IN THE MARKET

- Resist the appeal of advertising when it's just not logical for you.
- Learn how to put something down if you have reasoned that it is not the best for your wardrobe plan.
- Use a shopping strategy like the kind in the next *Style Profile*.

STYLE PROFILE #18

my shopping strategy

Use the sheet below to get what you need. Remember, you can't do this until you have planned out your wardrobe. Go back to chapter six to see if your wardrobe even needs new purchases. Otherwise, save this sheet for another wardrobe plan. Also, keep it as a record for your purchasing habits.

shopping strategy worksheet

DATE: ___________

season: (circle one)

cold weather   warm weather   transitional

For my ____________________________ wardrobe.

Base number = ___________

Total budget for this wardrobe = $___________

Dates for shopping: ____ / ____ , ____ / ____ , ____ / ____

ITEM #1

Need: __________________________ Color: _______________

Budget $_______ Where to check: ________________________

Results of search:

Found it at ____________________ for $____________

Found it at ____________________ for $____________

Purchased at ______________________ **for $**_____________

ITEM #2

Need: ______________________ Color: ______________

Budget $______ Where to check: ____________________

Results of search:

Found it at __________________ for $__________

Found it at __________________ for $__________

Purchased at ____________________ for $____________

ITEM #3

Need: ______________________ Color: ______________

Budget $______ Where to check: ____________________

Results of search:

Found it at __________________ for $__________

Found it at __________________ for $__________

Purchased at ____________________ for $____________

ITEM #4

Need: ______________________ Color: ______________

Budget $______ Where to check: ____________________

Results of search:

Found it at __________________ for $__________

Found it at __________________ for $__________

Purchased at ____________________ for $____________

ITEM #5

Need: ____________________ Color: ____________

Budget $______ Where to check: ____________________

Results of search:

Found it at ________________ for $__________

Found it at ________________ for $__________

Purchased at ________________ for $__________

ITEM #6

Need: ____________________ Color: ____________

Budget $______ Where to check: ____________________

Results of search:

Found it at ________________ for $__________

Found it at ________________ for $__________

Purchased at ________________ for $__________

ITEM #7

Need: ____________________ Color: ____________

Budget $______ Where to check: ____________________

Results of search:

Found it at ________________ for $__________

Found it at ________________ for $__________

Purchased at ________________ for $__________

ITEM #8

Need: ______________________ Color: ______________

Budget $______ Where to check: ______________________

Results of search:

Found it at __________________ for $___________

Found it at __________________ for $___________

Purchased at ____________________ for $____________

Total amount spent for this wardrobe: $___________

CHAPTER NINE

polished style
the power of poise

feel the power

Okay, I'll admit upfront that I was a hopeless tomboy as a child so grace never came naturally to me. I can remember my father attempting to teach me how to change brakes on our van while my mother called out the window, "Joe, don't do that. It'll make it worse!"

Once, in seventh grade biology class, a government scientist came to teach us about petri dishes, incubation, and how bacteria grow. He had us swab our mouths to see what kinds of things live in the typical adolescent human mouth. Well, I not only swabbed my mouth but I secretly scraped the floor under my desk as well. Boy did I think it was cool when I saw what grew in my petri dish! My classmates, on the other hand, did not think it was cool. Indeed, other adjectives came to their minds. I guess I hadn't grown out of the "gross is cool" phase even at the age of thirteen.

My poor mother did have a lot of work to do. But I, of course, had to eventually buy into the notion of femininity on my own. I think it happened sometime in high school, when I wanted to be taken seriously and grow into the woman I imagined.

Poise and elegance can mean different things to different people. I am no Grace Kelly and could never be, even after a diet and a dye job – and a radical facelift. I would never be able to fake the elegant voice, the smooth smile, or the graceful gestures. I'm just not her.

Adornment is never anything except a reflection of the heart.

COCO CHANEL

Once, a student of mine told me that I looked like a brunette Princess Diana. I was so thrilled that I ran off to tell the first person I could find. I told my husband and he said only if you squinted really hard – and switched off the lights – and turned the other way. Oh well, so much for that.

My poise is part of my style. While my clothing choices long ago ceased to be a struggle, I, like many women my age and younger (products of the 1970s), must continue to rediscover the power of poise. I am eternally grateful that poise no longer involves big hats or gloves, and, in our wonderful twenty-first century, poise allows room for personality (even mine).

OBJECTIVE: understand and develop poise.

I had poise once but lost it when my back went out (what poise is and isn't)

For the sake of finding common ground on our understanding of poise, a few clarifications are in order. First, remember the "polish and sparkle" of elegance in chapter one? That's poise!

Poise is

- femininity
- refinement
- modesty

Contrary to the unpopular rep it got in the past, poise is also

- Individualism
- Self-confidence
- Assertiveness

The only real elegance is in the mind; if you've got that, the rest really comes from it.

DIANA VREELAND

Poise is *not*

- aggression
- self-centeredness
- rudeness

Poise is *not*

- reactionism
- elitism
- stupidity

Finally, poise has two practical aspects that will be covered in this chapter:

1. fashion details (attention to details such as hair and makeup, hand care, and general fashion convention).
2. our interaction with others (body language and speech).

why poise?

So many women have found that poise helps them in so many ways. Poise yields

- enhanced personal style
- greater self-confidence
- greater personal appeal
- increased professionalism

who wants to look like a millionaire?

I'm not even going to dignify that question with a response. As my grandmother from Brooklyn would have said, "Who the heck are *you* trying to be?" or something a bit more colorful than that.

Clothes can suggest, persuade, connote, insinuate, or indeed lie, and apply subtle pressure while their wearer is speaking frankly and straightforwardly of other matters.

ANNE HOLLANDER

Friends like to point out to me books and fashion events that advocate learning from and imitating the wealthy. That goes against everything I have said in this book.

First, the wealthy don't necessarily have an edge in style. They may have sustained their past superiority only because clothes were so expensive. Now, clothes are relatively inexpensive. Quality requires money, but only to a certain extent. It would be nice to have a snooty handbag, but I think I'll avoid the temptation to go for the little drab one everyone has at the moment. Great personal style never means ostentation. It should never be a power thing or a way to make others feel less important. Great personal style should be your way to help other people feel as if they are more important because you look beautiful for them.

So, here's how! Below are some of the areas where you can try some new ideas and perhaps revisit some old ones. (You know, the ones your grandmother told you.)

aspire to feminine genius

makeup for heaven's sake

My best advice on makeup: Wear it. My second best advice: Learn how to apply it properly. As a fashion consultant, my best advice was often a revolutionary concept to clients. I think it was that whole casual-as-virtue thing. It was also partly due to the misconception that your children will be ragged and malnourished if you spend any time in front of the mirror in the morning.

Daily makeup application should only take *five minutes*. These five minutes should not be the accumulation of minutes in front of traffic lights. Makeup time should be soon after your shower; perhaps in your bathrobe if you'd like to keep your clothing stain-free.

I need to get control of this stuff so that I can take control of everything else in my life.

FASHION CONSULTING CLIENT

Don't take for granted the surface on which you are applying that makeup: your skin. Adopt a healthy skin care regimen that's right for your skin type and stick with it. Seek the advice of your dermatologist or read up on the current understanding of skin maintenance. Generally, your regimen should include cleansing, occasional exfoliating, and moisturizing. A great resource for serious dermatology information is the American Academy of Dermatology.

Generally, your makeup routine should go something like this (your face should be clean and appropriately moisturized before beginning):

1. Use a concealor on dark or red areas such as scars, blemishes, or right at the bottom of dark circles under the eyes. Also, as women age, areas around the side of the nose tend to redden so cover this if necessary.
2. Apply a liquid or powder foundation across entire face including eyelids and lips. Blend to the jaw line. (Makeup color should match the skin color of your neck, so blending there should be minimal.)
3. Apply a translucent powder if liquid foundation was used in step two.
4. Apply blush. Apply from center of cheek, up and out on the cheek bone; never below the cheekbone. Dap onto the tip of your nose and chin to get a sun-kissed look.

5. Apply eye shadow. Cover entire lid with the lightest color in a trio pack of color. Add color to just above the eyelashes. Add depth by applying the darkest color to the crease in the lid.
6. Draw along the eyelash line with eyeliner. Begin at center of eye for top lid; Begin a little further out for bottom lid. Draw outward.
7. Curl eyelashes with an eyelash curler if necessary.
8. Apply mascara to top eyelid. Apply to bottom eyelid if you don't have the habit of touching your eyes.
9. Apply lip liner to outside line of the lips and then fill in both lips. This will make lips look fuller and keep the lipstick on longer. Applying liner *inside* the lip line will make lips look smaller.
10. Fill in with lipstick of a matching color. Lip gloss can be appropriate for some occasions and makes a nice finishing touch.

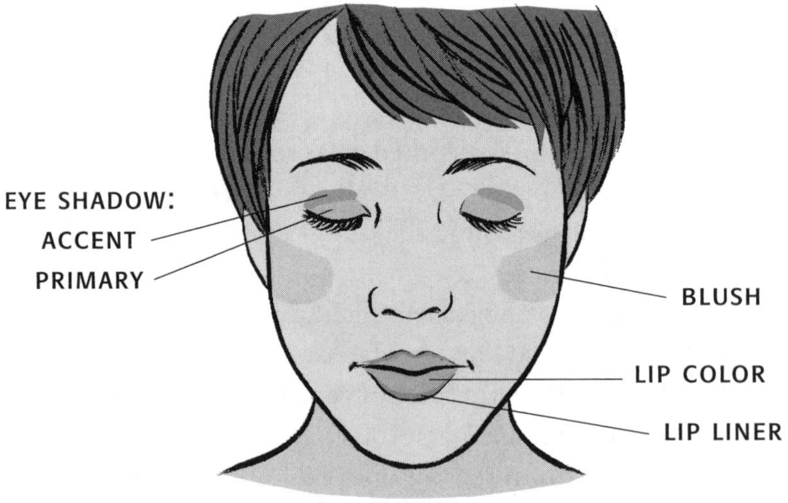

Voila! You are even more beautiful now. And the best part is it only took five minutes!

hair's the scoop

Facial hairs are never in style. Arched and thin brow styles come and go. So, always remove facial hairs from chin and lip, and groom brows to current style. Generally, thin and arched brows open the eyes and aid them as a focal point. (Find a salon that shapes brows rather than just removes hair.)

tips for making makeup simple and beautiful

- Have an area in your bedroom or bathroom where you can sit in a well-lit area – something like a vanity is best – and apply your makeup with care. For several years, while living in a cramped house, I would apply my makeup on the floor beside the bed. I got sick of it one day, so for $200 I purchased an antique art-deco vanity (the kind with the big circular mirror) and placed jars of cotton balls and cotton swabs on top. Afterwards, when I applied my makeup, I felt organized, methodical, and – best of all – confident when I finished.
- Limit your makeup choices for your morning makeup area. Have one foundation, one powder, one mascara, even only one or two lipstick colors.
- Go for some redundancy. Have two tubes of your best lipstick color. Place one where you do your normal morning routine and the other somewhere near the front door, like a bathroom or by a mirror in the closet. Go ahead and keep some blush there too. Apply as needed for touch ups right there instead of running up the stairs (which you probably wouldn't do anyway).
- Choose colors according to the colors of your color palette.
- Apply in a style that goes with the time of day and your fashion personality. Day time makeup is always a bit less

and lighter. Evening makeup can be darker and glitzy for special occasions.

- Keep your makeup in a small travel bag. Carry it in your purse if you are particularly mobile. I know women who keep two bags: one in the purse and one on the vanity and it works pretty well for them.
- Learn proper makeup *application* from a credible source like a book or makeup counter.
- Make it a point never to leave your house without makeup on your face.
- Refresh powder and lipstick throughout the day. Using a lip liner will help you to reduce the number of times you will need to refresh lipstick. My friend and mentor Patti carries straws everywhere she goes to preserve her lip color. Even at my home, I'll serve her some ice water and, sure enough, Patti will whip out a straw from her tiny purse!
- Modify your makeup routine for the weather seasons.
- Remember to remove your makeup at night with a good cleansing and moisturizing routine.
- Check out Paula Begoun's resources for makeup quality ratings. She provides a thorough critique for everything. She is known on the Internet as the *Cosmetic Cop.*[1]
- If you want to find information on the cosmetics industry in general and its regulations or lack of regulations, try the Food and Drug Administration's website and check out the section on cosmetics.[2]

fragrances

The use of perfume is at times controversial. In an effort to clean up the workplace environment, many business fashion consultants and business environment consultants suggest only minimal amounts of fragrance in the workplace. That's probably because there is a breed of woman who just can't stop the spray! They often have the greatest personalities, but the worst taste in perfume.

Learn how the art of fragrance can enhance your style.

- Remember how I said "less is better"? Well, this also applies to the use of fragrance in the workplace.
- Never use perfume to conceal bad odors. That's just not charitable to others.
- Where to place it? CoCo Chanel suggested putting it anywhere you want to be kissed. That's probably a good start. Avoid getting it on your clothing. Your neck and wrists are usually the best.
- You could also spray some perfume on your hairbrush to have it scent your hair.
- Pick your perfume according to your gut reaction and your fashion personality. You can also ask the people with whom you live how much they like it. (They are the ones who actually "experience" the scent.)
- While testing fragrances in a store, never test more than two or three as your nose can get confused and your brain can get discouraged.
- If you can, obtain some samples to see how you like it a few weeks later.
- Never spray perfume directly on to clothing and try to avoid getting any on jewelry, especially pearls.
- If you have overdone it with your scent, try dabbing some rubbing alcohol onto the area.
- Sure, change your perfume if you become bored with it, but if you absolutely love something, there's no reason to change. It could become a "signature scent" for you.

What dreadful hot weather we have! It keeps me in a continual state of inelegance.

JANE AUSTIN

- Check out the Fragrance Foundation's information. You can find them on the Internet. [3]

give me a hand please

Many wonderful stories have been told about the fancy lady who attempts to disguise herself as a commoner only to be given away by her elegant hands. These anecdotes reflect the fact that, in past eras, the upper class employed others to scrape their boots, boil their stews, and scrub their parlors. Hard-looking hands closed doors; soft ones opened them.

Fortunately, the hand-ethic-thing has changed. Don't get me wrong: soft and lovely hands are still valued greatly. It's just that even the well-heeled want to be hands-on in life, yet still keep them soft and young looking. Due to huge advances in hand care treatments, almost anyone can keep their hands graceful. We all just have to develop a few simple habits.

- Use hand lotion. Constantly. Morning and night is a good start, but you should place pumps of lotion by each of your sinks for everyone in the family.
- Wear latex or rubber gloves when you clean. I'm a total hypocrite here. I think I'm just impulsive about sticking my hands into things. My Granny-in-law once ceremoniously packaged up a few pairs for me and warned that it might not be *too* late to save my hands. I should have taken her advice, because it now may be too late!
- Do something with your nails. Either keep them short and clean or fashion them up with some polish (clear or color). A good habit to start is to gently push back your cuticles and file your nails just a little each night with your evening routine.

- If your polish is chipping, either repair the polish or remove it. Chipped polish is unsightly. (This is one of the reasons why I rarely polish my finger nails with color these days.)
- False nails are a nice short cut, but they can be expensive to maintain and will still break or fall off. Opt for shorter nails in a subtle color for a more professional appearance at work.
- Have only an hour to prepare for a special event? Try the drug store fakes. The glue is strong enough to get you through the event and weak enough to stay removable in the next few days. Just be sure to choose the right size fake for each of your nails.
- Nail art is one of those industries that exploded onto the scene during the economic boom of the 1990s. Beware of it. It is not a professional look, and in its wildest forms cheapens your appearance. If you have an expressive fashion personality and you are interested in adding a little glam to your hands, choose subtle themes for your personal time.

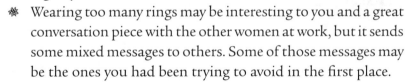

- A nice touch for hands is either a signature ring that flatters your hand or an interesting set of rings that you rotate according to your mood or the occasion.
- Wearing too many rings may be interesting to you and a great conversation piece with the other women at work, but it sends some mixed messages to others. Some of those messages may be the ones you had been trying to avoid in the first place.
- Keeping longer, polished nails will help elongate short fingers and will enable the hand to wear larger items of jewelry.
- A beautiful watch or a bracelet also adds elegance to hands. Choose them according to your fashion personality and the size of your hands. Women with large muscular hands and thick wrists should avoid jewelry that is either too large or too small. They should stick to medium sizes. Petite hands

and skinny wrists look best in small to medium sizes. Women with long fingers and naturally graceful hands can wear large or small items of jewelry.

do a do

Your hair (like your shoes) is so important for your style that it could ruin the beauty of an ensemble if it's radically out of date, unkempt, or unflattering. This is not to say that a bad hair day is always a bad style day. If you have the fundamentals set – like a really flattering and up-to-date haircut – then you will look spectacular even when your hair doesn't cooperate. Often, fashion consultants will develop relationships with really good hair stylists, and refer clients to these people as the need arises. A skilled stylist is the element of *this* style.

When I moved out to a Maryland suburb, I suddenly found myself in a position where I had to start from scratch. I not only had no relationships developed for the sake of the women who attend our services, but I had no clue as to where to get my own hair styled!

Once I calmed down and analyzed the situation, I decided to take my own advice: ask a woman with a really great do. I did, and I'm happy to say that I fell in love with my stylist. I use the same technique anytime I move.

Once you find a great stylist, remain loyal. Regularly schedule appointments and express your desires as your requirements change. (Sometime in January, I schedule a year's worth of appointments with my stylist because she is in such high demand.) A truly good stylist can work with your whims, so develop a relationship with this person in order to freely communicate these whims and have them tempered by good advice.

TIPS FOR GREAT HAIR

- Find a great stylist. Replace a stylist with another if you are not happy. Remember: you never signed a contract that binds you to her shears.
- Survey for styles. Look at other women, the television (especially news anchors), fashion magazines, and hair magazines. Be open-minded.
- Ask the stylist to show you how he or she is working with your hair. We often leave with a fantastic do, only to fail miserably in our own attempts to style with the next wash.
- Choose a style that suits your fashion personality.
- Choose a style that flatters your facial shape. (Just keep in mind the rules on strategies for creating the optical illusion of proportion.) How do you find your face shape? Stand in front of the mirror, pull back your hair, and trace the outline of the image of your face with a piece of soap.
    1. A pear-shaped face (larger mouth and jaw area, upper face is narrow) is flattered by a cut that has fullness at the top and less around the ears and neck. Width should be added to forehead and cheekbones.
    2. A heart-shaped face (pointed chin) is flattered by fullness around the jaw-line. A graduated bob with sweeping bangs and a side part is a nice option.
    3. A square-shaped face is best flattered by softer, layered styles. Curly styles can help soften the square.
    4. A short and round face is flattered by layered, sharper styles.
    5. A long face is flattered by shorter styles.
    6. An oval face can be flattered by most styles.

Why don't you get a haircut? You look like a chrysanthemum.

P. G. WODEHOUSE

- Use styling products that your stylist recommends. Don't invest a lot of money in experimentation.

FIVE TIMELESS HAIRSTYLES

These styles are always around and modified to meet current trends.

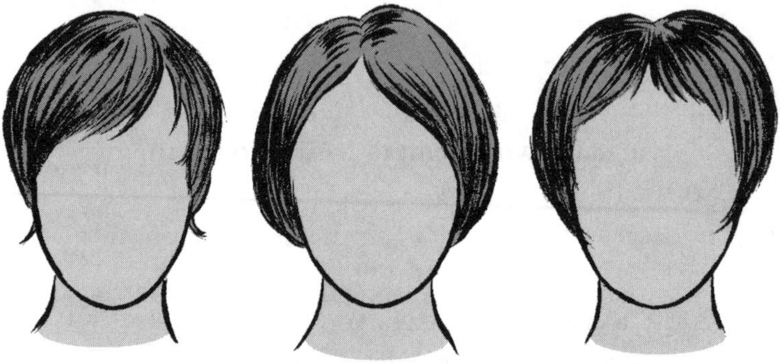

PIXIE — SHORT BOB WITH NO BANGS — SHORT BOB WITH BANGS

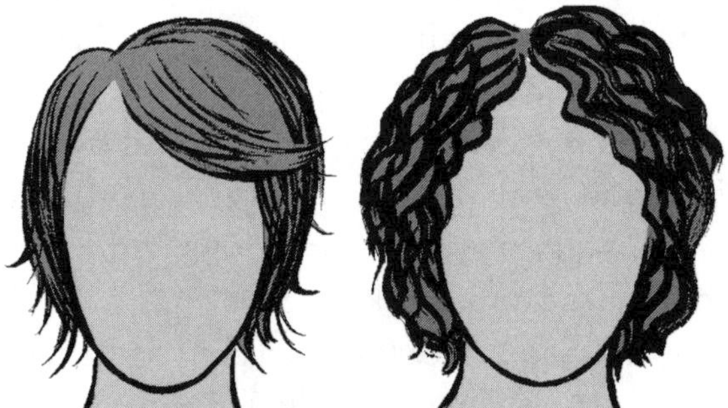

SHAG — CURLY

what a woman!

About two years into the life of our seminars, my colleagues and I decided to really polish up our main points on poise. Patti, who is one of these people to whom poise comes naturally (even with her very expressive fashion personality) would give presentations on how to give a really great job interview, how to introduce yourself to people, and how to conduct yourself in front of an audience.

Our seminar participants would be riveted. They couldn't get enough. Often, we thought we'd have a riot on our hands when we moved on to the next topic!

Years have passed, and we've found that the following tips are really the most important and the most effective.

she's got it together

- Maintain healthy posture. Keep your back straight and walk with your head held high.
- Avoid a sloppy silhouette. Keep your handbag neat and choose a strap length that allows the bag to swing above the hips. If you carry a briefcase, don't carry a purse. And, by all means, never carry accidental bags, such as plastic grocery bags, as substitutes for daily totes.
- Pay attention to the silhouette your overcoat creates. Go for clean, smooth lines. Stuffing pockets will add bulk to even the most streamlined of overcoats.
- When sitting, bend down and *slide* into the back of a chair.
- Sit with your knees together in some fashion.

Now when I bore people at a party, they think it's their fault.

HENRY KISSINGER

By way of illustrating the opposite of poise, and to make my point on the hard-to-describe quality of elegance, I must recall a scene from my early days with a technology company. In the midst of a heavy-duty business meeting, surrounded by hard hitting, image-crazy sales people, I pulled out my scheduling book and put it into the ready position. Suddenly, it was time to record an important date. Sure enough, tied to a piece of yarn secured to the metal ring of my book, my little yellow pencil presented itself in all its glory. "I'm so clever," I thought. But from the smirky smiles of my colleagues, I could tell that I had just made a major *faux pas*. (Now I carry a sleek electronic calendar.) My point: Strive to appear professional even in the smallest of things.

dear gentlest of readers

- While speaking, avoid touching your face with your hands.
- Eliminate crude gestures and hand signals.
- Avoid living with the cell phone or a set of headphones attached to your ear. Turn it off for important conversations, presentations, or shows.
- Establish eye contact with the person or persons with whom you are speaking.
- Practice a firm handshake with eye contact.
- Eliminate cussing. While in high school, I worked with a really tough kid who amazed me one day by admitting that he never cussed. Why? (Or "how" was really what I asked.) "Because cursing has no teeth. Everyone says them. I use originals" His "originals," as I found, were really obscure vocabulary words, probably from the SAT. He always got his point across!
- Think before you speak. Plan ahead. Slow down since you should continually think through what you are saying.
- Keep your breath fresh.
- If ever you chew gum, let no one catch on that you have it in your mouth. Avoid it altogether in a professional setting.

hi ho! it's off to work I go

how to make money, make friends, and influence people

After changing my life by knowing my style, dressing for work became a lot of fun. I really do revel in my wardrobe choices, and I never stress out about looking inappropriate. I know I look confident and capable, and my work reflects this.

John Malloy, the *Dress for Success* guru, claimed that women dress for failure. I can see that, even now. The difference now is that women *think* they are dressing for success, but make a lot of style decisions from years of bad habits and misconceptions. Many of these misconceptions are due to the fact that women don't have the long tradition of workplace wardrobe planning that men do – particularly at the higher corporate levels. Also, we get bad advice. Try this test: pick up a magazine (fashion or a woman's how-to) and find an article about creating a wardrobe for women's work wear. Note the styles. They tend to be inappropriate for all professional environments other than the fashion industry. Check the same magazine a month or two later: different wardrobe, similarly inappropriate items, and extra contradictory information.

Only God helps the badly dressed.

SPANISH SAYING

A serious fashion *faux pas* can actually repel people. Your choice of attire is your first decision in a work day and reflects your work ethic. No one wants to hang out with someone who appears to be unable to make competent professional decisions.

Now, try this test: look at the really successful women in your field or those women who are internationally known for their success (not their quirkiness). They not only make intelligent decisions about their wardrobes, but they incorporate a serious, professional ethic into their style. Here are some of the patterns of their behavior which you can use.

- Dress for your profession. Generally, law, business, and banking require the most conservative wardrobe choices. (The more money involved, the more conservative the suiting.) Engineering, art, architecture, education, and technology usually allow for wardrobes that consist of things other than suits. Geography determines tone as well. Take all this into account when planning.
- Know the dress code for your work environment. Many are unwritten, but you can play it safe with my tips for a business wardrobe on page 169.
- Don't try to compete with men in fashion. Wear suits and accessories designed for women. If you need help buying a suit, see page 278.
- Pay attention to your hands. Keep nails manicured. Use only subtle colors or no colors for finger nail polish.
- Fashion will come up as a topic at work. This is true even amongst the most serious professionals. Don't get tacky. Avoid discussing prices and, if you get a compliment for an outfit, say "thank you" without elaborating or faking modesty.

I matched my suit to my resume

Nothing tests your professional style like a job interview. While interviews are stressful for most people, women with style are often less stressed because one major aspect of the interview is part of their daily life anyway: polished style.

In regard to your total presentation, there are many details to attend to before an interview. First, understand not only the nature of the job, but the nature of the job setting. What is the dress code? (If there is one.) How do most people dress?

Think of the interview as a process that's more than the interview itself. Break it up into its before, during, and after stages. See the next *Style Profile* for details.

BEFORE THE INTERVIEW

- Find out if the job will require mostly business or mostly business casual attire. If the job requires business attire for even one day a month, choose a suit for the interview. If you decide that the job will be exclusively business casual, wear a higher level of business casual. For example, wear a skirt, white blouse, jacket, and medium heels.
- If you haven't a clue, ask people you know in similar positions or who are in the company. If you still don't know, wear a suit.
- Invest in a woman's briefcase. Choose a dark neutral that will go with your wardrobe.
- Invest in a leather portfolio. Fill it with clean paper, a calendar, and copies of your resume and references.
- Include two good metallic pens that work and don't leak.
- Invest in the perfect shoes. Go for a dark neutral (see below) and ensure that the shoes can be worn with your work wardrobe. Structured loafers go nicely with trousers. Pumps are best with skirts and pantsuits. Do not choose chunky heels or anything strappy. Also, be sure to choose a closed-toe shoe.
- Polish your shoes before the interview.
- Buy two pairs of neutral panty hose in case you get a run the morning of your interview.
- Check your trousers while you are wearing them in front of a full length mirror. Are there any panty lines? Do you need to cover yourself with a jacket? Be sure that it is a planned jacket and not an afterthought.
- Spend extra time refreshing your breath, but do not chew gum during the interview.
- Skip the perfume. Use a little bit of lotion or powder if you must. Don't forget the deodorant.

> ***What should work clothing symbolize? That the work is in the hands of responsible adults.***
>
> MISS MANNERS

- Remove any facial jewelry. Wear stud or small hoop earrings. Reduce the number of rings on your fingers and exchange loud bangles for a watch.
- Style your hair so that it doesn't distract either you or the interviewer. This is not a "big hair" day so if you have to, pull it back.
- Make sure your fingernails are cleaned and trimmed if not manicured and polished. Do not wear any nail art.

HOW TO CHOOSE A SUIT FOR AN INTERVIEW

- Remember your *elements of style.*
- Choose a dark neutral solid from your color palette: black, navy, charcoal gray, or dark brown.
- The buttons on the suit should be as dark or darker than the suit. (No metallic or novelty buttons)
- The lapel should be flat and unembellished.
- The shoulders should be structured with no exaggerated lines.
- The cut should be more conventional and less trendy.
- Try on the suit. The jacket sleeves should fall to the area between the nubby bone on your wrist and the beginning of your thumb. You should be able to move your arms with ease.
- The hem of your skirt should fall to just above, at, or just below your knees. The skirt should not cup your buttocks and the jacket should fall to a current length for suit jackets.
- Choose a white blouse (if you have cool undertones) or a cream blouse (if you have warm undertones) in a cotton or silk to go with your suit. The blouse should have no overwhelming embellishments and should not button or dip more than two inches below your collar bone.
- Choose hosiery to match your skin tone.

- Choose pumps with a one to two inch heel in either the same color as your suit, or a darker, neutral color. Make sure they are closed-toe.
- Coordinate your briefcase with your shoes.

STYLE PROFILE #19

twenty-four hours and counting: a checklist

About twenty-four hours before your interview you should conduct a countdown check. Twenty-four hours is a good point to do it because if you are missing something, you can find the information or get what you need.

- You know the time of the interview. (You better know this by Friday night!)
- You are arranging to arrive ten minutes before the interview.
- You know the address and have directions.
- The car functions and has gas.
- You know which bus to take and that it's running according to its regular schedule.
- You have childcare ready. You have emergency contact numbers ready for them.
- You have clean undergarments and a flesh-colored bra for under a light blouse
- Your suit or outfit is cleaned and pressed.
- The buttons are secure on the suit or outfit.
- Your appropriate shoes are polished.
- You have hosiery.
- You have a working watch.
- You packed a portfolio with extra copies of resume and references.

- You packed a portfolio with two good pens that don't leak.
- You packed a portfolio into your briefcase with directions and childcare numbers.
- Your nails are clean and trimmed.
- Your hands are moisturized.
- You have breath mints.
- You have chosen your jewelry.
- You have makeup.
- You have deodorant.
- You have your hair styling products ready.

DURING THE INTERVIEW

- Turn off your cell phone or pager or leave it in your car.
- Take a deep breath and smile.
- Provide a firm handshake with eye contact and a smile.
- Look for direction on where to be seated.
- Sit with your ankles crossed rather than crossing your legs.
- Sit up straight.
- Do not cross your arms or lean your face into your hands.
- Maintain eye contact.
- Answer questions honestly.
- Thank the interviewer for her or his time.
- Provide a parting firm handshake with eye contact.
- Smile!

AFTER THE INTERVIEW

- Breathe out.
- Jot down any necessary notes or dates, including experience notes.
- Hang up your suit. Dry clean it if necessary.
- Do necessary follow up.

STYLE PROFILE #20

Emma Lou's desk drawer emergency kit

All this talk about extra hosiery and breath mints makes me think of that life-saving measure the savviest of women keep in their workplaces: the *desk drawer emergency kit.* I remember a secretary I knew (her name was Emma Lou) who could supply anything at any time to anybody. That inspired me about as much as any genius in my field.

While you may not find latex gloves and burn ointment (as you would in Emma Lou's) you will undoubtedly use this kit often. It's simple to set up.

First, find a space in or around your desk that's discreet and at least the size of a shoe box. You could go out and buy a plastic case for this kit or simply convert a shoe box. Then, fill it with the following:

- breath mints
- extra hosiery
- tweezers
- lip balm

- facial wipes
- extra lipstick
- blush
- compact of translucent powder
- nail polish remover with a very reliable lid
- clear nail polish
- small, square neck scarf or a piece of jewelry for a special occasion
- deodorant
- hair spray or hair gel
- mirror
- aspirin
- liquid hand-cleaner
- lotion
- shoe polish wipes
- small bandages
- anti bacterial cream
- sanitary napkins or tampons
- emergency telephone numbers, especially for doctors and childcare.
- buttons, thread, needles
- safety pins

If you have a job that keeps you in the car a lot, be sure to store a kit there as well. Just don't put it in the glove compartment. This was my little trick once upon a time, but as I added things to my kit, I couldn't close the little door completely. That's a little embarrassing if you ever happen to drive your boss around. Trust me.

mom's in style

Motherhood brings with it so many challenges, not the least of which is the challenge for style. Moms who work outside of the home suffer from a severe lack of time and often can't get around to even *thinking* about a personal casual wardrobe, much less actually planning one. The challenge here is to pay some attention to at-home dressing by using all the strategies so faithfully followed for work time. Precious personal time deserves the same kind of care.

At-home moms face a challenge of a slightly different nature. Time is still a problem, but motivation is an even bigger one for many. The first time I went on maternity leave I just figured I'd slump it out in some old knits that would handle the little baby surprises of the day. No one was looking anyway, right?

By the time my second child had come, I had learned a lot about my style. This is one aspect of my life that changed dramatically. I realized that I had a lot more reason to have a great style. I simply dressed for the people I loved using the skills I had learned.

I continually remind myself that I am a walking mirror for everyone else in my family. I need to communicate to them how important and wonderful I think they are with my own appearance. Here are some personal-casual tips for any mom.

- Adhere to your *elements of style* especially when you are tempted to just settle for something.
- In working out a wardrobe plan, choose a combination personal casual and business casual wardrobe as you probably do get out now and then. (You tend to get out more often as your children get older.)
- Remember that your loved ones see you—and they see others. Your husband is at work surrounded by people who dress well (unless he works in a profession that prides itself on dressing badly). I had a client who realized that her husband, after

spending time in the office with a secretary who dressed to the nines, would come home to her totally scattered and sloppy appearance. She changed that as soon as she saw the implications. (Hey, a good marriage counselor would give the same advice!)

- Know that your time at home is part of your profession. Be professional in your dress.
- Avoid wearing cartoon characters or logos on your clothes. You are huggable and lovable in grown-up clothes as well.
- If you tend to spill things on your pants or if you find that you are always on the floor with paints and crayons, try a *spectrum* wardrobe that uses dark neutral colors in washable fabrics for your bottoms.
- Wear washable tops as well. Buy your tops in your most flattering colors. You do not have to wear muddy colors like those tired looking people in the playgroup.
- Wear an over-sized apron for heavy duty cooking or cleaning in your best color or dark neutral. What's fun is that children notice and remember these things.
- Throw on a charming neckline accessory for a bit of variety around your face. (If it suits your fashion personality.)
- Update when necessary. Check out fashion magazines or catalogues from time to time.
- Wear earrings. Babies can't pull studs out. (I wear my hoops around my babies anyway.)
- Wear makeup. Keep your makeup routine to five minutes.
- Gotta run out quick? Keep a pair of great shoes and a nice jacket or blazer by the door.
- Diaper wipes are good for more than just baby's backside! Use them to spot clean a shoe between polishes. This is especially handy if you are running out the door and you plunk formula on your boot.

- Stash lipstick and compacts around the house for quick touch ups before loved-ones come in.
- Get a really fantastic, *no-fuss* haircut.
- Stay healthy and vibrant and fun. Youthfulness does wonders for attitude; attitude does wonders for style.

SEMINAR FAQ

get with the times

QUESTION: I sort of get your point about being polished in general, but why do you advocate such conventional ideas? In our pluralistic society, isn't there room for breaking the old rules?

ANSWER: Many of the old rules have been broken. That really hasn't helped anyone. There is probably a lot more angst over what to wear for a wedding than there ever has been before. And how, pray tell, do you dress for an event that is billed "semi-formal"? Standards need to stick around to serve as a common language for smoother communication in a pluralistic society. So having manicured hands, placing your napkin in your lap, or saying "please" and "thank you" each serve as a baseline for civility. No one is guessing what to do next and everyone sees that you can keep yourself clean (manicured hands), anticipate the worst (napkin on your lap), and appreciate the effort of others (*please* and *thank you*). Sure, there may be other ways to communicate these things, but if the other way is an obscure one from Silicon Valley, no one is going to understand you. Being understood and respected is critical for success.

> We know from working with Success In Style clients that it's easy for people who have a lot to take it all for granted. Our clients (who are people without much) know they need a little poise and polish to get any where in this world. They have wisdom from the university of experience.

in style and in season

I've always suspected that women love fashion and homemaking magazines because features include both practical and timely information. You've read a lot of practical stuff in this chapter, but now let's focus on *timely*.

So many aspects of our style are related to the season in which we find ourselves. I'm often amazed at how much my self-image can vary from one season to the next. Much of this is due to the different kinds of demands that weather and climate can make on style.

Below is a checklist for both winter and summer. Scan it at the beginning of any season and enjoy how it cleans up your style. One very nice part of this ritual is completed at the end of the preceding season. Try this: While storing away clothes (only the ones you have actually worn!) write a note for yourself that lists suggestions and feelings about the wardrobe. You might write:

> "This winter wardrobe has way too much black in it; got really sick of it by February!"
>
> "Need a new purse."
>
> "Could use a couple new flesh-tone bras for all these white tops."
>
> "The grocery store had the lowest price on my moisturizer with sun block."
>
> "Could really use a hat for the pool."

"Need a button replaced on the pink and white sweater."
"I think a twin set would really complete this wardrobe."

Place the note with the clothes you will be taking out next year. It's kind of like a fashion time capsule.

planning for winter

- Read your note from last winter.
- Check all coats for wear and tear. Be sure to keep both a casual and dress coat. Repair or replace if necessary. See page 281 if you need to buy one.
- Check sweaters that have been in storage for unpleasant odors, pilling, and moth damage. Repair where necessary or discard anything that has been damaged too much.
- Check every shoe and boot in your wardrobe. Polish anything that needs it.

> *For everything there is a season, and a time for everything under heaven.*
>
> ECCLESIASTES

- Inventory hosiery, particularly the opaque or wool stockings. Replenish supply if necessary.
- Check that you are supplied with a coordinating hat, gloves, and scarf set for each coat.
- Place hand cream bottles at each sink.
- Invest in a really effective moisturizer for both face and body.
- If you tend to get pale in the winter, check that makeup colors are appropriate and replace if and where necessary. This is especially true for lipstick and foundation.
- Buy moisturizing conditioner for hair if static and harsh furnace heat is an issue.
- Check up on your hairstyle.
- At the end of the season, clean everything you own and store them in a clean and dry place (other than the attic or basement). Use cedar balls or blocks rather than moth balls for wool items.

planning for summer

- Read your note from last summer.
- Take inventory of your entire summer wardrobe. Use the *Style Planner* to ensure that the wardrobe works for you.
- Pull out your swimsuit and inspect. Hold it to the same standards as anything else. Spend time on this item and pay attention to all three *elements of style* when making a decision. (See tips for your body type when choosing one.)
- Get a coordinating wrap, beach bag, and towel for whatever swim suit you plan to use.
- Get a pedicure. Keep feet moisturized and scale-free. (This is a must if you wear sandals.)
- When washing feet, scrub with a buff pad instead of simply letting the water run over them.
- Check out each pair of shoes and sandals in this wardrobe. Sandals tend to wear badly but can be replaced inexpensively (relative to winter shoes). Replace if you can't repair.
- Inspect your shorts. Are they worn? Do they fit? Is it time to forget about wearing shorts? Make plans to replace them if your wardrobe plan calls for it.
- Inspect your summer purse. Clean out the one in storage if you plan on using that one. Organize everything in it for the lifestyle you have in the summer.
- Buy moisturizer with sun block.
- Buy sun block for the rest of you.
- If you do tan, buy makeup a shade or two darker as your skin darkens.
- Ease up on perfume use because it can overwhelm others in the summer heat. Stay well-stocked with deodorant.
- Ensure that your hairstyle is comfortable and workable in the heat.
- Make a plan for increasing your water intake.

I don't need to give out that kind of information

I once asked a class of inner-city high-school girls why you shouldn't sit with your legs spread. One girl chimed, "Because I don't need to give out that kind of information."

That's it. People don't need to see a private area of your body. But I would also add that a woman should be careful not to give out the wrong information about who she is and what she is trying to say about herself.

This is how poise comes together for a woman. It's the *tone* of voice in the language of fashion.

STYLE PROFILE #21
power fluctuations

So, how is your poise? Reviewing this chapter's ideas, reflect upon the strengths of your style. How could it be enhanced? What are your strong points for poise? How could you use poise to express your personality? In what areas could you improve? Write an action plan below. Pick maybe just a few, concrete things to change over the next week. Come back to this section a few weeks later and try again.

CHAPTER TEN

your gift of style

better than a million bucks

There are two types of women in the world: Those who pick up this book and read it through for their personal fashion enhancement; and, those who pick up this book, ignore the first nine chapters, and flip to this section with the objective of telling others how to pick their personal fashion.

If you are the latter type, read through everything up to this point and *then* read this section. You cannot share any ideas on personal fashion until your own style is developed and you have credibility.

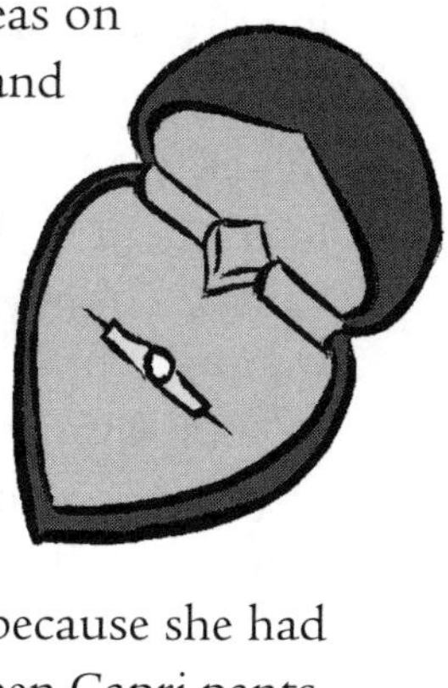

If, on the other hand, you have finished every *Style Profile* and you've faced all the *Fashion Moments of Truth*, you are now equipped to help others learn about the relationship between fashion and personal style. You know what it means to have successful style and you now have credibility.

My mother had credibility with her daughters because she had great personal style. I remember her stylish mint-green Capri pants, little woven handbag, and sassy bob hairstyle. She was so sharp. My friends thought she was very beautiful, and I did too. I loved to tell people that she was my mother.

My first fashion incident with her was when I was in Miss Riener's kindergarten. A girl in my class had a pink suede skirt and a pair of white lace-up go-go boots with two-inch heels.

I was hooked. I thought I would die without this exact same outfit. I distinctly remember begging my mother for these things, explaining that I would be a really good girl while wearing them.

Love is a great beautifier.

LOUISA MAY ALCOTT

My mother bought me a similar skirt, but she said no to the boots. "They're too old for a five-year-old girl," she explained, and I decided that she knew best.

A little later on, while in high school, I bought my own clothing and often asked my mother's opinion of an ensemble or two. I thought my mother had fashion sense, because, after all, who else's mother, after having ten children, could still wear a little black sheath and a pair of stiletto pumps?

Alas, time passed on, the designer jeans hit the scene. I knew what my mother would say to that: "Too tight and immodest. You'll look like a floozie."

So, I took great care to hide my jeans by wearing a coat and leaving the house as quickly as possible. Of course, I knew my jeans were too tight and very immodest. I knew that I was an idiot for blindly following my girlfriends. I simply thought that if they were going to make a pair of jeans look sexy, I would do a better job at it no matter what the cost. Perhaps other girls were less competitive and only wanted to fit in (talk about *fitting* in!), but all of us were unbelievably tolerant with that tight and pinchy feeling.

Then, one day during my sophomore year, my mother saw my rear end fully labeled with Jordache. "Get your backside in this house now and find something more appropriate," she hollered. I argued. I screamed. I even stormed away. I have no recollection whether or when I actually obeyed her, but in a way I was relieved that she was on to me.

Her objections did sink in, however, and I was appropriately embarrassed even if I didn't let on to it. Later on, in my twenties and long after Jordache faded away, I chose my fashion with the "floozie factor" in mind. (I knew that my fashion talks, and the last thing I needed it to say was "floozie.")

Now, *that's* a gift.

I want to help you pass on this gift and many others to the young women in your life. In my work as a fashion consultant, I get asked to work with teens on a continual basis. If I wanted, I could start a business just for the daughters of stressed-out mothers and make a heap of money. It seems as if for every one or two services I provide to middle-age women, I get at least one plea to work with the corresponding teens.

While I have never had a problem with heaps of money, I feel strongly that many of the extremes of adolescent fashion could be prevented early on. Note that I said *many* not *all*. As just about everyone knows, we don't have control over everything or everyone – especially adolescents.

I have three daughters, and I can only hope that I am communicating all of the positive things my mother so elegantly communicated to me. I feel so strongly about this that I want to share some practical ideas with other moms, grandmothers, aunts, friends, teachers, and older sisters on imparting a sense of personal style to the important young women in their lives. This chapter isn't necessarily just for moms (for convenience sake I use the words "mom" and "daughter"). It's for any woman who has a young girl in her life. In the long run, it will even help the boys too.

OBJECTIVE: learn how to foster the personal style of your daughter.

if I lock her up, I won't have to read the rest of this chapter

When you work with children, especially girls, you tend to develop your own slate of policies and ponderings in ways that would make a political think tank wish they had hired you. This can be a good thing if your theories are on the money. On the other hand, you could really cause headaches if you are wrong. Let's begin by dispelling some myths about girls.

myth #1: if you are both looking at the color red, you both see the color red.

FACT #1: If you are both looking at the color red, you see *stop sign* red and she sees *candy apple* red. For a short time during early adolescence, the red part may even be up for grabs. In other words, you cannot take anything for granted. You each have sensitivities which are the products of your own times, trends, and modes of thinking.

Once when I was in a Marshall Fields inspecting a display of plastic "bustier" handbags, a mother-daughter pair paused and carried on this little exchange in earshot:

"Look Mom! A purse in the shape of a shirt."

"That's not a shirt, dear; that's a bra."

"No, it's not a bra. It's a shirt. Don't you know *anything*?"

It was almost poetic. Her mother and I may have recognized the betrayed intimacy of the little novelty purse, (technically a bustier is neither a bra nor a shirt; it's its own kind of undergarment) but the teenage daughter had long become accustomed to these things as outerwear thanks to the likes of Vivienne Westwood, Jean Paul Gaultier, and others. To be fair, this gal was born *after* Madonna's "Blond Ambition" tour (1990).

Rather than becoming wholly flabbergasted by our daughter's declarations, it's best to keep our cool, clarify during the teachable moments, and always be willing to discuss appropriateness. When she's off seeing yellow in the sight of red, keep the light on for her; she will come back to you eventually.

Some helpful tips for seeing eye to eye (or at least some damage control):

- Experience what she experiences. Be there for her. Talk to her. Talk to her friends. Observe what they observe.
- Check out the section of the bookstore designed just for her age group. Note what the publishers know about the age group. They make money with this knowledge.
- Read what she reads. Discuss it with her.
- Check out the top retailers for her age group. Watch how they market their wares. Walk into their stores. (That'll get you going!)
- Watch what she watches on television – and then some. (It might reinforce the notion that you should set limits on entertainment!)
- Listen to her music. Listen to the lyrics.
- Even check out her school books. Note the layout.
- Check out her favorite websites. Then, check out other websites that are targeted to her age group. Note the content, the "voice" of the text, and the layout.
- Read her blog. Check to see what she's been doing online.
- Have her experience your world only when it is appropriate. (In other words, don't pull her in as your confidant; that's not appropriate.) Invite her to see the cultural things you enjoy. True, this is a one-sided experience because you as an adult are more willing to put up with her interests than she is to put up with yours. That's okay. Work with the little you have.
- Share with her one of your favorite books from high school and a favorite movie from childhood. Talk about them.
- Encourage Dad to do all of the above. Then, have him go through the next *Style Profile* with you.

STYLE PROFILE #22

everything about her

How well do you know your daughter (or sister, niece, granddaughter)?

Try answering the following questions. If you don't know an answer, make it a point to find out.

Her favorite color: ______________________________

Her favorite color to wear: ______________________________

Words she uses to describe her style: ______________________________

____

Words she uses to describe your style: ______________________________

____

Her favorite subject at school: ______________________________

She passionately believes in: ______________________________

____

Her favorite teacher: ______________________________

If she had a month off from everything she would want to:

____

____

Her favorite singer or band: ______________________________

Her favorite movie: ______________________________

Her favorite television show: ____________________

The names of three of her best friends: ____________________

____

myth #2: there's no harm in letting her have fun with wild teenage fashions – after all, she has the cute little body for it.

FACT #2: Let her have fun in healthy ways. In fashion that means color and theme. Cute little body or not, it's a body which belongs to someone with awesome dignity. (She's not a plate on which you're served humor or given a second chance at youth.) She does not have less of a right to respectful clothing than you do. If anything, she has *more* rights because of her vulnerability. This includes the right to be properly influenced by the adult in charge in ways that will inspire her to choose better clothing.

Remember, it's your duty to establish rules. Often, she craves rules because she knows that she needs them for her own protection.

Some helpful tips for encouraging fun with fashion:

- Reflect upon your attitude toward her fashion. Have you been permissive because you think it's cute or fun? Are you trying to live vicariously through her? I know, these are deep questions, but you have to correct your intentions if they are inappropriate.
- On the other hand, have you been completely intolerant of her tastes? You may be over-reacting because you know how bad you were with fashion. True, learn from your mistakes, but don't beat her up with your regrets. Let her know the areas that are acceptable for self-expression and fun.

- The areas which are acceptable for self-expression and fun? Color, theme, accessories, makeup, and even hair are all great palettes for self expression. Always, however, teach her to keep her focal point on her face. This starts at a very young age.
- Allow her to dress appropriately for her age group. Set your line of demarcation between acceptable and unacceptable clearly and explain *why*. See below.
- As always, discourage her from blindly following the trends of her peers. Point out her unique characteristics and affirm her dignity.

STYLE PROFILE #23
flashback

Name the one fashion item you really, really wanted in high school. What fueled your desire for this thing? Did you get it? Did it meet your expectations?

____
____
____
____

myth #3: she will think you are an idiot no matter what you say or how you dress.

FACT #3: Sure, she thinks you are an idiot sometimes. But it is possible to inspire her in the area of fashion (and in the other areas). This means your own fashion, not fashion for her age group. Inspiration is up to you.

Some helpful tips for inspiring your daughter:

- Know *your* style. Dress your best. Be elegant as a woman, not as a girl-wannabe.
- Laugh. Have a good sense of humor about all things fashion, especially your own fashion.
- Let her see your successes with your style. Let her see how fashion fits *your* life.

myth #4: if you send her to boarding school in Greenland, she will turn out fine.

FACT #4: You don't have to hide her to help her, but you do have to teach her the art of discernment. We live in a society that is saturated not just with sexual innuendo, but with sexual scenery. To spring it all upon her suddenly, without ever providing any explanation, is unfair to her and to everyone with whom she comes in contact.

Fashion is a particularly difficult area because current styles are, in the very least, so radically different from our own teen styles. Flesh is like the fabric of the times and fits right in with the scenery.

Feminist writer Joan Jacobs Brumberg agrees that things really have changed, but not necessarily for the better: "Life in the world of the micro bikini is obviously different from life in the world of the corset . . . but there are still constraints and difficulties, perhaps even greater ones."[1] So, girls may not be constricting their abdomens, but they are obsessing about their weight, their "bikini lines," and the perkiness of their breasts. That's really not progress, is it?

Keeping a code of modesty is a way of protecting a young body from unwanted attention. Without making her feel ashamed of her body, you need to teach her how to dress it with style and safety.

ANNA JOHNSON

In the face of all this, my mother had this very special way of editorializing through entire movies and while walking through the mall. As kids, we would become frustrated because it seemed like she was ruining the fun with her "that skirt is too short . . . he shouldn't touch her there . . . she walks like a floozie . . ." (We were also really embarrassed and knew she was right.) What she successfully did, however, was to make an impression on us.

The way you help her to discern is determined by your personality and communication style. (You may not be a narrator or social commentator, but you can do what comes to you naturally.) The critical factor is to keep that line of communication wide open. Talk with your daughter. Let her talk to you. Listen to her. Respond to her. Show her that you love her far more than anyone looking at her breasts or rear end. Encourage your husband to express his love for her as well and to tell her that she is beautiful. This introduces a whole new area for explanation. It's fundamental.

> *Diamonds are polished with diamonds and souls with souls.*
>
> ST. JOSEMARIA ESCRIVA

her life, her love, and her lipstick

We have dispelled a few myths, but that's just setting the stage. There are some very specific things you can do to help your daughter develop the three qualities you ultimately want her to have as an adult:

1. **AN UNDERSTANDING OF WHO SHE IS.** Remember chapter one? She has a dignity as a woman. So, her body is valuable and her sexuality is sacred.
2. **THE SKILL OF DISCERNMENT IN ALL THINGS FASHION.** She should be able to recognize the difference between appropriate and inappropriate fashion by using the standards of dignity and modesty.
3. **A FIRM SENSE OF PERSONAL STYLE.** She should see fashion as an art form and language and not as a chore. She should also be able to cultivate creativity, professionalism, and elegance into her look.

That little list may seem about as difficult as ensuring that your drooling toddler gets into Harvard one day. Fortunately, there is no comparison. Achieving these requires no genius, fanatical drive, or multiple savings accounts. All girls are capable of achieving these because they are intrinsic to all of us.

Indeed, it is a matter of justice to help girls toward these goals. Every single woman, no matter who she is, where she lives, the language she speaks, or the color of her skin, has the right to know the truth about her body.

an ounce of prevention is a pound of cure

As a teacher, I always like to see things laid out in a curriculum. That's a bit trite for our purposes, although I can't help but approximate one because, as with all things in child development, growth comes in stages. Growth in a sense of personal style has its own stages as well. Let's begin with the early years (age two until the beginning of adolescence).

An understanding of who she is (early years):

- Teach her that people are more important than things. That way she'll know what you mean later on when you say that her body is *not* an object.
- Use language with her that respects her body. I've known women who absolutely refused to use "bathroom" language with their children because it lacks respect. Refer to her body as a *gift* that needs to be taken care of like any of the most precious gifts. Sleep, food, and hygiene are properly justified with that rationale.
- As a child learns that her body is a special gift, she should also learn that the outer beauty reflects her inner beauty. True

beauty does lie inside, but it's wonderful when we take it outside as well.

- Affirm her innate sense of privacy. Make it a habit to close the bathroom door and train her to do this as well. Encourage her to wear a bathrobe instead of a towel.
- In keeping with the above, sensitize her to the concept of modesty. Show her that her sexuality is beautiful, sacred, and not something to take for granted. Also, begin this at an early age by avoiding ensemble and swimsuit choices that you wouldn't want her to choose when she has a fully developed body. For example, it's hard to adopt a no-bikini rule if she's been wearing one since she was two. (Hard, but not impossible.)
- Be on guard for how you "entitle" her with sayings on her t-shirt. If you caption her face with "goddess," "spoiled princess," "brat," or "dirty little diva," you may end up with a goddess, spoiled princess, brat, or dirty little diva.
- Compare her body to a miracle that can do a great number of amazing things: walk, run, climb, dance, work, etc. This is opposed to the idea of the body as something to put on display or on which one simply hangs clothing. Food intake should be mentioned in terms of how it energizes the body and helps to keep it working for her. Be on guard against how your own food neuroses are communicated to her, and change your vocabulary where needed.
- Encourage moderation in eating. Always refer to health rather than beauty while discussing food intake, exercise, or sleep. So, rather than saying, "You've got to get your beauty sleep," say instead, "Let's get some sleep so that we have energy in the morning."
- As her body develops, do not give her your latest critiques. Listen to her as she tells you about the changes and assure her that what she experiences is normal and purposeful.

The skill of discernment toward all things fashion (early years):

- Give guidelines for fashion choices based upon standards of modesty and appropriateness. These guidelines are often translated into boundaries or rules, depending upon her age. Don't be scared to say "no," but always give a reason. Generally, girls respond to the idea of the face as a focal point in fashion.

Everybody's fancy.
Everybody's fine.
Your body's fancy
and so is mine.

FRED ROGERS

- Choose retailers according to the success you both have had in the past. Using catalogues is very helpful at times because you can actually discuss what's on the pages in a private and even cozy setting. She may be more apt to tell you why she likes or dislikes something.
- Sensitize her to differences in taste. Not everyone likes the same thing. Not everyone looks great in the same thing. This may ease some of that adolescent herd mentality that she'll face later on.

A firm sense of personal style (early years):

- Sensitize her to beauty. Point out the variety of colors and breathtaking detail in nature, art, crafts, and fashion. An education in what is truly beautiful is a special gift for life.
- Talk about styles with her. Ascertain what she likes and dislikes. Engage her in conversation about very specific new fashions that appear each season.
- Rather than choosing for her, and certainly rather than offering her the full market of choices, allow her to choose from two to four acceptable options. Be sure that they are truly options and not just variations on a theme.
- When possible, give her freedom in color choices. Teach her about her color palette as she grows.

- Affirm her style by using adjectives to describe it: pretty, fun, soft, flowery, etc.
- Begin shopping with her at an early age to establish a rapport in the dressing room. I remember when my daughter was seven and helping me to decide on a top for me, she declared proudly, "This one has plenty of growing room, Mom!" I loved it. And I especially loved the laughter from the other women in the store.
- Show her that fashion is an art form and not a chore. Avoid complaining that you have to change your blouse because you have a guest coming over, or saying that you'll have to "give in" to some lipstick before going off to work. Revel in those lipstick colors and enjoy the refreshment of a changed outfit.
- Explain your reasons for your fashion choices. Model your justifications: "That's my best color," or, "These vertical lines are good for my body type."
- Explain your reasons for your fashion suggestions for her. Say, "This color really flatters your face," or "You'll be able to wear this with those pants we bought."
- Show her by example and by your purchases for her that less is more; less is better. This will help her distinguish between *needs* and *wants*. Use the money you save on higher quality items.

her style; not mom's

As a fashion professional, I found it not only easy but exciting to recognize, affirm, and even encourage the styles of other women. As a mother, I find that anything which isn't of my own tastes immediately suspect. Their music is tacky to me, their decorating ideas are a little too schmaltzy, and their clothing is, well, let's just say *interesting* at times.

Fostering a sense of style in your children, particularly your daughters, means recognizing, affirming, and even encouraging what passes for style or taste – *theirs*. But it also means gently guiding them away from things that are, shall we say, the learning curves of style education: for example, dirt, grime, stains, after-market coloring (with markers and paint usually), excessive glitter (that's *excessive* glitter), extreme mismatching, and what I like to call Barbie-esque fashion.

When my daughter was six, we spent most of the spring and summer battling over when to wear all those pretty dresses I had bought over the winter with fantasies of care-free scenes amongst the wild flowers, rabbits, and other little girls in the same kind of dress. I was practically tearing my hair out because she didn't like them and wasn't willing to ever wear *any* of them. It always came to a head on a Sunday morning, so I have to admit that I had some pretty rough weekends for a while.

I was pleasantly surprised to find out, however, that the issue was not simply a rejection of dresses *per se*, but her disdain for dresses with empire-style waistlines. Every darling little dress I had bought her was an empire style! She simply – and quite unexpectedly – explained that she much preferred the waistband around her waist. What a moment of revelation for me! Case closed. Problem solved. We moved on. (Now, we are tackling the jean thing.)

I have a friend in Los Angeles who is a classic with a flair for pretension, and she encouraged her daughters to subscribe to her classic tendencies. Once, while she was visiting me in Washington, she described her philosophy of fashion to me:

"I would die if my daughter wanted to wear purple! Butterflies? No way! No tackiness in my house."

"So, do your girls like being preppy?" I asked.

"I don't care," she answered. They're going to grow up and be classics."

Poor things. I never got the memo that purple is verboten. My guess is that if the girls can't assert their fashion personality and their style through color and innocent themes, they will find other, less acceptable ways to do so.

The most effective kind of education is that a child should play amongst lovely things.

PLATO

Style means choice. As I was growing up, the choices were simply the color and print variations contained on the pages of the *Sears* catalogue. Sometimes, that's enough for the very youngest girls. It seemed to be enough for me.

I do remember one visit to a department store to find a new winter coat. My mother immediately chose a red wool coat with gold buttons (that preppy thing again). In response, I held up a blue coat with silver buttons.

She argued with me. I cried.

Finally, my mother gave in to the blue coat, but only after my rainfall of tears. Why the tears? After all, red is in my color palette. In fact, I'd love to have a red coat now!

This incident was simply early evidence of my emerging sense of style. To me, red was forward, noticeable, and kind of ugly. I pictured myself walking around like a stop sign, cars braking suddenly as they neared me. The blue coat, on the other hand, was calm, conventional and pretty.

This is not to say that mothers should just give into children's shopping whims. Rather, all parents should dig around a little to find out what a child's tastes are in appropriate areas of fashion. Young girls need to learn the skill of designing personal style using personal taste so that they can do it at a later age with success. You must allow them to articulate this and it may involve cultivating their vocabulary for style: *flatter, optimize, accentuate, de-emphasize, focal point, fit, appropriate, inappropriate, coordinate, match, accessorize, harmonize, and style.* Save the furrowed brow for more serious issues such as modesty and appropriateness.

what to do about Barbie (and things of that nature)

I played with Barbie. In fact, I played with her a lot. I'm guessing that it didn't produce any harmful side effects, but I know she made her impression. Of course, my mother narrated her way through the Barbie years with "No one has legs like that" or "Her blouse is too tight," so the effects may have been cancelled out. No matter what Mom said, I thoroughly enjoyed those hours alone with my "Quick Curl" Barbie (1972), my bright yellow Barbie "Country Camper" (1972), and my Barbie "Town House" with moving elevator (1974). My mother never allowed Ken: "I don't know why *he* needs to be in the picture!" and I figured she knew best. (I found out much later that my mother never allowed my little sister Liz to own a Barbie.)

When I was a young adult, Barbie generally annoyed me. It's not like I ever joined the Barbie Liberation Organization (yes, a real group), but I always expressed my reservations when given the chance. Long before I was married I declared that whatever girls I had "would never play with such a stereotypical toy as Barbie," but I never had the chance to institute the policy. As soon as I gave birth to my first girl, the gifts which poured in included a Cinderella Barbie.

Barbie as a doll does pose some interesting challenges for our parenting. Her body is so very perfect (unreasonably so at 38-18-36 if she were a real woman). How do you ward off your little girl's comparisons with her own body? How do you teach that inner beauty is more important than outer beauty? And how do you explain that goodness, intelligence, and talent are important for a woman? Some moms recommend simply talking about it. Others have suggested even laughing at it all. One friend of mine played Barbie "going to physics class," or "arguing a case in court," or "caring for homeless children." To be fair, Mattel, the doll's maker, provides many accessories to accommodate that kind of play.

True, many girls never compare their bodies to Barbie's. This is probably because they are three and four years old. It might also be true that if a girl's relationship with her mother is very strong, she will more likely see her mother as the prototypical female form, thus developing a reasonable set of expectations for her own body. A comparison may become a ridiculous proposition to her.

Also, because Barbie's body so perfectly approximates the female form (even if it is dramatically idealized), it needs to be treated with a bit of dignity. How many times has a naked Barbie body fallen down the staircase or stuck out from under a couch? Even though she's just a toy, she is a *representation* of something which is actually rather sacred: a woman's body. I'd love to hot glue some undergarments to her because I can't help becoming disturbed when I see her in such a state. If indeed your daughter doesn't take notice of these things, think of what your son might be thinking. That may place it into perspective.

Barbie's fashion can be even more problematic. You may be telling her not to dress like a tart with your words, but you are buying clothes for her Barbie that all three of you know would never be allowed on those in the household who breathe. I've seen hot pants, micro miniskirts, bikinis, and fashions which inspired my brothers to call her "Hooker Barbie." (Oh, yes, I have had the interesting cultural experience of sharing a home with both Barbie and seven brothers . . . and a dog who loved to chew plastic things.)

This isn't the only world of Barbie. Happily, there are some gorgeous fashions for this kid. You might have to search a little, but a good guideline for Barbie is to dress her the way you would like to see your own little girl dressed. Barbie is a fashion tool. You can use words like *design*, *coordinate*, or *accessorize* to expand your daughter's fashion skills, and you can laugh heartily when Barbie pulls off a major fashion mistake. (Laughing at your daughter when she makes her mistakes is probably not as pleasant an experience.) Always use Barbie to your advantage.

There are many urban legends surrounding Barbie's origins, so in the interest of setting the record straight, let's go through some basic Barbie facts.[2]

- Barbie was introduced in 1959 at the Toy Fair in New York City by Elliot and Ruth Handler. Elliott Handler was a co-founder of Mattel.
- Barbie was the creation of Ruth Handler. The idea of a doll with womanly proportions had intrigued her, but she couldn't make clear what she wanted until she got a hold of the *Bild Lilli Doll*, modeled after a character with a sleazy reputation in a comic strip written by Reinhard Beuthien for the newspaper, *Bild-Zeitung* in Hamburg, Germany. The doll was marketed to men in tobacco shops. (This isn't such a great start for Barbie now, is it?)

- The conspiracy theories revolve around the true sentiments of Mrs. Handler's original vision, and it doesn't help that she had changed her account of the sequence of events a few times throughout the years.
- Just like the *Bild Lilli*, the very first Barbie had a coy side-ways glance and wore harsh red lipstick and a striped, strapless bathing suit. I'd wager that the typical 1959 parent recoiled in an act of decency, but bought her to please their wide-eyed little girls. Eventually, Mattel molded Barbie into a wholesome, American-style version, more suitable for child's play. (Ruth Handler's daughter's name was Barbara, nicknamed, *Barbie*.)
- Ken was introduced in 1961 and was named after the Handlers' son. He stuck around successfully, except for a few years

during the Vietnam War, when no one wanted to have to explain his whereabouts. (Yes, these are just dolls.)

- Just in case you are wondering, yes, the Barbie Liberation Organization really does exist. It is famous for replacing the prerecorded words "Math class is tough" of Teen Talk Barbie with "Vengeance is mine," in three-hundred dolls in 1989.
- Traditionally, feminist writings have condemned Barbie. Now they praise her for her independence and unabashed sexuality.
- Over the past forty years, over one billion Barbie dolls have been sold across the planet.[3]

What to make of the data? Well, for starters, if your daughter shows no interest in Barbie, don't force the issue. These girls get along fine without her. If and when your daughter does acquire a doll (or plays with her cousin's), use Barbie for what she does so well. Reinvent her into an image that is acceptable to you, and teach the basics of fashion. She is, after all, only a doll.

mom as ally and not as evil empire

Those blissful years of free-wheeling fashion moments finally become strained as your sweet little child becomes a teenager. It happens just as your fashion conversations become mutually productive.

Well, it's time to adapt the strategies to meet the needs of a more experienced, more questioning, and more emotional being. This is no time to turn your back or throw in the towel. Way down, deep inside her, issues are bubbling up like lava through a fissure. She suddenly sees "problems" with her appearance that are both there and *not* there. You may have been spending the last twenty years trying to forget about your own teenage years, so in the interest of jogging your memory, here are just a few of the things on her mind.

1. Her skin: "It doesn't look smooth and silky like the girl on the Noxema commercial. It looks like mushroom pizza."
2. Her hair: "It's the ugliest, most embarrassing thing in the school."
3. Her eyebrows: "They're raccoon tails."
4. Her teeth: "They're yellow, and one sticks out."
5. Her breasts: "Where are they?" For others, it's "Why do they do that?"
6. Her tummy: The dough boy's got nothing on me!"
7. Her bottom: "Why did I eat that brownie?"
8. Her feet: "My big toe is in the next zip code!"

With so much on their minds, it's a miracle that anyone ever makes it into advanced placement history.

Of course, all girls are different. Once in a while, I'll meet a sixteen-year-old who just rolls her eyes at the absurdity of obsessing over things that are going to change anyway. Most often, however, girls will cultivate their pet flaws, creating an entire subculture around them: specialized vocabulary, body language, poetry and prose, dietary restrictions, compensation techniques, and seemingly unreasonable styles (unreasonable, that is, unless you know what the pet flaw is).

It is my hope that by feeling confident with your physical looks, you'll develop the inner self assurance to do whatever it is you are most driven to do.

BOBBI BROWN

We could spend hours caught up into the awe of it all, but not only will it not go away overnight, it will be fueled by the pressures that surround her: peers, school, fashion and cosmetics advertising, television, cinema, music, dance, and even (sorry to say) the mothers and fathers of some of her friends. In many ways, your home might be the only safe haven from the bombardments of pressures "to get the perfect body and reject the very imperfect one you have now."

Admittedly, my oldest daughter is only beginning this stage. So I've talked to literally dozens of mothers (clients, friends, and relatives) who successfully brought their girls into adult fashion. Although some might form a stereotype of these women as a bunch of prudish goody-two-shoes in long corduroy jumpers, there are no grounds for any stereotype because the women are so very different from one another. (Several wear stilettos.) True, many are generally proactive and organized, but most just kind of took it as it came. Some moms were miserably uncomfortable with the teen environment, and some enjoyed the thrill of the entire teen subculture. In all cases, however, each woman understood the links between fashion, sexuality, self esteem, and personal success.

With time and patience
the mulberry leaf
becomes a silk gown.

CHINESE PROVERB

I've also spoken to many teens.

An understanding of who she is (teen years):

- Continue everything mentioned above. You may have to strain a little to stick to what you were doing before, but keep a smile on your face even when it hurts.
- Tell her that she's beautiful. Encourage her father to tell her she is beautiful. Make it deeper than a simple statement of physical beauty (although that's important too). Let her know that she has a great value to her that's worth more than anything she can comprehend, and that she is more important than many of the things that are happening in her culture at the moment.
- You probably have already had "the talk" with her, but touch base with her when the opportunities arise. Make it clear to her that she can bring all of her questions to you and that you will give her straight answers. You will find that many of these questions relate back to or imply fashion decisions as well.

- Continue to foster pride in her female body. Don't refer to menstruation as a curse and don't treat the bra as a dreaded punishment. Incorporate both into a beautiful rite of passage that's as simple as a heart-to-heart talk or as ritualistic as a shopping trip and lunch. Explain that while these things are uncomfortable now, they hold a purpose for her life as an adult woman. Although the adolescent brain doesn't often do this, always strive to pull her out of herself and into the bigger picture.

The skill of discernment toward all things fashion (teen years):

- Teach her the concept of focal point in fashion. Teach her the specifics such as color contrast, accessories, fit, or the play of fabric against skin.
- Clue her in to the fact that when she dresses in a sexually alluring way, she agitates the boys around her. (Mothers of sons count on the mothers of daughters to positively influence these girls' fashions.) Teach her that her sexuality should never be used as a weapon against males, or as a bargaining tool for getting what she wants.
- Express your boundaries early on and stick with them. If you weren't nit-picky or unreasonable to begin with, she'll probably come through and respect your opinion when it really counts. In turn, she should be able to express her own boundaries.
- Remind her that when she is out in public, she represents the family. How does *she* feel when Dad cuts the grass in his Bermuda shorts and black socks?
- Continue to shop with her. Make it an enjoyable experience. Don't go too early in the morning (for her sake) or too late at night (for yours!). Treat her to lunch if you can swing it, but never make a shopping trip too long.

- Be patient when she gets frustrated in the dressing room. (Let her go in there with some privacy, by the way.) Listen to what she is saying. Suggest ideas when appropriate, and bite your tongue when you are tempted to get snappy. Remember, she is trying to work out an understanding of her body and how it fits into the universe. She needs to know that you are the ally and not the evil empire.
- Teach her about the fit of garments. If something doesn't fit, point out that the garment needs to be either adjusted or returned. Never give her the impression that "she doesn't fit the garment." Tell her she's beautiful again.
- Talk to her about the specifics of fashion. Point out ensembles that you think are wonderful, even if she thinks they aren't. Point out ensembles that she thinks are wonderful, even if you think they aren't.
- Never give money or a credit card without a hard and fast spending limit. Make her pay back anything she has charged without permission.
- Involve Dad in fashion talk so that she can get the male view of fashion. Do this only, of course, if you think it would be helpful. Not every father feels comfortable dealing with typical adolescent fashion issues, but those who do and are successful create very warm and loving memories for a daughter. (Having him read this chapter will help.)

TRY THIS: While teaching your daughter to distinguish the appropriate from the inappropriate, note the retailers who repeatedly frustrate your efforts. Complain to them. Send the complaint in writing to both the store and the corporate headquarters. Or encourage your daughter to complain if she understands the situation. Entire marketing campaigns have turned on a dime due to the complaints of vocal moms and teens.

A firm sense of personal style (teen years):

- If she gets the opportunity to learn how to sew, go for it. Even a rudimentary class can cover the basics of fiber, fabric, stitching techniques, and quality.
- Get her a color analysis. Teach her about body type. Give her this book or any really good reference on fashion. I find that meeting with a fashion consultant or going to a fashion seminar is a really great way to introduce her to life-long skills. It will also make her feel like a woman.
- Give your daughter beauty secrets. If you don't know any, get some. My mom always told me never to wrinkle my brow. I don't know if there is a connection, but so far so good.
- Encourage her to maintain her own garments. Have her launder them (to the best of her ability), repair or seek repair for them when necessary, and maintain a somewhat organized closet.

Remember, teenage girls do grow up. The objective for you – one is that is even more important than avoiding the crazy extremes of adolescence – is to provide her with a foundation on which to return when she settles down in her twenties . . . or thirties . . . or forties.

mom and miss sophisticate

Older girls (women, really) begin to differentiate themselves from the others in ways they hope make them *chic*. It's actually the full blossoming of their fashion personalities. When you see this begin, seize the moment. Enjoy something new with her. For example, go on a special trip for shoes or visit a vintage shop for a unique piece of jewelry. Show her that you see the woman in her and give her the feeling that she's "in the club."

SEMINAR FAQ
prom queen

QUESTION: My daughter who is now in college put me through a nightmare shopping experience for her senior prom. Now my younger daughter is preparing for the prom season and I'm all stressed out about it. What can I do to ease the experience?

ANSWER: The short answer is "everything I've written in this chapter." No, maybe that's the long answer. Anyway, the more immediate answer is to do the three *A's*: *Anticipate, Authorize,* and *Affirm.*

Anticipate. Know what to expect. Figure out what it is she will be asking you to buy before she actually asks. That means doing a little fashion forecasting at all the basic retailers so that you can be prepared to set some guidelines. It will also allow you to find what's genuinely beautiful.

Talk to other moms. See what they are finding and positively reinforce any statements they may make about reigning in the amount of money being spent or floozie styles being explored. That may help everyone stand a little firmer.

Authorize. Once your daughter either approaches you about shopping or begins shopping herself, authorize her to choose only those options that adhere to certain objective standards. Remind her that the dress should keep the focal point on her face. So, for example, flesh should not be a major part of the ensemble. What they will probably argue about is the amount of back or leg that's exposed. Stay with your standards even then. Remember, you are the adult in the relationship and you can say no to what you *know* is inappropriate. (See p. 285 for tips on selecting a special occasion dress.)

How do you buy a dress in a market of mostly unacceptable options? Do a little reconnaissance of your own very early in the season, visiting both regular retail and most forms of alternative retail. Check many second-hand venues as well (your niece's high school had their prom two weeks ago).

If your daughter does not know her *elements of style*, this might be a great time to help her find out what they are. Then you can use what you both know to find the most flattering ensemble possible.

Place a limit on her spending. Explain to her that this is a one-time special occasion dress so it shouldn't cost an inordinate amount of money. (You'll save the money for her first suit, which she will use many times.) Don't forget to budget for the following:

- an appropriate bra
- hosiery
- shoes in which she can actually walk (have her test them out going up a flight of stairs)
- an evening bag
- a coordinated wrap
- the necessary makeup for the right amount of glam

Affirm. Affirm her beauty and tell her that you love her. Tell her that she needs to have standards for her own protection.

Finally, gently remind everyone that this is only one evening of her life. It may seem like a big deal now, but life will go on even if her makeup is smeared, her date is socially inept, or if she misses it entirely. Sometimes we adults can set expectations so high that teens can't help but get caught up into the hoopla.

warm fashion fuzzies

As you know from two chapters ago, women comprise a major part of the fashion and cosmetics market. This is true partly because of the gifts we give to others. Include your daughter on your list. Introduce her to the art form of *couture*. Try these for gifts:

- a book on fashion
- a biography of a woman with style
- a novelty purse
- a stainless steel manicure set in a stylish case
- a set of nail polish
- a professional manicure or pedicure now and then
- a facial or a makeover
- great smelling body lotion
- coordinated winter gloves, hat, and scarf
- a dresser or vanity (this is all my daughter wants!)
- a two-way lighted mirror
- warm and fuzzy slippers
- a bathrobe
- home spa equipment
- perfume
- monogram the things you buy her like towels, bags, or cases
- your time!

I can only find parkas with my mother's rules!

I have actually had a few young girls say this to me. At first I brushed it off. I thought maybe they were just being a little sullen. Soon after, however, I had to admit they were right! Some weren't sullen at all. Many of these girls actually agreed with their moms on fashion choices but couldn't find appropriate ones in the stores for their age group. What a terrible quandary. It really came to a head for me personally during a fashion seminar with a group of high-school seniors. I felt like a talk show host as they shared their stories about facing nothing thing but cheap knits that cling and provide no room for a bra (full-busted girls are particularly annoyed by this), finding a prom dress that didn't scream *Studio 54*, and locating jeans that didn't make bathroom visits difficult.

Manners and kindness are always in style.

MARY ANNE WAHLE

So I did a little homework to see if they were right. They were – but not completely. There are some beautiful things for teens but you just have to do a little digging around. The "vast array of choices" I mentioned earlier is a real asset in this department. Alternative shopping includes many of the same things older women use.

- The Misses department at any store
- Boutiques
- Catalogues, especially ones that pride themselves on customer satisfaction
- The Internet
- Consignment shops
- Vintage clothing stores (for prom dresses especially)
- Thrift stores

Of course, it's all luck of the draw, and some seasons are harder than others. For example, the spring and summer seasons are much tougher to find agreeable clothing choices than the fall and winter seasons. I advise my clients that once they find a favorite, they should buy three or four in different colors and stock up for next year if it is a workhorse item for a wardrobe.

ten gifts of style my mom gave me

There are some things you may distinctly remember about your childhood. A lot of them probably revolve around your parents and how they interacted with you. I consider myself fortunate to remember not only fun things about both my parents, but very specific lessons regarding fashion and style. My mother may not have consciously taught me all of them, but her example taught me as well.

1. Smile even when it's hard.
2. Look up-to-date. Clothes are kind of fun after all.
3. Skirts are one of the benefits of being a woman.
4. Have a totally cool jewelry box stocked with wonderfully exotic items. Don't yell at your daughter when she rifles through it.
5. Wear jewelry even when you scrub the toilet.
6. Wear lipstick. Brush your hair. Never look like Gravel Gertie. (Who is she, anyway?)
7. You have to have a few years behind you to wear black.
8. Always wear a pretty top in your best colors.
9. Wear heels when you can. Wear high heels when you can get away with it.
10. No one should ever spot your underwear under your clothing.

elegance In style

My Californian friend did make *some* good points on fashion.

She did eventually mention the word *elegance.* I agree with her completely that it is extremely important to pass that on to young women. It's like learning how to read; if you can't do it, a lot of doors are closed to you for the rest of your life.

Unlike reading, it's much harder to learn at a later age. (Believe me on this point: I am a trained reading specialist *and* a fashion consultant!) Elegance requires many habits, and many other habits go against it. Foster elegance in your daughter first by modeling it for her, and then give her a little direct instruction, maybe using role-play to make it really fun. Here are some basic areas.

- Greetings and handshakes. Teach her eye contact and smiling.
- Eating and table manners. Teach her the art of dining rather than the instinct of eating.
- Sitting and walking. Teach her about body language. My international students always had a little culture shock concerning the crude way that some American girls would walk, talk, and sit.
- Taking care of what she owns.
- Looking out for the feelings of others.
- Expressions and exclamations. Give her a few phrases to say other than the typical crude words and expressions.

STYLE PROFILE #24
my legacy

Reflect upon what you convey about yourself through your style to your daughter.

What do you convey about fashion?

What do you convey about the world?

What could you change?

What things could you specifically teach to your daughter so that she can develop her own personal style?

epilogue

You might be wondering about my title, *It's* So *You!*, and the benefits of fitting fashion to my own life. Has life changed beyond the closet? Is it better? Well, let's see . . .

- I know that I have dignity as a woman.
- I have more confidence about who I am because I know what's important.
- I am able to speak to anyone without becoming self-conscious about what I am wearing.
- I am more professional and appear more competent.
- I am more productive because I spend less time on my appearance and think less about fashion.
- I am ready for anything any time.
- I look in the mirror a lot less because I know I've done the groundwork early in the day.
- I save tons of money.
- I don't hide new outfits from my husband.
- My husband thinks I'm sexier now than when I was twenty-five.
- Friends and family seek my opinion on matters of fashion.

- Friends and family seek my opinion on matters of everything else.
- I feel confident in giving my opinion.
- I can see the back and sides of my closet.
- I can open the drawers to my dressers.
- My socks match, and I always have panty hose.

notes

INTRODUCTION

1. See Elegance In Style on the Internet, www.eleganceinstyle.com.
2. Success In Style has a boutique in Ellicott City, Maryland. Its mailing address is 2610 Turf Valley Road, Ellicott City, Maryland 21042. On the Internet, visit www.successinstyle.org.

CHAPTER ONE

1. Shalit, Wendy. *A Return to Modesty: Discovering the Lost Virtue.* New York, NY: Touchstone, 1999. Shalit illustrates how modesty works for women in a witty and intelligent way.
2. Markey, Kevin. *One Hundred Most Important Women of the Twentieth Century.* Des Moines, Iowa: Ladies Home Journal Books, 1998.
3. Robinson, Dwight E. "Fashion Theory and Product Design." *Harvard Business Review*, November-December, 1958.
4. Jones, Sue Jenkyn. *Fashion Design*. London: Lawrence King Publishing, 2002.
5. For the latest information on French fashion, you can contact *Federation Francaise de la Couture du Pret-a-Porter des Couturiers et des Createurs de Mode* rue du Faubourg Saint Honoré 75008 Paris tel 01 42 66 64 44 fax 01 42 66 94 63 or *Les Ecoles de la Chambre Syndicale de la Couture Parisienne,* 45 rue Saint Roch 75 0001 Paris. Tel: (33) 01 42 61 00 77. Or, visit www.modeaparis.com.
6. Lehnert, Gertrud. *Fashion, An Illustrated Overview*. Germany: Barrons, 1998.
7. Jones, Sue Jenkyn. *Fashion Design*. London: Lawrence King Publishing, 2002. Provides the current terms for inspirations in design and mentions "bubbling up" as term coined by Ted Polhemus.

8. Laver, James. *Costume and Fashion: A Concise History.* London: Thames and Hudson, 1995 (expanded from the original 1969 edition). Laver is thorough and very entertaining.
9. Laver, James. "Fashion: A Detective Story." *Vogue. Conde Nast,* January 1959.
10. ibid
11. Agins, Teri. *The End of Fashion*. New York, NY: Harper Collins, 1999.

CHAPTER TWO

1. Clark Keogh, Pamela. *Audrey Style*. New York, NY: Harper Collins, 1999.

CHAPTER THREE

1. For general fashion forecasting, visit Fashion Information Limited, 7 Mall Studios, Tasker Road, London, NW3 2YS,United Kingdom, www.fashioninformation.com. For information on color forecasting, see the *Color Association of the United States*, 315 West 39th St., Studio 507, New York, NY 10018, or visit www.colorassociation.com.

CHAPTER FOUR

1. Graphic artists will also use the words "hot" and "cold" when referring to color. Sutton, Tina and Whelan, Bride M. *The Complete Color Harmony*. Gloucester, MA: Rockport, 2004,
2. *The Fashion Book*, Phaidon Press, New York, NY: 1998.
3. Sutton, Tina and Whelan, Bride M. *The Complete Color Harmony*. Gloucester, MA: Rockport, 2004. *Ultimate Visual Dictionary of Science*. New York, NY: DK Publishing, Inc., 1998, and www.colormatters.com.
5. Check out www.crayola.com for more information on their color labels. It's fascinating.

CHAPTER SIX

1. The Fabric Institute is a non profit educational institution for the textile industry. They can be reached on the internet at www.fabriclink.com.

CHAPTER EIGHT

1. Garment Industry Development Corporation, 2000
2. Underhill, Paco. *Why We Buy: The Science of Shopping*. New York: Simon and Schuster, 1999.
3. Travis, Daryl. *Emotional Branding: How Successful Brands Gain the Irrational Edge.* Roseville, CA: Prima Publishing, 2000.
4. One great way to find a resale shop is to contact the National Association of Resale and Thrift Shops (NARTS) at www.narts.org.

5. Fashion industry news and fashion forecasting is easily found at www.apparelsearch.com or www.wwd.com (Women's Wear Daily)
6. Betzina, Sandra. *Fabric Savvy: The Essential Guide for Every Sewer.* Newton, CT: Taunton Press, 1999. Great resource for fabric information.

CHAPTER NINE

1. Begoun, Paula. *Don't Go to the Cosmetics Counter without Me.* Seattle, WA: Beginning Press. For information call 1-800-831-4088.
2. On the internet the FDA is www.fda.gov.
3. The Fragrance Foundation is at 145 E. 32nd St., New York, NY, 10016-6002. Tel: 212.725.2755. On internet they can be reached at www.fragrance.org

CHAPTER TEN

1. Brumberg, Joan Jacobs. *The Body Project: An Intimate History of American Girls.* Random House, NY: 1997.
2. Lord, M.G. Forever Barbie: *The Unauthorized Biography of a Real Doll.* William Murrow Co., NY: 1994.
3. Mattel posts many interesting facts about Barbie on their website, www.mattel.com.

index